Culturally Sustaining Policymaking in Indigenous Communities

Partnering to Promote Lasting Change

Aprille J. Phillips

Foreword by Teresa L. McCarty

TEACHERS COLLEGE | COLUMBIA UNIVERSITY
NEW YORK AND LONDON

Published by Teachers College Press,® 1234 Amsterdam Avenue, New York, NY 10027

Copyright © 2024 by Teachers College, Columbia University

Front cover illustration and design by Peter Donahue.

All rights reserved. No part of this publication may be reproduced or transmitted in any form or by any means, electronic or mechanical, including photocopy, or any information storage and retrieval system, without permission from the publisher. For reprint permission and other subsidiary rights requests, please contact Teachers College Press, Rights Dept.: tcpressrights@tc.columbia.edu

Library of Congress Cataloging-in-Publication Data is available at loc.gov

ISBN 978-0-8077-6956-0 (paper)
ISBN 978-0-8077-6957-7 (hardcover)
ISBN 978-0-8077-8232-3 (ebook)

Printed on acid-free paper
Manufactured in the United States of America

Contents

Series Foreword *James A. Banks*	ix
Foreword: Toward a Praxis of Indigenous Education Sovereignty *Teresa L. McCarty*	xiii
Acknowledgments	xix
Introduction	1
Democracy and School Reform	3
Grounding Terminology and Conceptual Framing	4
School Policy Reform in Indian Country	8
Policy Culture and Culturally Sustaining Policymaking	9
Methodology and Positionality	10
Overview of Chapters	12
1. So What? Lessons Learned and Why They Matter	15
Accountability: What Came Before	18
No Child Left Behind	20
NCLB Limbo	21
The Role of State Departments of Education	25
SDEs, Policy, and Power	27
Spatial Tactics as Resistance	28
2. Welcome to Flyover Country	29
Accountability and Nebraska's AQuESTT	30
The Nebraska Way	31

	A Nebraska Way of Education Governance	33
	The Nation's Only Unicameral	33
	A Bill's Journey Through the Unicameral	34
	A Brief History of Schooling and Governance in Nebraska	35
	Policy Landscape and Key Figures	36
	The Shifting Roles of NDE	40
3.	**A Broader Story Than the Village of Santee**	**43**
	Early Interactions with Colonizers	44
	A Dakota Education	45
	"Big Knives" and the "Physical and Moral Degradation" of Reservation Life	47
	School as a Policy Tool	48
	Sovereignty, Self-Determination, and Self-Education	50
	Agency, Survivance, and Schooling	52
	What's a "Good" Education?	53
	Culturally Sustaining and Responsive Pedagogy	54
	Culturally Sustaining/Revitalizing Education Policymaking	55
4.	**Policy Crafted on the Legislative Floor**	**57**
	The Introduction of LB438	58
	Public Hearing: A Better Way to "Fix" Schools	59
	LB438 and the Second Session of Nebraska's 103rd Legislature	61
	LB438 Becomes Law	69
5.	**Nebraska's AQuESTT: Bolder, Broader, Better**	**71**
	The SBOE Hires a New Commissioner of Education	72
	From Vision to Plans on Paper	76
	Codifying AQuESTT	79
	Sketching out AQuESTT's Implementation	80
	Bolder, Broader, Better	81

	Inching Closer to Classification/Designation	83
	The First AQuESTT Classification and Designation	85
	A Retrospective View	88
6.	**Run by Outsiders**	**91**
	Initial Thoughts About Improvement in Santee	92
	A Diagnostic Review	95
	State Plan Development	98
	Priority Schools: Developing Progress Plans	100
	Progress Plan Approval and Initial Implementation	106
7.	**Compliance, Kind Of**	**115**
	Reporting First-Year Progress	122
	Continued Compliance, Kind of . . . and Incognito Improvement Efforts	124
	Incognito Improvement Acts Endure	129
8.	**Wait, What Just Happened?**	**133**
	The "Consultocracy"	134
	Sovereignty and Who Gets to Define Educational Quality	136
	Everyday Tactics and Incognito Acts of Improvement	138
	The Decolonizing Work of Culturally Sustaining Policymaking	139
	Conclusion	141
	Afterword	**143**
	A Final Trip to Santee	143
	The *iSanti Ozuyapi* at State	143
References		**145**
Index		**161**
About the Author		**171**

Series Foreword

This copiously researched book details the efforts by state educational leaders in Nebraska to "turn around" or reform a school on the Santee Sioux Reservation, which they considered failing. This K–12 public school was established on tribal lands in 1976 and was governed by reservation leaders. The ways in which state educators outside the Santee Sioux community tried to control the school exemplifies what Hopkins (2020) calls colonizing education, which results in the "control of the minds, bodies, and lands of Native children, peoples, and communities . . . [as well as] Indigenous survival and resistance" (p. 3). Phillips also describes how state-imposed educational policies implemented in iSanti Community School colonized and confined and "attempted to eliminate [the] identity, culture, and community" of Indigenous peoples in the United States (p. 30).

The case study that Phillips describes in this book took place in Nebraska among the Santee Dakota Sioux. However, it is a cautionary tale that has implications for other educational interventions in diverse communities. Phillips concludes that the educational intervention in the iSanti Community School "undermined local trust and further marginalized a community with a colonizing history of outside 'experts' determining what schooling should be like in Indian Country" (p. 31). These interventions also denied agency to Native communities, resulted in cultural erasure, and evoked resistance.

The case study of school reform and its demise described in this book illustrates how standardization (Sleeter & Carmona, 2016), deficit theory (Gorski, 2018), and the silencing of the voices and aspirations of marginalized groups can result in failed educational reform. Consequently, this book is an important contribution to the Multicultural Education Series. The major purpose of the Multicultural Education Series is to provide preservice educators, practicing educators, graduate students, scholars, and policymakers with an interrelated and comprehensive set of books that summarizes and analyzes important research, theory, and practice related to the education of ethnic, racial, cultural, and linguistic groups in the United States and the education of mainstream students about diversity. The dimensions of multicultural education, developed by Banks (2004) and described in the *Handbook of Research on Multicultural Education* and in the *Encyclopedia of Diversity in Education* (Banks, 2012), provide the conceptual framework for the development of the publications in the Series.

The dimensions are *content integration*, the *knowledge construction process*, *prejudice reduction*, *equity pedagogy*, and an *empowering institutional culture and social structure*. The books in the Multicultural Education Series provide research, theoretical, and practical knowledge about the behaviors and learning characteristics of students of color (Darling-Hammond & Darling-Hammond, 2022; Conchas & Vigil, 2012; Lee, 2007), language minority students (Gándara & Hopkins 2010; Valdés, 2001; Valdés, Capitelli, & Alvarez, 2011), low-income students (Cookson, 2013; Gorski, 2018), and other minoritized population groups, such as students who speak different varieties of English (Charity Hudley & Mallinson, 2011), LGBTQ youth (Mayo, 2022); and students with disabilities (Waitoller & Thorius, 2022).

Structural and institutional racism is a significant factor that causes the forced assimilation and deculturation that Indigenous groups experience in the United States. A number of books in the Multicultural Education Series focus on *institutional and structural racism* and ways to reduce it in educational institutions. These books include Özlem Sensoy and Robin DiAngelo (2017), *Is Everyone Really Equal? An Introduction to Key Concepts in Social Justice Education* (Second Edition); Gary Howard (2016), *We Can't Teach What Do Don't Know: White Teachers, Multiracial Schools* (Third Edition); Jabari Mahiri (2017), *Deconstructing Race: Multicultural Education Beyond the Color-Bind*; Zeus Leonardo (2013), *Race Frameworks: A Multidimensional Theory of Racism and Education*; *Racial Microaggressions: Using Critical Race Theory in Education to Recognize and Respond to Everyday Racism* by Daniel Solórzano and Lindsay Pérez Huber (2020); and *Seeing Whiteness: The Essential Essays of Robin DiAngelo* (2023).

This is the fourth book in the Multicultural Series that focuses on the education of Native American students. The others are *"To Remain an Indian": Lessons in Democracy from a Century of Native American Education* by K. Tsianina Lomawaima and Teresa L. McCarty (2006); *Indian Education for All: Decolonizing Indigenous Education in Public Schools* by John P. Hopkins; and *Unsettling Settler-Colonial Education: The Transformational Indigenous Praxis Model* edited by Cornell Pewewardy, Anna Lees, and Robin Zape-Tah-Hol-Ah Minthorn. These interrelated and reinforcing books provide insightful analyses of the problems of educating Indigenous groups in the United States and describe visionary interventions for school reform.

Phillips describes a number of important lessons she derived from her case study of school reform at the iSanti Community School on the Santee Sioux Reservation. School reform guided by standardized criteria, tests, and practices are rarely successful (Sleeter & Carmona, 2016). Effective school reform must be grounded in and guided by the characteristics of specific cultural communities, students, teachers, and parents. Effective school reforms must also be culturally responsive and culturally sustaining and incorporate the voices, hopes, dreams, and visions of the people who live in the community and work in the school. School reform that is conceptualized and designed by outsiders with little and no input from the people in the school and the community will fail in part because of cultural resistance by the people for whom the educational intervention is designed. The prodigious research and empirical conclusions about school reform that Phillips describes in this book merit serious reflection and consideration by policymakers and school leaders.

—James A. Banks

REFERENCES

Banks, J. A. (2004). Multicultural education: Historical development, dimensions, and practice. In J. A. Banks & C. A. M. Banks (Eds.). *Handbook of research on multicultural education* (2nd ed., pp. 3–29). Jossey-Bass.

Banks, J. A. (2012). Multicultural education: Dimensions of. In J. A. Banks (Ed)., *Encyclopedia of diversity in education* (vol. 3, pp. 1538–1547). Sage Publications.

Charity Hudley, A. H., & Mallinson, C. (2011). *Understanding language variation in U. S. schools*. Teachers College Press.

Conchas, G. Q., & Vigil, J. D. (2012). *Streetsmart schoolsmart: Urban poverty and the education of adolescent boys*. Teachers College Press.

Cookson, P. W. Jr. (2013). *Class rules: Exposing inequality in American high schools*. Teachers College Press.

Darling-Hammond, K., & Darling-Hammond, L. (2022). *The civil rights road to deeper learning: Five essentials for equity*. Teachers College Press.

DiAngelo, R. (2023). *Seeing whiteness: The essential essays of Robin DiAngelo*. Teachers College Press.

Gándara, P. & Hopkins, M. (Eds.). (2010). *Forbidden language: English language learners and restrictive language policies*. Teachers College Press.

Gorski, P. C. (2018). *Reaching and teaching students in poverty: Strategies for erasing the opportunity gap* (2nd ed.). Teachers College Press.

Hopkins, J. P. (2020). *Indian education for all: Decolonizing Indigenous education*. Teachers College Press.

Howard, G. (2016). *We can't teach what we don't know: White teachers, multiracial schools* (3rd ed.). Teachers College Press.

Lee, C. D. (2007). *Culture, literacy, and learning: Taking bloom in the midst of the whirlwind*. Teachers College Press.

Leonardo, Z. (2013). *Race frameworks: A multicultural theory of racism and education*. Teachers College Press.

Lomawaima, K. T. & McCarty, T. L. (2006). *"To remain an Indian:" Lessons in democracy from a century of Native American education*. Teachers College Press.

Mahiri, J. (2017). *Deconstructing race: Multicultural education beyond the colorbind*. Teachers College Press.

Mayo, C. (2022). *LGBTQ youth and education: Policies and practices* (2nd ed). Teachers College Press.

Pewewardy, C., Lees, A., & Minthorn, R. Z. (2022). *Unsettling settler-colonial education: The transformational indigenous praxis model*. Teachers College Press.

Sensoy, Ö., & DiAngelo, R. (2017). *Is everyone really equal? An introduction to key concepts in social justice education* (2nd ed.). Teachers College Press.

Sleeter, C. E. & Carmona, J. F. (2016). *Un-standardizing curriculum: Multicultural teaching in the standards-based classroom*. Teachers College Press.

Solórzano, D. & Huber, L. P. (2020). *Racial microaggressions: Using critical race theory to respond to everyday racism*. Teachers College Press.

Valdés, G. (2001). *Learning and not learning English: Latino Students in American schools*. Teachers College Press.

Valdés, G., Capitelli, S., & Alvarez, L. (2011). *Latino children learning English: Steps in the journey*. Teachers College Press.

Waitoller, F. R. & Thorius, K. A. K. (2022). *Sustaining disabled youth: Centering disability in asset pedagogies*. Teachers College Press.

Foreword

Toward a Praxis of Indigenous Education Sovereignty

In 1976, the Congressionally mandated American Indian Policy Review Commission (AIPRC) published its 400-plus page final report on the state of American Indian education and federal Indian education policy. Among the scores of testimonials from Native education leaders across the United States was this clear directive from Cree educator Dorothy Small of the Rocky Boy School District in Montana: "Our people believe that control of education is a natural and inherent right" (AIPRC, 1976, p. 261). The Commission's Final Report is replete with similar, unequivocal testimony. As we learn from the compelling yet troubling story told by Aprille Phillips in this book, it is also the long-held belief of the Santee Dakota Nation, whose public school was founded just 5 years before the Commission published its report. An education system to be governed by local Dakota people, the new public school would be "organized around the Dakota virtues of *Wokspace* (wisdom), *Woohitika* (bravery), *Wowacintanka* (fortitude), and *Wacantognaka* (generosity)," Phillips explains (p. 50). This was the beginning of the Santee Community Schools (SCS), "a school for the Tribe" and the focus of Phillips' perceptive ethnographic account.

Although it takes place decades later, the story that unfolds is one that would surely be recognizable to SCS founders, as Santee Dakota sovereignty confronted relentless settler state surveillance and the "Nebraska Way." Mvskoke scholar K. Tsianina Lomawaima sums up the larger history of American Indian education of which this story is part, with "three simple words: battle for power" (2000, p. 2). As Phillips recounts, the Santee Dakota People have been waging that battle for centuries—and Santee Community Schools for more than 50 years—with schooling as the "policy tool" (p. 48) for land theft and intended Indigenous identity erasure. But this is also a story of Indigenous refusal, persistence, and de facto policy-making; the ongoing struggle between Santee Dakota sovereignty and settler state control is the heart of it. The terrain of that struggle is the euphemistically named ground of education reform.

Aprille Phillips takes us into this story through a clear, accessible, and often personal narrative. As a critical ethnography of education policy, the book is a welcome contribution to Indigenous education scholarship in public schools (Benally, 2019; Hopkins, 2020; Sabzalian, 2019), and the anthropology of education policy (Castagno & McCarty, 2018; Hamann & Rosen, 2011; Levinson et al., 2020; Sutton & Levinson 2001). By documenting ethnographically the disjunction between top-down policy formation and local, bottom-up policy implementation, Phillips's study also contributes to a long and generative stream of scholarship in the ethnography of language policy (Hornberger, 1988; Hornberger et al., 2018; McCarty, 2011). In this intellectual genealogy, policy is conceived not as disembodied text, but as a dynamic, power-infused sociocultural process. Illuminating that process, Phillips shows how education policy in Nebraska, influenced by neoliberal national trends, "*traveled* from the floor of Nebraska's Legislature, across tiers of the education system in the state, and was *actualized* on the Santee Sioux reservation" (p. 4, emphases added). Known as AQuESTT—Accountability for a Quality Education System, Today and Tomorrow—this statewide school labeling and sanctioning regime moved wave-like across unequal systems of power.

As an employee of the Nebraska Department of Education (NDE), Phillips had a "front-row seat" to the policy's development and implementation (p. 30). Through fine-grained qualitative detail, she takes us into the state's unicameral legislative chamber, showing how policy agents—legislators and state-level bureaucrats—constructed a deficit-driven policy culture that positioned Native communities "as needing guidance and 'correction'" (p. 56). Here Phillips amplifies the critical scholarship of Sandra Stein (2004), revealing the complex and consequential ways in which policy rhetoric constructs taken-for-granted ways of seeing—and occluding—education problems, solutions, and "target" communities. SCS was positioned within the state's bullseye as one of three AQuESTT targets, discursively rebranded "priority schools."

Demographic data bring this raced and classed policy culture into sharp focus. At the time of the study (2016–2023), SCS served a student body identified as 84% Native American and 16% Hispanic (Latinx). All students qualified for free and reduced lunch, a federal poverty indicator. Although the school was staffed with paraprofessionals and other staff from the Dakota community, students' teachers were mostly White. Over the 7 years of the study, SCS had a revolving door of six superintendents and five high school principals, all but one of whom was White; the single Native superintendent was placed on leave 6 months into her contract and did not return. The external consultants and legislators who wielded power over all these individuals, the school, and its constituent community, were predominately White (Aprille Phillips, personal communication, October 12, 2023). As Phillips relates in the book, these racialized policy dynamics and

Foreword   xv

their consequences were not confined to SCS. "For example," she writes, "all schools on American Indian reservation lands and a high proportion of schools serving historically marginalized students would be labeled as needing improvement . . . every single school on American Indian reservation lands was classified in the lowest classification" (pp. 85, 88). Deficit-based policy logics subjected these schools to White settler sanctions and "best practices," which, readers may not be surprised to learn, did not include any form of culturally responsive or sustaining pedagogy (Ladson-Billings, 1995, 2021; Paris, 2012; Paris & Alim, 2017). Indeed, local Indigenous knowledge was explicitly eschewed by the dominating White external consultant as inadequate to the task of "school improvement."

Phillips's study also makes important methodological contributions. As a non-Dakota researcher and NDE's designated liaison to the Santee school, Phillips had a tremendously challenging role. "I was keenly aware of the freighted history of those who had come before me in this kind of liaison role," she notes (p. 11). Throughout the account she grapples transparently with the ethical dilemmas she encountered, as the state, via its highly paid fly-in/fly-out consultant and the bulwark of settler bureaucracy, consistently misrecognized Santee Dakota knowledge, sought to override Santee Dakota sovereignty, and dismissed the community-engaged efforts of school personnel to craft a self-determined path toward "improvement." Midway through the study Phillips's role became increasingly difficult as it shifted from "relationship bridge between SCS and NDE to that of responding to the consultant's directives and interacting with SCS administrators and staff at her request" (p. 115). In a final climax of colonial manipulation, Phillips "realized that this would likely be my last trip to Santee in an official capacity" (p. 123). She left NDE with the sobering recognition of the inability of the state education agency, as an arm of Anglo-American imperial power, to live up to the lofty official rhetoric of collaborative policy implementation. Taken as a whole, the book offers an exceptionally candid portrait of researcher reflexivity and ethics, through Phillips's critical assessment of her positioning and positionality (Boveda & Annamma, 2023) and the implications for relational accountability in research with Indigenous Peoples (Tuhiwai Smith, 2012; Wilson, 2008).

In 2006, K. Tsianina Lomawaima and I introduced a theoretical framework intended to address shifts in federal Indian education policy, which we called Safety Zone Theory. Our premise is that, over more than 2 centuries, federal and state governments have, in coherent and empirically discernable ways, sought to distinguish "safe" from "dangerous" Indigenous cultural practices, using schooling as the chief "policy tool" to proscribe and contain practices deemed threatening to state interests. This is the metaphoric safety zone—a political and pedagogical space of intended Indigenous containment (Lomawaima & McCarty, 2006, p. 6). In 2014, we clarified and elaborated this theory, adding Lomawaima's notion of Zones of Sovereignty to denote Indigenous "practices of creative self-determination toward the goals of equity, justice, tolerance, and mutual well-being" (Lomawaima & McCarty, 2014, p. 66). In Phillips's account, AQuESTT is a prime example of safety zone containment tactics. But those tactics did not go uncontested. As Phillips relates, SCS personnel engaged in "incognito improvement acts" (p. 129), carving out a Santee Dakota education sovereignty zone.

Culturally Sustaining Policymaking in Indigenous Communities provides the fields of education, anthropology, and Native American/Indigenous Studies with a richly described, thoughtful, and timely account of the innerworkings of education "reform," laying bare the ways in which state-level safety zones serve to reinscribe systems of oppression, and revealing the policy improvisation and push-back of Indigenous nations, communities, and schools. While we might wish for an anti-oppressive finality in this carefully crafted account, we have instead something more grounded and nuanced: a forthright witnessing that honors the vision and perseverance of the Santee Dakota Nation in affirming its "natural and inherent right" to education self-determination. In this regard, Aprille Phillips's book is reciprocation to those whom it matters most: the Santee Dakota and other Indigenous Peoples who imagine a future of collective well-being through the praxis of Indigenous sovereignty.

Teresa L. McCarty
University of California, Los Angeles

REFERENCES

American Indian Policy Review Commission (AIPRC). (1976). *Report on Indian education. Task Force Five: Indian Education. Final Report to the American Indian Policy Review Commission.* U.S. Government Printing Office.

Benally, C. (Guest Ed.) (2019). Indigenizing the curriculum: Putting the "Native" into Native American content instruction mandates. Special Issue, *Journal of American Indian Education, 58*(3).

Boveda, M., & Annamma, S. A. (2023). Beyond making a statement: An intersectional framing of the power and possibilities of positioning. *Educational Researcher, 52*(5), 306–314. https://doi.org/10.3102/0013189X231167149

Castagno, A.E., & McCarty, T.L. (Eds.) (2018). *The anthropology of education policy: Ethnographic inquiries into policy as sociocultural process.* Routledge.

Hamann, E.T., & Rosen, L. (2011). What makes the anthropology of educational policy implementation "anthropological"? In. B.A.U. Levinson & M. Pollock (Eds.), *A companion to the anthropology of education* (pp. 461–477). Wiley-Blackwell.

Hopkins, J.P. (2020). *Indian education for all: Decolonizing Indigenous education in public schools.* Teachers College Press.

Hornberger, N.H. (1988). *Bilingual education and language maintenance: A southern Peruvian Quechua case.* Foris.

Hornberger, N.H., Anzures Tapia, A., Hanks, D.H., & Kvietok Dueñas, F. (2018). Ethnography of language planning and policy. *Language Teaching, 51*(2), 152–186. https://doi.org/10.1017/S0261444817000428

Ladson-Billings, G. (1995). But that's just good teaching! The case for culturally relevant pedagogy. *Theory Into Practice, 34*(3), 159–165.

Ladson-Billings, G. (2021). Three decades of culturally relevant, responsive, and sustaining pedagogy: What lies ahead? *The Educational Forum, 85*(4), 351–354, https://doi.org/10.1080/00131725.2021.1957632

Levinson, B.A.U., Winstead, T., & Sutton, M. (2020). An anthropological approach to education policy as a practice of power: Concepts and methods. In G. Fan & T. Popkewitz (Eds.), *Handbook of education policy studies: Values, governance, globalization, and methodology, vol. 1*. Springer. https://doi.org/10.1007/978-981-13-8347-2_17

Lomawaima, K. T. (2000). Tribal sovereigns: Reframing research in American Indian education. *Harvard Educational Review, 20*(1), 1–21.

Lomawaima, K. T., & McCarty, T. L. (2006). *"To remain an Indian": Lessons in democracy from a century of Native American education.* Teachers College Press.

Lomawaima, K. T., & McCarty, T. L. (2014). Revisiting and clarifying the safety zone. *Journal of American Indian Education, 53*(3), 63–67.

McCarty, T. L. (Ed.) (2011). *Ethnography and language policy.* Routledge.

Paris, D. (2012). Culturally sustaining pedagogy: A needed change in stance, terminology, and practice. *Educational Researcher, 41*(3), 91–97. https://doi.org/10.3102/0013189X12441244

Paris, D., & Alim, H. S. (Eds.) (2017). *Culturally sustaining pedagogies: Teaching and learning for justice in a changing world.* Teachers College Press.

Sabzalian, L. (2019). *Indigenous children's survivance in public schools.* Routledge.

Stein, S. J. (2004). *The culture of education policy.* Teachers College Press.

Sutton, M., & Levinson, B.A.U. (Eds.) (2001). *Policy as practice: Toward a comparative sociocultural analysis of educational policy.* Ablex.

Tuhiwai Smith, L. (2012). *Decolonizing methodologies: Research and Indigenous Peoples.* Zed Books.

Wilson, S. (2008). *Research is ceremony.* Fernwood.

Acknowledgments

I would first like to acknowledge the many individuals in the Santee community and *iSanti* Community School who have become teachers, colleagues, and friends. I see the way you practice everyday acts both inside and outside of the school to bring alignment between your vision of a school for the Dakota people and reality.

I have been researching for this book for more than a decade and conducted fieldwork for more than 7 years. Along that journey, the number of individuals who shared academic wisdom, engaged in dialogue, offered feedback, and encouraged me to keep thinking through writing are too numerous to name individually. Particularly, I would like to acknowledge mentors Ted Hamann, Bryan Brayboy, and Roni Adams. Over coffee or over the phone you listened, asked questions, and offered crucial insights along the way. I also acknowledge my colleague and friend Tricia Gray. I know for certain that this book would not exist without our Friday morning "start of the week" meetings and your encouragement and constructive feedback. I wish to acknowledge Freida Lange, Matt Heusman, and Sue Anderson whose observations were essential to understanding the dynamics of state policy and its implementation in Santee. I would also acknowledge former Nebraska Commissioner of Education, Matthew Blomstedt, who encouraged me to study AQuESTT for my dissertation over lunch back in 2014. I also acknowledge the circle of friends whose encouragement included coffee and wine far away from my laptop. Faith, Liz, Sarah, Heather, Alicia, and Amber, thank you. Finally, Dad, Mom, Daniel, Alycia, Isaac, Eleanor, and Willa, you have lived with this book as long as I have, and I am grateful for the encouragement and support you offered throughout its development.

Introduction

> Today, education is perhaps the most important function of state and local governments. Compulsory school attendance laws and the great expenditures for education both demonstrate our recognition of the importance of education to our democratic society. It is required in the performance of our most basic public responsibilities, even service in the armed forces. It is the very foundation of good citizenship. Today it is a principal instrument in awakening the child to cultural values, in preparing him for later professional training, and in helping him to adjust normally to his environment. In these days, it is doubtful that any child may reasonably be expected to succeed in life if he is denied the opportunity of an education. Such an opportunity, where the state has undertaken to provide it, is a right which must be made available to all on equal terms.

Chief Justice Earl Warren, in his (1954) written unanimous majority decision of the court in *Brown v. Board of Education* (above), highlighted both the hoped-for role of states and communities in ensuring an equitable education to all, and the aspirational role of education in sustaining democratic society in the United States. Making schools equitable has long been a preoccupation of policymakers, practitioners, and scholars of education, but that talked-of intent too often falls short in practice (Au, 2009; Lashaw, 2010; Peck & Reitzug, 2014; Trujillo & Renée, 2013). As a result of the influence of *No Child Left Behind* (NCLB) and its replacement, the *Every Student Succeeds Act* (ESSA), and their associated school accountability requirements, Nebraska, like all states, is host to a number of schools that have been labeled as consistently low-performing. Schools are compared with each other using the same test score metrics. Those that rank poorly in the school comparison data for each state are then labeled and identified for improvement interventions. Schools serving Indigenous communities are frequently among those schools labeled failing or persistently low performing. Since NCLB, state legislatures have established parallel state accountability systems with similar comparison methodologies and approaches to intervention in local schools. It is against this larger backdrop of school accountability reform that *Culturally Sustaining Policymaking in Indigenous*

Communities scrutinizes the ways leaders and intermediaries involved at various tiers of policy development and reform conceptualized and implemented school accountability policy. Particularly, I explore state-led school turnaround efforts in a school on the Santee Sioux Reservation consistently labeled as "failing" and persistently experiencing intervention from individuals hired as outside experts.

Nebraska is unlike states like Montana, Oregon, or Washington, that have recently implemented state-level policies to reimagine the way that public schools include the teaching of Native history and culture in public schools. In the case of Montana, for example, the state education system works in collaboration with tribal entities to ensure the inclusion of Native cultures through culturally responsive/sustaining approaches (Hopkins, 2020). Nebraska differs from states like Arizona, Oklahoma, Alaska, or South Dakota that have large geographic regions of sovereign tribal land or concentrations of Native people per capita (Office of Minority Health, n.d.). Nebraska's American Indian/Alaska Native population, according to state data, is 1.5% (Office of Health Disparities and Health Equity, 2020), which contrasts with nearby states like South Dakota at 8.57% (Office of Health Disparities and Health Equity, U.S. Department of Justice, 2023) or Oklahoma 9.4% (U.S. Census Quick Facts, 2022). As such, political power in shaping policy is proportionate to a small Native population dispersed across the state. Policymakers have not engaged tribal nations or public schools located on reservation lands to collaborate and coconstruct culturally sustaining policy with the *UMÓⁿHOⁿ* (Omaha), *iSanti* (Santee), Ponca, or Ho-Chunk (Winnebago) tribes in the state. Unlike those in its neighbor to the north, South Dakota, with federally governed Bureau of Indian Education (BIE) schools, public schools located on or near tribal lands in Nebraska are state public schools governed by locally elected school boards. Santee Community School, renamed *iSanti* Community School in 2021, was established in 1976 as a K–12 public school on tribal lands governed by representatives from the reservation. In these ways, Nebraska represents a subset of states within flyover country that have been nearly invisible as compared with the places and narratives most frequently featured in articles and books on Indigenous education like Arizona, Oregon, or Montana (e.g., Hopkins, 2020; Lomawaima & McCarty, 2006; Sabzalian, 2019).

It is important to attend to the narratives of what is happening in education policy and practice in states with few square miles of reservation lands or low incidence per capita. With this case of state school accountability education reform in Nebraska, I offer such a perspective. Granted, a single case of education reform and its implementation in a public school on tribal lands in flyover country feels so specific that one may wonder what kind of broader implications might be found in the following chapters. The development and implementation of education policy is complex, and its study must be grounded within the sociohistorical, sociocultural, and

Introduction

sociopolitical contexts of a place while at the same time being comparable (Sutton & Levinson, 2001), so that we might uncover examples of what works and what does not work in Native contexts in flyover country.

From one perspective, this book could be just another study that illustrates the ways that policy intention meets or does not meet its intention when implemented. The project could be yet another example of colonialist, external state intervention in a school serving Native students. Conversely, I argue that context and its particularity matters. Recording and attempting to deeply understand what happened in Nebraska's school accountability education reform and its implementation in Santee teaches several lessons about culturally sustaining policymaking that have applicability beyond flyover country, as I discuss in Chapter 8.

When writing about Santee and *iSanti* Community School, I envision a brick school building near the banks of the Missouri river with jagged bluffs rising out of the water on the South Dakota side. While the early chapters describe some of the backdrop of education policy efforts and the histories and legacies that endure in Indian Country, the school, and the people for whom it is a community hub, are central to the story. To bring them in, we must explore some essential concepts like tribal sovereignty, expressions of agency and survivance, and why these terms matter within a larger framework of democracy and the pursuit of equity.

DEMOCRACY AND SCHOOL REFORM

I begin with the broad scope of education reform as an attribute of democracy that evolves as perceived societal needs shift and what is demanded from the education system also shifts. As the epigraph above points out, a core commitment of the education system, according to U.S. law, is equity. Equity in schooling is understood to support equity in society as a whole. Moving a democratic society toward greater inclusion requires attention and persistence. Paulo Freire (1998) describes this kind of society-building as "serious democracy," grounded in social justice and reconfiguring structures of power. Visions for what democracy and school reform or democratic education should look like is contested, particularly by those who desire to maintain power, privilege, or even to profit from the system of education (Dryzek, 2000; Gutmann, 1999; Mira & Morrell, 2011; Noddings, 2013). Because the educational system has failed so often to fulfill society's expectations for everyone, educational reform policy is always available as a field to contest (Cuban, 2003; Labaree, 2010; Lomawaima & McCarty, 2006; Parker, 2003).

Education reform policy identifies challenges or problems that exist in schools or in the system of education and proposes solutions (Cuban, 2003; Hall & McGinty, 1997). One problem that remains a focus of more recent standards-accountability education reform is how to help "low-performing schools," those schools that serve a concentration of students who are not demonstrating proficiency on high-stakes accountability assessments or in complex federal or state school accountability formulas. Education policies, according to Hall and McGinty (1997), are "vehicles for the realization of intentions" (p. 441). These vehicles of intention travel throughout the system to reach those for whom the policy was intended (Stein, 2004). Policymakers across the education system, from Congress to local school boards, have made attempts to fix schools through the implementation of new policy and intervention in local schools. Subsequent chapters detail the way education policy, influenced by national trends, traveled from the floor of Nebraska's Legislature, across tiers of the education system in the state, and was actualized on the Santee Sioux reservation.

Education policy is developed and implemented through democratically constructed structures and democratic participation (e.g., legislature, state board of education, local school boards). Thus, the work of policy development and implementation illuminates how democracy operates in education policy among the structures of power that have been sociohistorically, sociopolitically, and socioculturally produced. French philosopher Michel Foucault (1977) elucidated the ways that individuals in a society function to construct and maintain systems of power, identifying them as either "subjects of communication" or "objects of information"(p. 200). *Subjects* act upon the world around them and *objects* are acted upon, according to frameworks of power. In education reform, locating the subjects and objects of policy illuminates the structures of power and how the voices of objects are included (or not included) in democratic policy development. I attend to policymakers, intermediaries, and the intended policy recipients and document the ways they function within constructs of power in a particular place and time with an intention of making visible the machinations of power and whether they move society toward or away from the kind of serious democracy Freire (1998) described. I also attend to expressions of agency and ways that individuals remake policy spaces, particularly the ways people push against constraining policies and practices. The case of legislatively mandated school accountability reform and its implementation in Santee underscores the challenging nature of complex school reform efforts that include stated intentions to advance equity in real and meaningful ways.

GROUNDING TERMINOLOGY AND CONCEPTUAL FRAMING

It is requisite that I provide clarity around definitions and concepts related to American Indian education in the United States that ground this work. In doing so, I acknowledge the enduring reality of colonization and its ongoing oppressive legacy that extends to the way we name and describe people. The people who lived on the lands now called the United States named themselves and constructed ways of knowing and being long before colonizers arrived from Europe and imposed new names and ways of knowing and being.

Terms used to describe Native peoples are contested and continue to change. In naming and defining terms, I acknowledge that I am choosing some terms and not choosing others that people use to name and refer to themselves or their shared understanding of community. As Lomawaima and McCarty (2006) point out, "Personal identity among Native peoples is often layered: rooted in a particular tribe; encompassing a shared American Indian identity and expressed in intersecting layers of tribal, state, and national citizenship" (p. 8). Like Brayboy et al. (2015), I acknowledge that on its own, the term "Indigenous" does not describe the unique histories of each people group or the relationships they have to the land that existed "long before the United States and any political relationship between it and tribal nations existed" (p. 8). When I use the terms "Indigenous" or "Native" when referring to the people and people groups who inhabited what is now the United States prior to colonization, I recognize the shortcomings of such general terms and acknowledge the array of unique peoples and histories that the terms describe. There will also be times I will use other encompassing terms like "Native American" or "American Indian," particularly when these terms are used in policy or in the context being described. When possible, I refer directly to the Dakota people and use the terminology individuals in Santee used to name and describe themselves.

When describing the lands currently governed by a Native people group in the United States, I will use the term "Indian Country" or "tribal lands," which includes reservations. I will also use terms like "tribal nation" when referring to the body of people to self-identify as part of an Indigenous tribe, whether Indigenous individuals live in Indian Country or not. It is important here to also acknowledge that there are many tribal nations that are not recognized by the U.S. federal government and many that do not have designated reservation lands.

Tribal Sovereignty

Each tribal nation has a particular history and culture that includes language, tradition of governance, education, and a specific history of its relationship with the colonizers who arrived in North America, and later, relationship with the U.S. federal government and state governments (Brayboy et al., 2015; Hopkins, 2020). Not all tribes are recognized by an official relationship with the U.S. government. Those tribes that are recognized have a government-to-government relationship that acknowledges the tribe as a sovereign nation (Brayboy et al., 2015; Castagno et al., 2016). The acknowledgment of sovereignty and its "right of a people to self-government, self-determination, and self-education" sets apart Indigenous peoples from other minoritized people groups in U.S. history (Lomawaima

& McCarty, 2006, p. 9). In short, as sovereign nations, "Native peoples possess governmental, political, and economic control over their own lands and communities" (Hopkins, 2020, p. xvii). These rights, however, do not mean that a tribe is completely independent. As Wilkins and Lomawaima (2001) point out, the status of tribal nations, embedded within the United States and functioning in interdependence with federal and state governments, does not nullify the inherent right to sovereignty. These relationships among tribal nations and state and the federal government remain contested today, as evidenced with the release of the Supreme Court decision in *Oklahoma v. Castro-Huerta* at the time of this writing (2023).

Education

Tribal sovereignty includes the right to self-education (Brayboy et al., 2015; Brayboy & Castagno, 2009; Castagno et al., 2016; Manuelito, 2005). I draw a distinction between the term "education," describing a holistic experience of teaching and learning that takes place inside and outside formal school structures in a community, and the term "schooling," describing students' experiences in K–12 public and private schools (Goodlad et al., 2004; Hopkins, 2020; Lomawaima & McCarty, 2006; Pewewardy et al., 2018). In Indigenous communities, an education is inclusive of Native ways of being and knowing that have been passed down across generations as well as the schooling requirements set forth by the state and federal governments. Balancing the desires and expectations among tribal members to educate young people in the tribe with schooling mandates external to the tribe is a complex task that has been and continues to be mediated in unique and context-specific ways. Adding to this background is the reality that most Native students (nearly 90%) attend public schools that are governed by local school boards and state government (Brayboy et al., 2015) rather than by the federal government or a tribal government. What seems to be common across tribal communities, however, is a belief that education in its most holistic sense is essential to ensuring the future of tribal nations, and an ongoing challenge for Indigenous children to access high-quality, culturally responsive schooling experiences (Anthony-Stevens, 2017; Brayboy et al., 2015; Castagno et al., 2016; Pewewardy et al., 2022).

Decolonization and Space

Undergirding these questions of access and cultural-responsiveness is the ongoing legacy of settler colonialism. I draw on both Nayar (2010) and Tuck and Yang's (2012) definitions of settler colonialism or the seizure of Native peoples', lands, cultures, and their exploitation by European colonizers. Wolfe (2006) distinguishes between violent examples of settler colonialism and the strategies employed in the cultural genocide of Indigenous peoples in the United States (e.g., forced removal, military invasion) with "softer" examples (e.g., policy, state intervention) that gradually diminish tribal knowledges, identities, and ways of being. Tuck and Yang (2012) assert that settler colonialism remains reflected in educational organizations (e.g., governance, curriculum, assessment) and the knowledge and data used to validate educational structures that perpetuate inequities. In these ways the influence of settler colonialism endures in the current federal education policy toward Indigenous peoples in the United States. Education policy efforts with each generation have included more examples of affirming practices that have welcomed Indigenous languages and ways of being along with ever-persistent efforts to oppress, marginalize, and attempt to erase. In his study of education policy intended to decolonize indigenous education in Montana, Hopkins (2020) describes the ongoing presence of settler colonial influence in education policy as the *dominant colonizing voice*. Like Hopkins, I assert that within state education policy, this dominant colonial influence endures and must be disrupted. Decolonization reflects the agency and tactics employed to resist and dismantle colonizing systems of power and oppression and to claim space, identities, culture, histories, and territories (Grande, 2015; Hopkins, 2020; Tuck & Yang, 2012). Throughout this book I highlight the colonizing and decolonizing policy strategies employed, the ways that policy shaped schooling spaces in Santee, and the tactics used to reconstitute power and space during policy implementation.

I draw upon Low and Lawrence-Zuñiga's (2003) and Low's (2009, 2014) works in urban anthropology to consider space and the way power manifests in policy spaces. Low (2014) asserts that spatial analysis is a tool that surfaces social injustice, and thus the lens of space allows us to consider the constructs and distribution of power in "contested spaces" (Low and Lawrence-Zuñiga, 2003, p. 18) and the "spatial tactics" (Phillips & Gray, 2021) actors employ to author and reconstitute space in the pursuit of "spatial justice" (Soja, 2010). I use the term "space" to describe physical places (e.g., land, school buildings) as well as figurative ones (e.g., decision-making, policy, values).

Schooling is an institution and by its very construction is a space containing power and constraint (Goffman, 1959). Within Indigenous communities and contexts, school has been used as a tool of colonialism, control, assimilation, and cultural genocide on one side of the pendulum swing and as one of revitalization and self-education on the other (Lomawaima & McCarty, 2006). Documenting the state's intervention in a public school on the Santee Sioux Reservation illuminates policy spaces (physical and figurative) that both colonize and confine, and the agentic decolonizing tactics practiced by educators and community members to redistribute power and reconstitute space. Kuper's (1972) foundational explorations of the politics of space delineated between "the concept of space" and the "experience of space," highlighting the values, experience, and culture that is woven within the fabric of space. As I have done previously (Phillips, 2021) I draw upon Kuper's notion of figurative space as both concept and experience in Indigenous education policy.

Survivance

Survivance is one strategy Native students, families, and communities have practiced to confront the enduring legacy of colonization in the schools and to act to decolonize public schooling spaces. In a conversation with scholars Eve Tuck and K. Wayne Yang (2014), Indigenous scholar Gerald Vizenor described *survivance* as "an intergenerational connection to an individual and collective sense of presence and resistance in personal experience and the world, or language, particularly through stories" (p. 107). The term itself, a combination of the words *survival* and *resistance*, carries a deeper connotation that includes creative practices of agency, or as Morrill (2017), describes, "Indigenous creative approaches to life beyond genocide, beyond the bareness of survival" (p. 15). Indigenous survivance, first defined by Vizenor (1999), acknowledges colonialism while also acting to decolonize spaces through an "active sense of presence" (p. vii) that rejects deficit framing or pathology and celebrates strength, history, culture, and vitality.

Leilani Sabzalian, in *Indigenous Children's Survivance* (2019), highlights the persistent and creative ways that students, educators, families, and community members in Indian Country assert agency as they practice survivance in schooling contexts. As Sabzalian points out, survivance is expressed in the macro and micro, from larger policy reforms like the Indigenous education efforts in Western states like Montana and Oregon or in "the small, everyday, and future-oriented acts of Native students, families, and educators negotiating the colonial contexts of public schools" (Sabzalian, 2019, p. xv). I explore stories of survivance in the context of the state's oversight in rapid school improvement in Santee. I also borrow from John P. Hopkins's (2020) book *Indian Education for All*, where he describes the importance of "decolonizing conversations" as a practice of survivance. Extending the idea of "decolonizing conversations," I (a) consider Indigenous voices in policy spaces, the possibility of culturally responsive policymaking as a creative expression of survivance, (b) explore critical moments of policymaking and implementation that continue to colonize, and (c) surface the possibilities and practicalities of policymaking and implementation that are culturally sustaining (McCarty & Lee, 2014).

SCHOOL POLICY REFORM IN INDIAN COUNTRY

Broadly, education policy toward Indigenous peoples in the United States has attempted to eliminate identity, culture, and community (Lomawaima

& McCarty, 2006; Noel, 2002; Wilkins & Lomawaima, 2001; Wyman, 2012). However, there are strong examples chronicled in the literature about policy done *with*, rather than *to*, Indigenous peoples (e.g., Barnhardt & Kawagley, 2005; Nelson-Barber & Johnson, 2019; Sabzalian et al., 2019). Top-down, external improvement mandates and their associated prescriptions to "fix" schools have resulted in narrowed, less culturally responsive educational experiences for American Indian students (Castagno & Brayboy, 2008). In the standards-accountability reform era, schools have placed performance on standardized tests above pedagogically sound or culturally based instruction, which harms Native students' academic achievement (Brayboy & Maaka, 2015; Castagno & Brayboy, 2008; Demmert, 2001; McCarty & Lee, 2014; Nelson-Barber & Lipka, 2008). This kind of approach also "compromises tribal sovereignty and Indigenous community choice" (Beaulieu et al., 2005, p. 4) over time. Since the colonization of American Indian lands, tribes have fought for recognition of their sovereignty, the right to self-govern, and the right to determine what constitutes a good education (Brayboy et al., 2015; Lomawaima & McCarty, 2006).

A federally recognized American Indian Tribal Nation, the Santee Dakota Sioux have a unique relationship with both federal and state government entities. Despite stated intentions among legislators and policymakers in Nebraska to improve failing schools for the sake of every child every day, and to glean lessons that might be applied to support schools in similar contexts, the "policy culture" (Stein, 2004, p. 19) that developed in Nebraska's state school accountability and school turnaround implementation efforts undermined local trust and further marginalized a community with a colonizing history of outside experts determining what schooling should look like in Indian Country. This case of legislatively mandated school accountability reform in Nebraska underscores both the challenging nature of complex school reform, the possible roles for state departments of education (SDE) to advance equity in real and meaningful ways, and the survivance stories of Indigenous students, families, and educators asserting agency and reclaiming space. These are realities that are hardly unique to one flyover state.

POLICY CULTURE AND CULTURALLY SUSTAINING POLICYMAKING

A growing body of evidence indicates that culturally responsive models are improving outcomes for American Indian students (Brayboy & Castagno, 2009). Policy approaches responsive to cultural context affirm both language and culture as foundational to constructing knowledge (Balter & Grossman, 2009; Castagno & Brayboy, 2008; Lipka & McCarty, 1994). There were critical moments throughout the development and implementation of school accountability and state-directed school improvement efforts in Nebraska that provided glimpses of the possibilities of culturally responsive policymaking. It is worth scrutinizing how policy cultures develop in order to consider practical implications for cultivating culturally responsive policymaking (Castagno & Brayboy, 2008). In this way, I extend Sandra Stein's (2004) *Culture of Education Policy* and the necessary commitment to overcome a policy culture that frames beneficiaries as "other."

Like Stein (2004), I too followed an implementation from a piece of complex school accountability reform in its legislative drafting, debate, and codification into law, to its development and implementation. Stein asserts that policy has often framed its beneficiaries as the "other," employing deviant or deficit frames and positioning the government (or in this case the SDE) as a "corrective force" (p. 19). She describes the othering approach as a "policy culture" (p. 19). *Culturally Sustaining Policymaking in Indigenous Communities* scrutinizes how individuals throughout the strata of policymaking and implementation viewed individuals at other tiers. Like Stein (2004), I posit that if equity is going to be advanced through educational reforms, the policy cultures of these reforms must evolve in their commitment to equity through "purposeful work on the cultural dimensions of schooling [that] address[es] complex considerations of students' strengths and needs" (p. 24–25), rather than pointing to "policy beneficiaries as deviant" (Stein, 2004, p. 17).

Nebraska's foray into state accountability and its intervention efforts in Santee provide a glimpse into the policy culture of an SDE in one state, in one window of policy development and implementation. However, SDEs working alongside Native communities to support schools is hardly singular to one state or a single education policy reform effort. As such, this case highlights policy questions around who should get to define what a good education looks like, what support for schools in sovereign Native spaces looks like in practice, and what implications from the case in Nebraska might have relevance beyond the state's borders.

METHODOLOGY AND POSITIONALITY

Studying a single case of school accountability policy reform allows deep exploration and the opportunity to interrogate nuance and establish patterns with germane meanings for other places. For me, Nebraska's case provided proximity and access, and yet situating myself in this book is complicated professionally and personally.

Professionally, I worked at the Nebraska Department of Education (NDE) between 2014 and 2017, and served as NDE's liaison to Santee Community School from January 2016 until I left NDE in August 2017. In those years I spent more than 200 hours in the village of Santee and many more engaged with school personnel and local school board members through emails, phone calls, text messages, and Zoom sessions. Navigating the role of liaison and researcher presented challenges. I am not Dakota, and my participation could only be partial, not only as an outsider, but an outsider who represented the state. I was keenly aware of the freighted history of those who had come before me in this kind of liaison role. I was transparent with educators and community members in Santee and with my colleagues and supervisors at NDE about the tensions inherent to my liaison and researcher roles. I also raised questions and critiques of the state's implementation with NDE based on my observations from SCS during the months I served in the liaison role.

I was authorized to chronicle what I observed in the NDE's implementation in the local school, and I made my dual roles of NDE employee and researcher clear when in Santee, in my interactions with individuals in the school and community. While my role provided access, making it possible to be present in public meetings and to document what unfolded as policy moved across tiers of the education system, from the legislative chambers, to the state board of education and NDE, and eventually to the hallways and classrooms in Santee, it is also important to acknowledge that there were conversations and meetings for which I was not present. Like anthropologist Laura Nader (1972), I contend that "most Americans do not know enough about, nor do they know how to cope with, the people, institutions, and organizations which most affect their lives" (p. 294). Thus, my approach attends particularly to the institutions and organizations that make policy, the people who make them up, and the culture that is developed along the way. Nader (1972) called this "studying up." (For more detailed information about my methodology, I would point readers to Phillips [2017].)

Personally, I also have struggled to know where to situate myself in relation to the state's intervention at *iSanti Community School.* Until two generations ago, my family lived in northeastern Oklahoma, active citizens of Cherokee Nation. I grew up with stories about my grandmother's family, about our long history educators across generations. That her father was Cherokee was known but not discussed, and it was not until I was an adult that I learned that he taught and served as a principal in Pryor, Oklahoma, before moving his family to Tulsa where he began work with the postal service. In decisions or circumstances lost to time, sometime in my great-grandfather's generation, he distanced himself from his Cherokee identity. I have found it complicated to publicly incorporate Cherokee among my identities two generations later, hesitant to be considered a "racial shifter," one who reclaims or even appropriates Native identity, as Circe Sturm (2011) describes in *Becoming Indian: The Struggle Over Cherokee Identity in the Twenty-first Century.* Privately, just as I have my great-grandfather's Oklahoma teaching certificate, issued in 1923, hanging on the wall of my office, I cannot separate my educator heritage from the knowledge that his schooling and teaching happened in Indian Country. I carry this history and the knowledge of this legacy with me, and did so with each visit to Santee and through the writing of each page of this book.

OVERVIEW OF CHAPTERS

Chapter 1: So What? Lessons Learned and Why They Matter

The first chapter provides a broad overview of recent education policy and the shifting role of state departments of education as a result of federal policies as they intervene in local communities and try to turn around schools that are identified as struggling. It provides a foundation on the construct of "policy culture" (Stein, 2004) that supports ongoing analysis of the policy culture in Nebraska's case. It explores the intersections of space, power, and agency (Phillips & Gray, 2021) and includes a critique on the limitations of what a state department of education can do to transform schools.

Chapter 2: Welcome to Flyover Country

Nebraska came to be known as an education policy renegade state following the passage of *No Child Left Behind* and the state's resistance to enacting the federal legislation (Gallagher, 2007; Ruff, 2019). The second chapter situates the reader in the context of the state's recent education policy history and the policy cultures that developed as a result. It explores the role of the legislature, the state board of education (SBOE), and the Nebraska Department of Education and the dynamics among state and federal education policy and its impact on local school districts. This chapter also describes a rationale for why the lessons learned in flyover country in a state with a small American Indian population relative to other Plains states (e.g., South Dakota, North Dakota, Oklahoma) matter outside the state's boundaries, particularly in relationship to pursuit of "serious democracy" (Freire, 1998).

Chapter 3: A Broader Story Than the Village of Santee

Chapter 3 explores the sociohistorical and sociopolitical relevance of this particular policy implementation through the juxtaposition of the chronologies of American Indian history at-large with the Santee Dakota Sioux. The goal of this chapter is to explore the relationship between education policy done *to* rather than *with* Native peoples and concepts like sovereignty, self-determination, self-education, and survivance. It also examines the ways agency has been asserted and power contested in the face of policy constraint. It discusses what constitutes a "good education," who should define what that means in schooling spaces in Indian Country, and the imprudence of ignoring local voices and knowledge.

Chapter 4: Policy Crafted on the Legislative Floor

This chapter explores legislative policy spaces, recent education policy reforms, and their neoliberal influences on the roles of SBOEs as they intervene in local school districts. The chapter traces the development of school accountability policy and its evolution in the Legislature; it describes an evolving policy culture that encompasses a shift away from a culture that once reflected a measure of resistance to federal policy aims and a dedication to a "Nebraska Way" of engaging multiple voices in the co-construction of policy. It describes how it came to pass that a state board of education intervened in local schools, how schools in Indian Country were considered in the evolving legislation that led to intervention in Santee, and whose voices were present and invited to participate in official policy spaces.

Chapter 5: Nebraska's AQuESTT: Bolder, Broader, Better

Chapter 5 discusses the state's role in local school improvement as a pursuit of democracy through the enactment of school accountability policy and turnaround efforts. The new Accountability for a Quality Education System Today and Tomorrow reform effort came to be known as AQuESTT in the state. Specifically, the chapter includes an analysis of the roles of the SBOE and the state department of education. It scrutinizes critical moments that shaped the policy culture as it moved from statute to implementation. The chapter explores concepts of governance and sovereignty and interrogates policy aims and intentions in contrast to the intended as well as unintended consequences of enacting policy, particularly in Indian Country.

Chapter 6: Run by Outsiders

This chapter chronicles the intersections (and incongruity) of policy when it becomes practice in local contexts. It discusses intervention in Santee and the structures of power within the implementation, scrutinizing how state leaders, intermediaries, and hired consultants conceptualized local educators and community members in Santee whether they were viewed as co-decisionmakers or as objects of mandates they had no voice in developing. The chapter details how external intervention collided with local visions for a good education. It critiques the ways the improvement efforts in Santee reflected or did not reflect a policy culture committed to social justice and discusses the possibilities for culturally sustaining policymaking and implementation.

Chapter 7: Compliance, Kind Of

The seventh chapter analyzes agentic practices among students, teachers, and community members to both comply with and, at the same time, resist state-led efforts in Santee. It discusses the remaking of policy spaces and systems of power through the agentic acts at the local level and what that means to democracy and education. It also revisits the themes of survivance, sovereignty, and self-determination that are foundational to cultivating culturally sustaining policy and practice in Indian Country.

Chapter 8: Wait, What Just Happened?

The final chapter in the book includes a synthesis and reflection on the lessons that can be gleaned from Nebraska's state-led intervention in Santee and discusses the relevance of lessons learned to places beyond flyover country. The chapter concludes with future education policymaking and implementation implications for culturally responsive/sustaining policymaking committed to democracy.

As you read, you will see that individuals with publicly named roles (e.g., senators, school board members, Commissioner of Education) are frequently mentioned by name; these names are in the public record. Conversely, policy intermediaries employed by NDE, or public school district personnel, are often referred to by their role (e.g., Principal, Consultant) or by a pseudonym. Some of the pseudonyms used come directly from the common ways individuals in Santee described particular external actors coming into the school (e.g., The Lady from North Carolina). I make this distinction because those in public roles are acting in public; their actions are part of the public record and, in Nebraska, their meetings are subject to open meeting laws intended to provide transparency to the public. While it would be possible to identify many education department or school district employees from the public record or newspaper and media accounts, these individuals are not public actors; they are policy actors and educators. Naming these individuals by role or pseudonym provided anonymity in the writing of this book while also illuminating how actors negotiate policy throughout the education system.

I am aware my critical analysis may not frame all the actors in the most favorable light. I write from the "posture" (Wolcott, 1988) that I do, convinced both that there is a value in revealing the hidden processes of hegemony and that the actors depicted did want what was best, even if their concept of what that might be was more the product of longstanding, potent national policy currents than a considered understanding that honored self-determination and, broadly, what schools *should* do. In short, I write to illuminate the structures of the larger systems at work and interrogate how they function in advancing or not advancing equity and social justice in local contexts like Santee.

CHAPTER 1

So What? Lessons Learned and Why They Matter

Just as democracy in the United States ever evolves, the institution of public education has been directed toward a range of purposes, including the preparation of democratic citizens, the development of a competitive workforce, and ensuring equity and access to opportunities in society, among others (Labaree, 2010). As perceived societal needs shift, what is demanded from the education system also shifts, and thus the landscape of education policy is ever-changing (Berliner & Biddle, 1995). With each wave of school reform, policymakers and reformers offer proposed solutions to the perceived problems of the era. Policymakers (e.g., legislators, elected boards), are usually democratically elected or appointed; along with education reformers, they design policy solutions and mobilize coalitions to make changes happen (Cuban, 2003). This notion of intention and design is central to the reform I will describe in Nebraska, as the following chapters will describe the way policy was developed in view of national trends in education policy, state-level policy considerations, and perceived local needs, and how that policy was actualized in Santee.

Education policy travels throughout the system to reach those for whom the policy was intended (Stein, 2004). What makes the movement of policy across tiers of the system to local implementation even more complex is the loosely coupled education system in the United States (Labaree, 2010). Power is diffused across 50 states with different state constitutions and school governance models, and a range of control over policy, curriculum, and practices from the state to local level (Heck, 2004, p. 38). These structures shape how school reform policy is developed and implemented across a policy continuum covering federal, state, and local levels. While Nebraska's state accountability policy effort affected every school in the state, placing each school and district in one of four classifications based on outcomes (described more in Chapter 5) in order to hold schools accountable for student achievement, its core stated intention was to intervene in schools that were "failing" to succeed according to the accountability system's formula.

Before moving on to discuss the case of school accountability reform in Nebraska, however, it is requisite to think about the structures of power that exist in policymaking and the way policies are implemented throughout the education system, particularly when a state has the power to label and rank schools in the public space. Policymakers and intended recipients of policy act within a policy power construct. My approach to policy study is decidedly critical, attending to the structures of power within and across systems and the agents across those systems (e.g., legislators, SDE intermediaries, teachers, students, community members).

While policy is developed and implemented within systems of power, policy is also an expression of democracy. Education policy requires that people act collectively to agree on a common course of action. Understanding the processes that allow people to come together and act is central to understanding how policy will move across the system and ultimately be implemented in local contexts (Heck, 2004). Policymaking and policy implementation are more than utilitarian processes or simply governmental actions focused on a particular problem; they are socially constructed activities where actors engage in dialogue, negotiation, and compromise (Cuban, 2013; Heck, 2004; Ozga, 2009). While some policymakers believe that the system of education can easily be mapped and policy implementation drafted into a flowchart, schools and reform efforts require the engagement of humans who bring their own positionality, opinions, expertise, and agency to policy.

Honig (2006) used the metaphor of waves to describe policy development and implementation with the periodic rising attention on a perceived public problem, the efforts of individuals to craft and implement a plan to address the stated problem. The formal study of these waves of educational policy and implementation began in the 1960s as the federal government sought to ensure that the investments in programs outlined in federal policy were implemented effectively (Berman & McLaughlin, 1978). Much of the early policy studies focused on understanding why a particular effort was successful or failed (Smylie & Evans, 2006). The next wave considered the ways that context influences implementation in an effort to avoid patterns of policy pitfalls and to develop better policy (Honig, 2006). The following wave shifted from study of a policy and its delivery toward "the ways in which local actors influenced implementation" (Smylie & Evans, 2006, p. 187). Following the release of *A Nation at Risk* (1983), policy implementation study concentrated on "ensuring full implementation" and "demonstrable improvements in students' performance" (Honig, 2006, p. 8). Policy implementation study then shifted to examining education as a system and ensuring alignment and coherence between and across levels of the system (Clune, 1993; Coburn & Stein, 2006; Jenkins, 2008; O'Day & Smith, 1993).

In recent decades, however, much dissatisfaction has been directed at dominant methods of studying political, organizational, and educational processes. Criticism suggests that these lenses have not been entirely satisfactory either in understanding policy activities or assessing education reform's impact on social change (Heck, 2004). As a result, the field of education policy research has widened to include critical theory as well as methodologies from anthropology (e.g., Hamann & Rosen, 2011; Honig, 2006; Sutton & Levinson, 2001; Ozga, 2009). With new analytical tools, education policy implementation study can be situated within sociocultural and sociohistorical contexts (Dumas & Anyon, 2006). Accordingly, implementation study now aims to "reveal the policies, people, and places that shape how implementation unfolds and provide robust, grounded explanations for how interactions among them help to explain implementation outcomes" (Honig, 2006, p. 2). This is my approach to studying policy development and implementation, an approach that considers the nuances of the people, places, and dynamics that shaped Nebraska's school accountability policy and implementation in Santee. The education policy dynamics in Nebraska are influenced by recent policy trends in the United States. Thus, we must first zoom out to chronicle education policy history since No Child Left Behind (NCLB) and more recent trends in education reform as it will relate to the way reforms came to be expressed in Nebraska education policy, as described in Chapter 2.

I borrow Honig's wave metaphor and map it onto the history of education policy in the United States, particularly policy related to complex school reform and the role state departments of education have assumed in these reform efforts. Historically, schooling in the United States has been a local and state-level endeavor, with state constitutions requiring the establishment of public schools (Greene, 1985; Russell, 1929). Only within recent decades has the federal government assumed a more significant role in public schooling. State departments of education (SDEs) bear the responsibility of carrying out federal requirements (a shift following the passage of NCLB) while they also develop and implement their own policies and reforms. While some SDEs have more centralized control over public schooling in their states, Nebraska has maintained a long tradition of local school district control governed by elected local boards of education. On a range from local to national, local boards have historically governed schools, districts and state departments of education have assumed a regulatory role, and the federal government had very little role until the mid-20th century (Cantor, 1980; Fuhrman & Elmore, 1990). In recent decades, the federal role in education has grown and SDEs have become mediators of federal funding and policy mandates as well as enactors of state-level policy, particularly when it comes to accountability (Hamann & Lane, 2004; Lane & Garcia, 2005; Mehan, 2005). Districts and local boards have maintained some local control in states, but these schools and districts must also navigate wide-ranging reporting, accountability, and policy mandates and strive to bring coherence to divergent policy aims.

A shift in policy approach to school accountability at the federal level has led to a shift in the role of policymakers and policy intermediaries (employees) at state departments of education (discussed briefly in the Introduction). Individuals at the SDE and in local districts and schools, where policy is transformed into practice, act in a space of sensemaking, where individuals create, interpret, and remake policy (Weick, 1995). The iterations of sensemaking continue as people move ideas into practice in sociocultural spaces such as board rooms or classrooms. Actors appropriate reform policy and make it their own (Sutton & Levinson, 2001). It is by examining educational policy implementation through a sociocultural lens that we illuminate the ways that people make sense of policy and re-author it as they enact it. It allows us to gain understanding of the ways policy impacts people and how we can better inform future policy and make policymaking and implementation more democratic (Datnow et al., 2002; Sutton & Levinson, 2001). Again, I borrow from Freire (1998) when I define democracy in education as meaning both education for democracy and democracy for education. I also borrow from philosopher and democratic theorist Amy Gutmann (1999) who states that democracy is built upon dialogue, deliberation, and consensus. Gutmann's descriptions of deliberative democracy, when extended, include more critical ways of thinking about democracy and invite a greater diversity of voices in democratic processes while challenging extant structures of power. Thus, my explorations of policy, power, space, and agency provide insight into the way democracy is being expressed.

ACCOUNTABILITY: WHAT CAME BEFORE

Calls for accountability and this shift along the national to local continuum resulted from a perception that U.S. schools were falling behind. Beginning with fears that the Soviet Union was surpassing the United States with the launch of Sputnik in 1957 to the release of A Nation at Risk in 1983, and ongoing federal education accountability legislation with No Child Left Behind and the Every Student Succeeds Act, America's fixation on measuring and ranking its education system against other nation states endures. One lens of accountability draws upon a neoliberal narrative that holds that schools function to produce skilled workers ready to enter the economic machine of a society. A contrasting narrative regards schooling as a way to ensure equitable entrée to a democratic society where a citizen is prepared to engender democratic dispositions. In considering accountability systems, one must ask questions such as: What is the purpose of schooling? For what outcomes ought educators in school be held accountable? How can such outcomes be measured or assessed?

Where schools were once accountable to their local community and governing board, schools in the United States today are accountable to state and federal accountability systems. Conversations about the purpose of schooling and how to measure outcomes are now being held on legislative floors in Washington, DC, and in state legislatures and departments of education across the United States. Following complex school reform initiatives that came about in the 1990s, much of the focus of school reform has been on reforming the system, rather than implementing stand-alone programs targeting specific schools or the student groups they serve (Lane & Garcia, 2005; Lusi, 1997). Systems reform efforts continued to expand as the federal influence on local education increased under NCLB as states implemented school improvement grants tied to the law and developed their own state accountability systems and interventions aligned to both *Race to the Top* and Requests for ESEA Flexibility. These second-generation accountability systems, along with the federal government situating itself as responsible for the kinds of interventions in local schools through school improvement grants (SIGs) implemented in states demonstrated a new federal role in education and a new role for state departments of education in mediating federal policy in local school districts.

The federal role in school accountability advanced in the late 1980s and early 1990s, as a new reform wave emerged following a meeting of President George H. W. Bush and the nation's governors in Charlottesville, Virginia, in September 1989. This meeting was the impetus for the drafting of the National Educational Goals (Cohen, 1995; Elmore, 2003; Vinovskis, 2003). Two years later, under the direction of Secretary of Education Lamar Alexander, President Bush unveiled *America 2000*. It proposed a series of systemic reform initiatives including voluntary national standards and assessments and "break the mold" schools established through the federal grants through the American Schools Development Corporation (Fuhrman, 2003; Vinovskis, 2003).

The objectives of *America 2000*, with its emphasis on a standards-based approach to school reform and market-based strategies, continued under both the *Goals 2000: Educate America Act,* signed into law by President Bill Clinton in 1994, and the reauthorization of ESEA, the *Improving America's Schools Act,* passed that same year (Fuhrman, 2003; Linn, 2007). *Goals 2000* called for standards-based reforms that would include creating content standards and assessments at the state level (Vinovskis, 2003). In this phase of standards-based reforms, policymakers proposed greater local school autonomy coupled with higher levels of accountability. Those schools that demonstrated their effectiveness were rewarded with increased autonomy; those schools that struggled would experience greater oversight (Fuhrman, 2003).

In response to these national policy trends, SDEs employed a standards-assessment approach that rewarded successes or punished teachers or principals if schools did not demonstrate improvement, under a belief that if educators were held to a high standard of academic expectation while implementing standards-aligned curricula, they would get students to demonstrate their mastery on standardized assessments (Cuban & Usdan, 2003). This resulted in states adopting content and performance standards and high-stakes tests, except in cases like Maine, which created "a 'low-stakes' test" (Hamann & Lane, 2004, p. 436) or Nebraska, which developed local assessments (Dappen & Isernhagen, 2005; Gallagher, 2007). While a movement to standards reform was celebrated by business and industry (Cuban, 2003), others warned that the prescribed reforms would oblige schools to focus on teaching to the test and would only exacerbate bias against schools serving poor and minoritized students (Berliner & Biddle, 1995).

NO CHILD LEFT BEHIND

After a decade of district and state reform efforts that leveraged systemic reform around either common standards and assessments or, conversely, more decentralized, district-level reform, legislators in Washington, DC, debated a more prominent federal role with the drafting of the 2001 bill to reauthorize the *Elementary and Secondary Education Act* (ESEA): *No Child Left Behind*. Before this time, lawmakers were hesitant to centralize educational reform or accountability, recognizing the diversity of communities, unique needs, and governance structures across states and local districts that presented a challenge to prescribing educational reform that could adequately meet the needs of such contrasting contexts with a singular prescribed solution (Cohen, 1995; Gordon, 2003; Labaree, 2010).

With bipartisan support and under the leadership of President George W. Bush's administration, the *No Child Left Behind Act* was signed into law on January 8, 2002, drastically changing public education in the United States (Vinovskis, 2003; Weiner, 2007). For the first time, the federal government was "the chief enforcer of performance-based accountability at the state and local level" (Elmore, 2003, p. 27). NCLB provided more funding for Title I; called for stricter accountability; included penalties for schools that did not meet expectations; and emphasized performance standards, assessments, and research-based interventions and reforms (Cuban, 2003; Linn, 2007; Vinovskis, 2003). It called for annual public reporting of school performance. Data were to be disaggregated by targeted sub-groups including poverty, race, ethnicity, disability, and English learners to ensure that no group was left behind (Sleeter, 2007). In a similar approach to state accountability efforts in the 1990s, policymakers believed that if held more accountable, teachers and principals would ensure that students met higher standards while also closing achievement gaps (Hall & Parker, 2007).

Some of the unintended consequences of NCLB included emphasizing the "deficiencies of schools and students while deemphasizing collaborative and proactive interventions at the school level" (Hall & Parker, 2007, p. 132). Schools were labeled as "failing" for not meeting performance benchmarks included in the law such as adequate yearly progress (AYP). Schools employed a variety of responses to boost test scores, including remediation for students not meeting proficiency, increasing instructional time in tested areas such as reading and math, changing instructional strategies, selecting new curriculum, allocating time for test preparation, bringing in outside coaching or expertise, creating rewards or sanctions for teachers not meeting performance goals, and (unfortunately, in a few cases) cheating (Dee et al., 2012; Weinbaum et al., 2012). Over time, this exacerbated the contrast between the curriculum and instructional approaches available to more privileged students in schools not worried about looking good on annual assessments and those offered to students in schools on the low end of assessments that risked sanctions (McNeil, 2000).

NCLB LIMBO

As the clock ticked toward a 2014 100% proficiency requirement for all students under NCLB, pressures on Congress to pass a long-overdue reauthorization of ESEA increased.

During this NCLB limbo, school reform efforts included charter school and choice movements supported by the Obama Administration's *Race to the Top* competitive grant program, the implementation of rigorous college- and career- ready Common Core State Standards, as well as Requests for ESEA Flexibility also extended under the Obama Administration.

Charter Schools and Choice

Milton Friedman's 1955 essay "The Role of Government in Education," which proposed that families should be able to select a school of their choice and use a voucher from the state to support their attendance at their chosen school, became a foundation for school choice advocates (Ravitch, 2010). For those who saw public schools as failing, school choice through vouchers, which would allow students to carry funding to a school of choice, offered parents an option to choose a private school over a public one (Noddings, 2013). Under the Reagan administration there was support for vouchers for low-performing students, but national teachers' unions opposed vouchers and school choice, seeing it as a neoliberal threat to public education (Ravitch, 2010). Minnesota was the first state to implement an open enrollment program, allowing students to transfer into any district by the 1990s. This policy shift followed the publication of Chubb and Moe's

Politics, Markets, and America's Schools, for the Brookings Institution, where school choice was positioned as the panacea for an education system that was seen as "incapable of reforming itself" (Ravitch, 2010, p. 118). The school choice movement was built upon the notion that the marketplace is more efficient at promoting school effectiveness, providing greater accountability for schools.

Charter schools emerged as part of the school choice movement. Often publicly funded but operating with less oversight or accountability to rules and regulations than their public school counterparts, charter schools have had bipartisan appeal (Noddings, 2013). Under NCLB, charter schools were often seen as a remedy for areas where schools were labeled as failing. The idea grew from a vision that teacher-led schools under a charter could innovate in working with students that historically had not been served well by schools (Ravitch, 2013). Out of this initial vision, however, grew the private sector's investment in charter schools. Both charter schools and large charter school management organizations expanded under the Obama Administration. While CREDO's 2012 study of charter schools across the United States highlighted modest gains in student performance on English language arts assessments, overall comparisons between charters and traditional public schools show little evidence that charter schools provide better educational experiences or outcomes than public schools that enroll similar student populations (Brighouse & Schouten, 2014; Ravitch, 2013; Zimmer et al., 2012).

The school choice movement became one way that Native families asserted agency in choosing a school governed by tribal members or one implementing culturally sustaining practices. This approach that takes into account the sociohistorical and sociopolitical contexts present in Indigenous communities differs from school choice arguments framing parental and student decision-making as an individual choice primarily influenced by access to high-quality educational environments (Anthony-Stevens, 2017; Cullen et al., 2005). In Indian Country, families centered cultural tribal affiliation and academic performance when choosing a school (Anthony-Stevens, 2017; Castagno et al., 2016; Phillips, 2021).

There is a caveat when we describe school choice on American Indian reservations. Schooling has "not historically been centered upon offering youth and families *choices*. Instead, it has been about *control*—control of the schooling offered to Indigenous youth" (Castagno et al., 2016, p. 227). The research literature on school choice has not attended to the way choice is used in Tribal communities, and existing studies focus primarily on charter schools and not on other ways that families practice choice (Anthony-Stevens, 2017; Castagno et al., 2016; Fox & Buchanan, 2017). Native families consider children's academic success, but also their cultural membership and affiliation with the Tribe as core elements that guide their school choices (Anthony-Stevens, 2017; Castagno et al., 2016). Even when one school might be rated higher than another by state or federal accountability measures (e.g., higher test scores and graduation rates), Native families sometimes assert their agency in defining what a good school choice means for their children. Nebraska does not have charter schools or vouchers; however, students are able to option into a district outside their attendance catchment one time during their K–12 schooling. In this way, the state offers family choice. In Santee, this choice option means that many families on the reservation send their children to a neighboring school district off the reservation.

Race to the Top

Race to the Top (RttT), a voluntary, competitive grant, was offered to states by the U.S. Department of Education under the Obama administration in 2009–2010, providing $4.35 billion to awarded states (McGuinn, 2011; Onosko, 2011). RttT, according to McGuinn (2011) had two primary objectives: encouraging states to innovate in their school improvement reform efforts and supporting states in developing the capacity to implement their innovations. States' applications were evaluated using a 500-point scale related to how well the reforms proposed aligned with the U.S. Department of Education's priority areas: (a) developing common standards and assessments; (b) improving teacher training, evaluation, and retention policies; (c) creating better data systems; (d) and adopting preferred school-turnaround strategies (U.S. Department of Education, 2012). The theory of action behind the reform was built upon extending incentives and awarding winners or adopters of reform strategies that might motivate other states as well. In its implementation, RttT opened doors for states to implement charter schools, educator evaluations tied to merit pay, school choice programs, and turnaround models for low-performing schools, and invited private-sector actors and venture philanthropists to enter the education marketplace (McGuinn, 2011; Ravitch, 2010, 2013; Russakoff, 2015). Not only did the U.S Department of Education extend these grants to states, but also awarded $361 million to two assessment groups, Partnership for Assessment of Readiness for College and Careers (PARCC) and SMARTER Balanced Consortium, to "design and deliver national assessments aligned to the common national standards" (Onosko, 2011). According to Ravitch (2013), RttT demonstrated that there was bipartisan support for a new kind of education reform directed by the U.S Department of Education, philanthropic foundations, Wall Street, and major corporations. Without the reauthorization of ESEA, the Obama Administration's next reform effort intended to bypass NCLB, building upon what Secretary Duncan had unveiled in *Race to the Top*.

Common Core

The Common Core State Standards (CCSS), developed through the collaboration of the National Governors Association Center for Best Practices and the Council of Chief State School Officers (CCSSO), were released for English language arts and mathematics in 2010 (Porter et al., 2011). Developed to provide common expectations across states for grades K–12 that could be compared to other national and international standards, the standards also intended to create a common assessed curriculum (Porter et al., 2011). The standards, which were not field-tested prior to their implementation or their incorporation into RttT, were also supported by the private sector, because with a more standardized approach to schooling, there was greater scale to make money in a growing education marketplace (Butler, 2014; Ravitch, 2013). States selected which of the assessment groups (PARCC or Smarter Balanced) they would implement for statewide assessments. At one point, 46 states had adopted or partially adopted Common Core State Standards, with only four states never adopting the standards: Alaska, Nebraska, Texas, and Virginia (Ravitch, 2013). Berliner and Glass (2014) cautioned that CCSS were just another one of the prescribed policy solutions to "fix" a crisis that did not, in fact, exist and will further narrow the curriculum to what is assessed. Yong Zhao (2009), in his book *Catching Up for Leading the Way*, concurred, stating that even after 20 years of standards reform, the results were yet to be seen. The public also expressed concern as CCSS were implemented. Controversy regarding the standards caused some states to back out of their testing consortia and to return to their own state standards (Coburn et al., 2016).

State Requests for ESEA Flexibility

In an effort to provide states relief from the increasing sanctions of NCLB, the U.S. Department of Education under the leadership of Arne Duncan, Secretary of Education in the Obama administration, offered each state department of education an opportunity to request flexibility from some of the requirements of NCLB. These waivers were first introduced in September 2011, and required states to outline reforms aligned to four principles: (1) Raising expectations with college- and career-readiness standards and assessments; (2) implementing state-differentiated accountability systems for schools and districts; (3) implementing teacher and principal evaluation systems based on multiple measures that include student performance on assessments; and (4) reducing burden on local school districts (U.S. Department of Education, 2014). College- and career-ready standards incentivized states to continue their implementation of the Common Core and associated assessments. State-differentiated accountability systems brought about a wave of second-generation accountability in states intended to provide a parallel accountability system to what was required under NCLB. New accountability systems were still required to include student performance as measured by statewide assessments as well as reporting and measurable goals by federally reported sub-groups. Principle 3 required states to have both teacher and principal evaluation systems in place based on multiple measures, one of which must be tied to student performance on assessments in tested areas. The final principle incentivized states to continue to develop robust data and reporting systems intended to reduce burden on local districts (CCSSO, 2013; Polikoff et al., 2013; U.S. Department of Education, 2012). When ESEA was finally reauthorized in 2015 with the *Every Student Succeeds Act*, 45 states and the District of Columbia had approved waivers, with California, Montana, Nebraska, North Dakota, and Vermont the only non-waiver states.

THE ROLE OF STATE DEPARTMENTS OF EDUCATION

The design of school governance and structure in the United States places state departments of education (SDEs) in an important policy role in the allocation of state resources, the promulgation of rule, the regulation of local districts' adherence to rule and statute, and in more recent decades, the mediation of federal policies passed down from Washington, DC. (Heck, 2004). Since federal policy has reached further into state education systems (particularly since NCLB), the role of the SDE has shifted to meet new policy aims. The primary role of state departments of education had been the regulation of the state system to ensure that schools met a set of common requirements (accreditation), that teacher certification went forward appropriately, and that funding was disseminated to local districts (Cantor, 1980). As is evident in the reform chronology outlined above, the roles have shifted as federal policy has increasingly reached into state and local policy. What makes state-level mediation of federal policy development and implementation even more complex is the diversity of governance structures in place across 50 states. SDEs are a vital site at the intersection of policy and practice. According to Hamann and Lane (2004), this makes SDEs an important site for study, because they are "dominant within the hierarchy of K–12 education; hence, paying explicit attention to them allows for the examination of policy as the practice of power" (p. 429).

Drawing upon Susan Follett Lusi's (1997) case studies of complex school reform initiatives in Kentucky and Vermont 2 decades ago, I explore the engagement of the Nebraska Department of Education (NDE) in legislated school accountability reform. At the time of Lusi's study, the role of SDEs was shifting from sites of state regulation to support for system improvement and federal education policy mediation. Until the mid-1990s there had been little empirical study about what state departments of education do in relation to policy change. While an empirical focus on the SDE has increased (Hamann & Lane, 2004; Lane & Garcia, 2005; Mehan, 2005; Nichols & Cuenca, 2014; Phillips, 2017; Timar, 1997), it has not increased by much, despite the reality that the role of SDEs has continued to evolve.

I extend Lusi's work as I examine the shifting role of an SDE authorized by school accountability legislation to intervene at the building and classroom level, reaching across the education system in ways that it had not previously done in Nebraska. Complex reform policy development and implementation is messy. In the socially constructed and contested spaces where policymaking occurs, "policy actors compete, negotiate, or compromise and cooperate over time in integrating diverse interests to create coalitions in support of policy actions" (Heck, 2004, p. 7). Such policymaking or implementation is hardly linear or straightforward and it requires states to approach their work in very different ways than they have historically done.

Lusi's study focused on systemic, complex reforms around standards, curriculum, and assessment implementation in Kentucky and Vermont. She stated that in examining each state in its reform development and early implementation, she expected to see the work of the department change to reflect an innovative culture where the formal structures of organizational hierarchy were flattened, organizational boundaries were made more fluid in order to create streams of communication, the organization would be more mission- and vision-driven rather than driven by rules and regulations, individuals across all levels would be placed in the position to be decision-makers through collaborative processes, and the culture of the organization would promote trust, risk-taking, questioning, and seeking even better ideas (Fullan & Hargreaves, 1996; Lusi, 1997). Lusi also pointed to the complex and often ambiguous work of states engaged in such broad reform efforts. Like Madsen (1994), Lusi (1997), and Hamann and Lane (2004), who all describe ways SDEs made sense of and mediated education policy implementation, I approach the study of the SDE and its policymakers (State Board of Education and Commissioner) and policy intermediaries (SDE employees) with attention toward the human dimensions of the individuals who mediate, adapt, and redefine policy, "and thereby become coauthors of the ultimate policy that becomes practice" (Lusi, 1997, p. 447). Inevitable in the human dynamics of policy development is the cultivation of a policy culture, as first described by Sandra Stein (2004). As mine does, Stein's study of education reform and the culture that emerged as a result unfolded against a backdrop of a broader national policy context. Similar to Stein's approach, I describe the crafting of school accountability policy on the legislative floor and trace the way that policy moves and is enacted across tiers of the education system, from SBOE meetings to implementation in Santee.

SDEs, POLICY, AND POWER

I also rely on Stein (2004) as one template for how to study the policy culture of a SDE in the midst of responding to legislated reforms. As Stein pointed out, policy has historically framed its beneficiaries as *the other*, employing deviant or deficit frames and positioning the government (in this case the SDE) as a corrective force. She described this as a "policy culture" (p. 19) and asserted that overcoming this kind of policy culture requires an authentic commitment to equity. According to Stein, demonstrating a commitment to equity that transforms a deficit policy culture requires "purposeful work on the cultural dimensions of schooling [and the] language and rituals of practice" that invites the voice of the school in actively pursuing policy that "address complex considerations of students' strengths and needs" (Stein, 2004, pp. 24–25).

In this framing, discussions about school accountability policy, and its stated aim to make the education system more equitable, cannot occur without an interrogation of power. I ask whether Nebraska's school accountability legislation was truly about advancing equity and favorably changing the educational trajectories of students at three struggling schools. I ask whether it is the product of a political technology at work where individuals (irrespective of noble intentions and dedication to do the right work) function as objects of this technology in ways that undermine rather than advance equity, democracy, or sovereignty. By their very premise, efforts to turn around troubled or "failing" schools are supposed to be challenging the structures of power (by helping students accrue and develop social capital), so the policies being studied here are intertwined with "serious democracy" in ways that raise questions about poverty and low achievement, and the expectation that schools shoulder the primary responsibility for social amelioration (Apple, 2013; Gorski, 2014; Labaree, 2010).

An exploration of the ways that power is expressed in policymaking and policy implementation raises questions about space, particularly when studying spaces where state and sovereign tribal powers come into contact. Hilda Kuper was one of the first scholars to theorize and explore space as a construct in politics. Kuper's foundational piece distinguished the "concept of space" from the "experience of space" (Kuper, 1972, p. 411), which I would compare to the spaces of policy intention and the spaces where policy is actualized. While Kuper's work focused on physical sites (e.g., buildings, structures), French social theorist Henri Lefebvre (1991) distinguished between material and conceptual constructs of space, describing space as "both a field of action and a basis for action" (Lefebvre, 1991, p. 191). Lefebvre also acknowledged the relationship between space and power as contested and full of meaning, and a resource for social actors. When describing policy and the social actors engaged in its design and implementation, spaces can be those of constraint or those that are being remade through agentive actions. A policy culture is intertwined in the policy spaces and the value-mediated ways in which social actors interpret, participate in, and construct spaces (Phillips & Gray, 2021). Policy spaces and educational spaces are socioculturally and sociohistorically constructed and institutionally maintained (Phillips & Gray, 2021; Sexton, 2008).

As was true in Stein's policy culture and seen in the chapters ahead, individuals demonstrate the ways that they both are authored by structures and systems and find ways to author themselves (Goffman, 1959) and remake spaces through the assertion of individual and collective agency. It matters who inhabits policy spaces, who is not included, and who resists power and asserts agency in those spaces. Low (2014) asserts that the lens of space and place "provides a powerful tool for uncovering material and representational injustice and forms of social exclusion" (p. 34). I will use the lens of space in this way as I explore Nebraska's policy spaces (both physical and figurative), in order to investigate structures of power and expressions of agency (Ahearn, 1999; Barth, 1969).

SPATIAL TACTICS AS RESISTANCE

Individuals in policy and schooling spaces are mobile spatial actors, acting upon or being acted upon by structures of power. When considering power and the tactics (de Certeau, 1984) individuals use to act upon space, I rely on Foucault (1977), who described the way power worked in the system to constrain or create a "docile body" (p. 198), and Rabinow (1982), who asserted that space (physical, figurative, embodied) is a mechanism for deciphering the relationships among knowledge, power, and control. Acting on space requires agentic action, or what Phillips and Gray (2021) refer to as "spatial tactics," borrowing from Low and Lawrence-Zúñiga (2003). The next chapter will describe Nebraska's particular policy context and the policy cultures that emerged and evolved during the standards reform movement post-NCLB. I will also describe central elements of AQuESTT's policy development and implementation spaces, including the structures of governance and official policy actors. Then, in Chapter 3, I will focus specifically on American Indian education; policy; agency and space; and tactics that have been and continue to be effective in remaking spaces of power in Indian Country.

CHAPTER 2

Welcome to Flyover Country

From a window seat on my flight to Nebraska, I find myself pausing, glancing away from my writing to gaze at the scenery far below. The flight has moved beyond snow-capped peaks to an expanse of open prairie, like a patchwork quilt of irrigation circles and ribbons of rivers and roads extending as far as I can see. The land between coastal cities is often called flyover country, "a conception that envisions the country as divided geographically and culturally between only two regions: 'places that matter' and 'places that don't'" (Harkins, 2016, p. 97).

Despite perceptions of a relative sameness across states that make up the middle of the United States, communities represent the varied nature and cultures in the regions and states that make up flyover country. Essayist and humorist Roger Welch opened a particular portal into life in flyover country in his "Postcards from Nebraska," on *CBS Sunday Morning*. What I offer in this book is different from Welch's postcards; however, I share a similar aim—to illustrate that what happens (here, in education policy) in flyover country has broader relevance. Nebraska's position is uniquely interesting to interrogate. It has a small American Indian population relative to other Plains states (e.g., SD, ND, OK). It contrasts with a state like Montana, where there is greater Native representation and therefore greater political will to pass legislation like *Indian Education for All*.

It is with this juxtaposition that I posit that what unfolded in Nebraska, a state known for its renegade approach to resisting external national education reforms, and strong public engagement in and support for public schools has relevance. If school accountability implementation directed from the state in a local school were going to work, it would have worked in a state that until recently, had rebuffed "failing public schools" narratives that have eroded trust in a pillar of American democracy. Throughout the development and implementation of the school accountability policy at the center of this book, the state largely maintained trust and collaboration among the SDE, the state educators' and school administrators' associations, regional service agencies, local districts, and communities. Nebraska is a place where the customary attitude among citizens, when faced with a challenge or reform movement, has been, "Let's get the key players from the education system at the table and hash it out," and it's a place where getting everyone around the table is possible. If external, state-directed local school improvement were going to work in a local school anywhere in flyover country it likely would have been more likely to work in this particular prairie flyover state where a school like Santee might have benefited from Nebraska's collegial and trusting policy culture.

ACCOUNTABILITY AND NEBRASKA'S AQuESTT

When new statewide school accountability legislation was proposed and debated across two legislative sessions, and eventually passed and signed into law in 2014, I recognized that I had a front-row seat to its implementation as the newly hired Student Achievement Coordinator working in the Nebraska Department of Education. Within my first week, I was assigned to work on the accountability project. The statute authorized the State Board of Education (SBOE) to develop a statewide accountability system that would classify schools and districts in performance levels and identify and intervene in up to three priority schools.

Nebraska joined a list of states tasked with "taking over" the improvement effort of specific schools, a significant shift to Nebraska's most recent state-level policy trajectory. As the SBOE developed a new school accountability system that came to be AQuESTT, they relied primarily on student performance on summative statewide assessments and graduation rates to classify schools into performance levels. In an additional school accountability role, included in the legislation, the SBOE identified three priority schools (from 87 schools in "Needs Improvement," the lowest performance classification) and authorized the Nebraska Department of Education (NDE) to intervene in each priority school, bypassing local school boards and school districts. Not surprisingly, the three priority schools reflected the types of schools commonly identified as low-performing across the country. One, in North Omaha, had a predominantly low-income African American enrollment; one school was in a mostly White, predominantly rural community with declining enrollment; and one was on an American Indian reservation: Santee Community School. As of the writing of this book (2023), Santee is the only remaining school district with a state priority school and is still subject to state-directed intervention intended to improve student outcomes.

At each tier of policymaking, people stated their intention of practicing collaboration and listening to people; nevertheless, the policy culture that developed with AQuESTT was top-down, in a departure from a grassroots way of developing and implementing education policy in the state. It was influenced by national neoliberal education policies privileging the interests of the private sector rather than the public good. Historically, Nebraska had been a state that resisted national policy trends like state intervention in local schools. For example, it bucked the statewide assessment requirements under *No Child Left Behind* (NCLB) and was one of only seven states not to authorize charter schools. Policymakers described a tradition of dialogue among individuals and opportunities for direct participation among citizens in design and development across all tiers of the education policy system, from local people to the Commissioner and decision-makers in both the legislature and SBOE. This approach was affectionately called the "Nebraska way" by several state-level policymakers. The shift in the state's approach and structuring of AQuESTT's policy implementation and the influence of national policy trends ultimately impacted the efforts to improve local schools in communities like Santee.

THE NEBRASKA WAY

Just as Nebraska has prided itself on its unique style of state governance with a one-house legislative body called the Unicameral, state education policy around school accountability displayed a similar originality in its grassroots resistance to national policy trends, a stubbornness seen in many situations and often referred to as "the Nebraska Way." Under NCLB, when faced with meeting Average Yearly Progress (AYP) requirements, every state but Nebraska identified or developed their own high-stakes assessments (Dappen & Isernhagen, 2005). Following the passage of LB812, the *Quality Education and Accountability Act,* in 2000, Nebraska's department of education (under the leadership of then Commissioner of Education Doug Christensen and Deputy Commissioner Polly Feis) instead developed its own local assessment and accountability system: STARS (School-based, Teacher-led, Assessment and Reporting System) (Nebraska Department of Education, 2004). Narrative in a STARS Summary report (2004) articulates this commitment to local knowledge and approaches to teaching and learning in partnership with state entities:

> The underlying philosophy that supports Nebraska's School-based Teacher-led Assessment and Reporting System emphasizes a partnership between the local school districts and the Nebraska Department of Education. Keeping decisions about student performance on standards at the local classroom level provides a balance between state level guidance and local decision-making. Partnership and balance are the two crucial elements in making changes in schools that will result in improved learning for all students. (p. 1)

Nebraska's approach to standards, assessment, and accountability encouraged the state to focus more on teaching and learning and teachers' professional assessment literacy rather than centering high-stakes assessment (Dappen & Isernhagen, 2005). It also allowed the control of curriculum and assessment to remain at the local level, where accountability was on the teachers working directly with students and instruction that might better meet the needs of students (Sleeter, 2007). Statewide professional development focused on assessment literacy, and the state partnered with the Buros Center for Testing housed at the University of Nebraska–Lincoln in order to demonstrate the validity and reliability of the state's assessment approach for the U.S. Department of Education.

However, increasing federal pressure, and frustrations expressed by local educators concerning the amount of time and professional development necessary to maintain the STARS assessment system, escalated discussions about Nebraska's approach to the legislative level (Isom, 2012). In 2008, the Nebraska Legislature passed LB1157, which required that a single statewide assessment of reading, math, and science be phased in and, by the year 2013, replace the STARS system of locally developed assessments. These statewide assessments came to be known as NeSA (Nebraska Statewide Assessments). In response to this legislative pushback, Commissioner Christensen resigned, stating,

> I believe that state testing is wrong and is not in the best interests of students, teachers and other educators, and schools. I cannot uphold the constitutional responsibility of being a Commissioner who is to uphold the "law of the land" and put in place something that I believe is so dreadfully wrong as education policy and so destructive as public policy about education. (Cody, 2008)

Beyond mandating the implementation of statewide assessments, LB1157 also required the SBOE to develop a way to "determine how well public schools are performing in terms of achievement of public school students related to the state academic content standards" (Nebraska Revised Statute, § 79–760.03).

In January 2012, with statewide assessments fully implemented in the state, Sen. Greg Adams, a former schoolteacher and representative from the central part of the state, introduced LB870, which authorized the SBOE to develop and implement an accountability system for schools and districts by the 2012–2013 school year. The bill allowed the board to incorporate multiple measures into a single performance score for each public school and district in the state. The bill was passed and signed into law and on August 9, 2012, in its first foray into state-level school accountability, the SBOE adopted the Nebraska Performance Accountability System (NePAS), which provided multiple scores and rankings for school districts in Nebraska state assessments of reading, math, science, writing, and by graduation rate (NDE, 2014a). Thus, since 2008, Nebraska has experienced a major shift. Education policy that was once done with great public participation has moved inside legislative chambers and SBOE and SDE meeting rooms.

A NEBRASKA WAY OF EDUCATION GOVERNANCE

According to Nebraska's schooling governance structure, an elected SBOE mediates state law and sets policy. The state department of education actualizes that policy under the leadership of a Commissioner of Education who is hired and authorized by the SBOE. These layers of the system comprise the state. To clarify further, "state" here does not refer to the nation-state. In the United States, the federal government (the nation-state) is not the traditional locus for education policy-setting and governance. The state legislative body in Nebraska is a single house, nonpartisan body. With the introduction of LB438, a bill that would extend Sen. Adams's (2012) legislation, elected representatives in the Unicameral and elected SBOE members (none of whom were necessarily education experts) set education policy and may (or may not) have relied on the expertise of the Commissioner and NDE (the experts) in the process. This setup, in which amateurs can tell the experts how to make policy and implement it, is not restricted to education governance in Nebraska or elsewhere. Having a basic understanding of the way that Nebraska governs schools and the processes for developing school policy is necessary to understand the state's policy culture and its evolution over time. Nebraska's unique education governance, situated in a framework with the country's only unicameral legislature, matters to this particular policy history.

A policy's development and its implementation contain many decision points. Education policy is crafted by people whose perceptions and experiences shape the policy they create and the legislative decisions they make. Policy moves from Washington, DC, to state capitols and among them, and then to the school down the street. It is within a broader context of national education policy reforms (e.g., Common Core Standards, charter schools, vouchers) and Nebraska's reluctance to follow prescribed neoliberal trends in order to maintain a "Nebraska Way" of doing things that discussions about statewide school accountability (LB438) took place. This context also included memory (particularly for senators not yet affected by term limits established in 2000 in the state) of recent disputes over whether education policy would be controlled in the legislature or by the department of education.

THE NATION'S ONLY UNICAMERAL

Nebraskans pride themselves on their nonpartisan governing body, maintaining that the single house structure provides more straightforward procedures, greater privileges to the press, and allows for greater public access than does the bicameral legislature of every other state (Nebraska's 10th Legislature,

2016). The 49 members of the Unicameral, each of whom can serve a maximum of two consecutive, 4-year terms, each represent around 40,000 people; while geographically large, Nebraska is really just a small, tightly networked state as far as population goes. The state's Unicameral is one example of a "Nebraska Way" of imagining the the state's governance as inclusive of great public input and making itself available through great public access and transparency. What follows is an overview of the way that policy is legislated, a brief history that provides background on Nebraska's education system, and some introductions to key figures whose roles and actions influenced the way that school accountability policy came to be and how it came to be implemented.

A BILL'S JOURNEY THROUGH THE UNICAMERAL

Before a bill is introduced, a senator and staff research legislative remedies between legislative sessions. A senator drafts of a bill and introduces it by filing it with the Clerk of the Legislature. When a bill is on file, a budget or fiscal note process estimates the financial impact of the bill. Following this first phase every bill is assigned to a legislative committee and goes to a public hearing. The accountability legislation was assigned to the Education Committee, and the public had a chance to present opinions on the proposed legislation to the senators on the committee.

Once a hearing has been completed, a committee can choose to advance, hold, or take no action on the proposed bill. If a bill is advanced, it is placed on General File. The full legislature will debate a bill on General File and vote on it. It is at this stage that senators consider amendments. For an amendment to be adopted, it takes a vote of the majority of the Unicameral (or 25 votes). If the bill advances in the General File vote, it goes to Select File, which allows for a second debate and opportunity for further amendments or compromises. A bill on Select File may be returned to committee for further review, postponed, or advanced to Final Reading. At Final Reading, the bill (which cannot now be amended or debated) is read aloud by the Clerk of the Legislature. Senators may elect to vote on the bill for Final Reading or return it to Select File for consideration of a specific amendment. A final vote on a bill can only be taken after a bill has reached the Final Reading.

When a bill is passed, it goes to the governor, who has five days to act on a bill, either signing it into law or vetoing it. A signed bill goes into effect three months after the Legislature adjourns for the session; however, if a bill has an emergency clause (as did LB438), it can go into effect immediately. (A vetoed bill can be overwritten, but that procedure does not further pertain here.)

A BRIEF HISTORY OF SCHOOLING AND GOVERNANCE IN NEBRASKA

In 1855, twelve years before statehood, the Territorial Legislature passed the *Act to Establish the Common Schools of Nebraska*, instituting local school governance through three-member boards consisting of a president, secretary, and treasurer. Local boards were responsible for governing decisions around textbook selection, teacher hiring, curriculum, and school regulation (Beggs, 1939). Fourteen years later, the newly formed Nebraska State Legislature passed an *Act to Establish a System of Public Instruction for the State of Nebraska* (Nebraska Legislature, 1869), putting in place a State Superintendent of Instruction and county superintendents who were elected every 2 years. School supervision and accountability was provided through visits from both the county superintendents and the State Superintendent of Public Instruction. An early State Superintendent realized the need for common policies and procedures and a Department of Public Instruction in order for Nebraska's children to receive a quality education. Over time, local leaders came to accept the role of Nebraska's Department of Public Instruction as a regulatory body but maintained local control over schools and districts. The State Superintendent and Office of Public Instruction were included in the state's constitution of 1875.

Nearly 75 years later, in 1947, State Superintendent Wayne O. Reed proposed updates to the role of the State Superintendent and the Office of Public Instruction. As the state had grown, there was a to move from a network of common schools with a simple set of statutory guidance to a complex public school system that included 10 classes of schools and hundreds of laws (Limoges, 2001). Reed suggested that the complexities inherent in the current system necessitated a State Board of Education and an appointed Commissioner of Education that would be better able to provide for the varied and complex needs of the schools in the state.

Nebraska voters agreed, and in 1952 a constitutional amendment reorganized the state's education functions into a Department of Education in place of the old Office of Public Instruction and transferred the authority of the State Superintendent to the newly established State Board of Education and Commissioner of Education. Laws passed in 1953 outlined a six-member, elected, non-salaried structure. In 1968, the number of state board members increased to eight, and in both 2011 and 2021 the district boundaries were redrawn. The Nebraska State Board of Education (SBOE) is, at the time of this writing (2023), an eight-member elected body that serves as the policy-forming, planning, and evaluative body overseeing the state's school program, deliberating, and taking action with the professional advice and counsel of the Commissioner of Education (Neb. Rev. Stat. § 79–301). It is responsible for appointing the Commissioner of Education and, since 1953, it has ensured that the Nebraska Department of Education (NDE) functions effectively under the Commissioner's leadership. The Legislature has, over the past 60 years, set forth numerous duties for the SBOE, including coordinating educational activities related to accreditation of schools, academic content standards (Neb. Rev. Stat. § 79–760.01), assessment (Neb. Rev. Stat. §§ 79–760.02–03), and accountability, most recently updated with the passage of LB438 (codified as Neb. Rev. Stat. § 79–760.06-.07).

The Commissioner of Education serves as the executive officer of the State Board of Education and, together, the Commissioner and board mediate education policy issued by the state and federal legislation and create policy through rule and regulation for public and private schools in the state. While NDE has responsibilities for "general supervision and administration of the school system of the state" (Neb. Rev. Stat. § 79–301.01) and actualizes policy under the leadership of the Commissioner of Education and the SBOE, local school boards maintain their primary authority over the operations of schools within each district.

It is according to this governance structure that statutory requirements, regulation, and policy is developed and implemented in Nebraska. Unlike many states, where a chief education officer may be appointed by a governor or elected by the people, or where an SDE may be a code agency under the direct authority of a state's legislature or governor, Nebraska's education governance is overseen by the eight elected officials of the SBOE, who appoint a Commissioner that leads and oversees a state department of education that is a constitutional agency (i.e., NDE) and thus separate from the direct governance of the executive branch. Each SBOE member serves on 4-year terms, with a 2-year cycle where half the board is up for election.

POLICY LANDSCAPE AND KEY FIGURES

Education policy is socially constructed and implemented and thus includes an array of key actors that require introduction. Heck (2004) describes policy actors as either "insiders" who set the agenda and move policy forward; the "near circle," who can persuade insiders; the "far circle" who have less direct influence but can influence implementation from their organizational role; and "forgotten players," which are groups on the fringes that have influence at particular times but "generally do not influence the agenda" (p. 65). This way of framing policy actors is helpful when exploring the way the education system acts on local schools and individuals in those schools and the communities they serve. The following brief biographical sketches provide introductions to some of the individuals serving in formal, institutional roles during the development and implementation of the school accountability legislation that eventually made its way to Santee, Nebraska.

Discussions of sovereignty, self-education, and the history of education policy toward Native peoples will take place in more detail and nuance in Chapter 3. When describing the political landscape that contributed to the shaping of LB438, I again highlight that school governance on or near American Indian reservations in Nebraska are governed by locally elected school boards. In the case of Santee, where the school is located in the village of Santee, the largest community on the reservation, the locally elected school board is most often composed of members of the Tribe, which was the case between 2014 and 2022.

According to state statute, a local school board in Nebraska is responsible for (a) forming policies, rules, and regulations around the operation of the schools and district, (b) hiring and evaluating the superintendent, (c) providing oversight to ensure that the district is following state and federal law, and (d) developing an annual budget that covers the personnel and operations of the school district. Despite these local powers, public school districts remain under the oversight of the state's regulatory agency (NDE), the SBOE, and state and federal law. The combination of a local school board of tribal members and oversight from governing bodies outside the reservation sets up a tension already taut with a long history discussed in the next chapter.

Below, I provide introductions to the key policy "insiders" who played roles in the governing bodies away from Santee, whose actions ultimately led to the state's intervention on the reservation. Note that public figures who are part of the public record are listed by name, while "near circle" or "forgotten players" (Heck, 2004) are named by role or a common pseudonym used to describe them. I differentiate between public figures doing public jobs from policy intermediaries or intended beneficiaries through this naming structure. While it is possible to identify latter actors by name in the public record, my intention is to interrogate the system and the roles individuals played within those systems, rather than to critique individuals.

Unicameral

Greg Adams: Former Nebraska Senator Greg Adams represented District 24. He began his career in York, Nebraska, where he taught for 31 years. He served as the mayor of York, a town of just under 8,000 located right on I-80 in the south-central part of the state, for 10 years before running for the legislature. During his tenure in the Unicameral (2007–2015), he spent 4 years chairing the Legislature's Education Committee. In 2013, he was elected speaker of the Legislature, the same session in which he introduced the school accountability legislation at the core of this book: Legislative Bill 438. Due to term limits, Adams left the Unicameral and went on to serve as executive director of Accelerate Nebraska, a nonprofit focused on improving education outcomes and connections to career.

Kate Sullivan: First elected to the Legislature in 2008, Sullivan represented the 41st District, in the central part of the state. She chaired the Education Committee when LB438 was introduced and worked with Sen.

Adams on proposed amendments to the bill before its final reading. She served until 2017.

Scott Lautenbaugh: Appointed to the Legislature in 2007, Lautenbaugh represented District 18 in northwest suburban Omaha (the largest city in the state). During his time in the Legislature, Lautenbaugh introduced several charter school bills, and in 2014 he introduced LB972, which would have allowed charter schools in the state (McDermott, 2014). Facing term limits, Lautenbaugh stepped down from his term early to become a lobbyist at the end of the legislative session in 2014.

State Board of Education

The membership of the SBOE changed over the course of the 8 years from 2014, when LB438 became law, through 2023, the writing of this book and the end of the fifth year of state intervention in Santee. While the faces on the SBOE changed, the board's public meeting format remained consistent, meeting the first Thursday and Friday of each month. Board committees scheduled meetings beginning on Wednesday of the week and prior to Thursday's work session or following Friday's business meeting. While both the work session and business meeting were subject to open meetings law and therefore open to the public and livestreamed on public television, committee meetings and executive sessions were closed to the public. Key board figures were primarily engaged in the implementation of LB438 (which came to be known as AQuESTT) between 2014 and 2017, with annual updates on accountability ranking and priority school implementation each year following. These actors included:

District 1: Lillie Larson. Serving a portion of Lancaster County, including Lincoln, the second-largest city in the state, Lillie Larson was first elected to the SBOE in 2013 after serving many terms on the Lincoln Public Schools Board of Education. Larson began her career as a public high school social studies teacher. She served on the board until 2016.

District 2: Glen Flint. Flint was appointed by Governor Heineman to represent District 2 on the SBOE on March 28, 2014, following the resignation of Omaha attorney Mark Quandahl. Flint was a software developer with Northrop Grumman in Bellevue, Nebraska. He served on the board until 2016.

District 3: Rachel Wise. Wise was elected to the SBOE in 2013, representing rural, Northeast Nebraska. A retired educator whose teaching and administrative experiences included work in rural districts, Omaha Public Schools, and in an Educational Service Unit (a regional education organization that supports a consortium of schools), Wise was elected president of the State Board of Education in January 2014. She retained this role until 2016 and served on the board until 2021.

District 4: John Witzel. Witzel was also appointed by Governor Heineman to the SBOE in March 2014. A retired Air Force veteran, Witzel served for 14 years as a board member for Educational Service Unit #3 serving Douglas and Sarpy Counties prior to joining the State Board. He served the SBOE until 2021, serving as its president in 2019–2020.

District 5: Patricia Timm. First appointed to the SBOE in 2004, Timm represented Southeast Nebraska until 2021, when she resigned due to health issues. Timm began her career as a kindergarten and K–12 art teacher. As the member with the longest tenure with the board, Timm served as board president in January 2013, when LB438 was first introduced and prior to Wise's election in 2014, and then again in 2017–2018.

District 6: Maureen Nickels. Nickels was first elected to represent central Nebraska in 2015. Nickels taught for Grand Island Public Schools for 26 years before joining the Nebraska State Educators' Association (NSEA). Following her election to the board, questions were raised by opponents as to whether it was constitutional for her to maintain her employment with NSEA; it was determined that she could maintain her job with NSEA and her position on the SBOE. She became president of the SBOE in 2020–2021. Her term ended at the end of 2022, and she did not run for re-election.

District 7: Molly O'Holleran. Elected to the SBOE in 2010 and representing the largest region (over 72,000 square miles), across western Nebraska, O'Holleran also began her career in education. Prior to joining the SBOE, she served on the North Platte Public Schools Board of Education. O'Holleran served as the chair of the Accountability Committee when LB438 was debated and passed. She served on the SBOE until 2019.

District 8: Patrick McPherson. McPherson was elected to represent a portion of the Omaha metro area in 2015. Upon assuming his role in January 2015, McPherson was the focus of controversy and pressure to resign after a post on his blog, the *Objective Conservative*, referred to President Obama as a "half breed" (Reist, 2015). McPherson deleted the post and stated that the post had been written by a contributor to his blog, acknowledging that he needed to do a better job monitoring content. Despite ongoing pressures from political officials including the state's Congressional delegation and governor and a State Board of Education 6–2 vote requesting his resignation, McPherson made it clear that he had no plans to resign his position. McPherson served on the SBOE until 2019.

Nebraska Department of Education

While there are many names of individuals from across NDE who played significant roles throughout this study, the individuals listed here were key in the decision-making throughout the development of AQuESTT and direction-setting throughout its implementation.

Matthew L. Blomstedt. Blomstedt was appointed Commissioner of Education by the SBOE on January 2, 2014, to replace Roger Breed (who had been in office since 2009). Prior to taking this position, Blomstedt served as the Executive Director of the Educational Service Unit Coordinating Council, the Executive Director of the Nebraska Rural Community Schools Association, and as research analyst for the Education Committee in the Legislature. Unlike his predecessors, Blomstedt's prior roles did not include experience as a classroom teacher, building principal, or district superintendent. He continued to serve as Commissioner until January 6, 2023.

Deputy Commissioner Deborah A. Frison joined NDE in August of 2015 as the Deputy Commissioner of School Improvement and Support. An educator with more than 38 years of teaching and administrative experience, one of her core responsibilities was overseeing the work to develop and implement LB438. She remains in her role at the time of this writing (2023) and is serving in an interim role as the SBOE completes its search for the next Commissioner of Education.

The Accountability Coordinator joined NDE in August 2014. She had previously worked at NDE in the early days of Nebraska's writing assessment and then returned to coordinate activities related to LB438. The Accountability Coordinator served in her role until 2017.

The First Consultant (a.k.a. The Lady from North Carolina) was hired as a contractor by NDE in February 2016 to work with the state's identified priority schools (i.e., three schools identified through AQuESTT). She had worked as a contractor for the Omaha Public Schools in previous years and most recently with Druid Hill Elementary, which was one of the three priority schools, in the 2015–2016 school year. A former Assistant Superintendent of Instructional Design and Innovation who retired from a school district in North Carolina in August 2015, The Lady from North Carolina was hired to help the state develop a model for intervention and support that could be used to support all schools in Needs Improvement. She retained contracts from NDE at the time of this writing (2023); however, her work in Santee ended in 2019.

THE SHIFTING ROLES OF NDE

The individuals listed above were central to the implementation of legislated state-led improvement efforts in three school districts, a shift in the role of policymakers and NDE. Their new roles are situated within a broader shift in what is expected from state departments of education in order to respond to federal and state education policy legislation.

Drawing upon Susan Follett Lusi's (1997) case studies of complex school reform initiatives in Kentucky and Vermont 2 decades ago, this study examines how a state department of education (SDE) in Nebraska involves itself in a legislated school reform effort. Lusi provided a model for the study of an SDE engaged in complex legislated school reform. Nebraska's case is an example of an SDE mediating legislated policy and shows the disconnect that can occur when noneducators are the ones crafting education policies and educational experts are the ones mediating policies. While SDEs in the mid-1990s were grappling with their roles as intermediaries, this case chronicles NDE's attempt to figure out how to transform legislated policy into practice in ways that aligned with stated intentions, a common challenge for SDEs across the United States.

Intention and context are fundamental to understanding the nuances of policy implementation, why some things work for certain people in particular contexts and the same kind of policy implementation fails someplace else. Intention and context are also fundamental to interrogating education policy toward Indigenous peoples in the United States. Education policy has long been designed to systematically "erase and replace" identity, culture, and community (Lomawaima and McCarty, 2006, xxi–xxii) in Indian Country. It is rare that Indigenous sovereignty, right to self-education, and ways of knowing are centered in education policymaking or contextualized in policy implementation. Rarely are Native voices, histories, or knowledges present at state policy decision–making tables.

Whether intentional or not, a series of policy decisions throughout this study undermined the Nebraska Way of engaging local voices in policymaking and implementation in significant ways. For example, before the legislation even made it across the street to the SBOE, the legislature amended the bill (that became AQuESTT), removing provision for a "community operating council" intended to ensure local voice and oversight in priority school improvement. Then, during the AQuESTT development and implementation, the Commissioner of Education (with the approval of the SBOE) reorganized the department of education in ways that isolated upper-tier decision-makers from broader public access and voice. Finally, when the Commissioner of Education and SBOE authorized a private consultant with a one-size-fits-all approach to command the "turnaround" efforts in each of the three priority schools, they enacted a policy culture that bypassed local voice and expertise and privileged external knowledge.

CHAPTER 3

A Broader Story Than the Village of Santee

A small, twisty road rises and falls, connecting the village of Santee with the highway. The land is craggy, with deep folds and shallow valleys freckled with hay bales and tight outcroppings of scrawny trees. A cluster of houses and buildings sit near the river's edge, a contrast from the Minnesota forests and lakes the Dakota people once called home. As I passed a few buffalo on a ridge, it was a reminder that despite the policies meted out on the Dakota people by the U.S. Government, the people endure, with a resilience grounded in the stories of survivance. The people persist.

American Indian people groups have fought for recognition of their sovereignty and the right to self-govern and self-educate since the plunder of their lands (Lomawaima & McCarty, 2006; Brayboy et al., 2015). The Santee Sioux are a federally recognized sovereign American Indian Nation. As a result, they have a special relationship with both federal and state government entities. I borrow from scholars Lomawaima and McCarty (2006), who define Tribal sovereignty as the "inherent right of a people to self-government, self-determination, and self-education" (p. 9). I also rely upon Castagno and Brayboy (2008) who describe sovereignty and the right to self-education as Indigenous peoples' right to "determine the nature of schooling provided to their youth" (p. 949).

The current contexts that exist in American Indian education reflect the histories of Native peoples and their ongoing relationships with the United States since its inception (Brayboy et al., 2015; McCarty & Lee, 2014). Broadly, policy crafted by the U.S. and state governments and enacted upon Indigenous peoples have been sweeping and have failed to account for the wide diversity, histories, and societal organization of Indigenous nations. While there are patterns and commonalities shared across American Indian groups, particular policy relationships and legacies are unique to each Nation.

This chapter briefly chronicles a history of the Dakota Sioux, and the ways schooling was used as a policy tool for the U.S. government and state governments. Schooling on the Santee Sioux reservation reflects the ways broader schooling policies were implemented and the ways their legacies endure in other Native communities.

EARLY INTERACTIONS WITH COLONIZERS

The Dakota people had intermittent interactions with Europeans beginning in 1660, when French explorers Pierre Esprit Radisson and Médard Chouart, Sieur des Groseilliers, were met by a group of eight warriors and their wives who carried with them gifts of wild rice and corn. It was not until 1679, however, that White men visited the Dakota people on their lands in what is now Minnesota. Two French missionaries, Daniel Greysolon, Sieur du Luth, and Father Louis Hennepin visited the village of Izatys (the source of the name Santee). They were the first of many French explorers, trappers, and traders throughout the rest of the 17th century. After the French and Indian War, also called the Seven Years War (1754–1763), British presence in the region replaced the French. During the American Revolutionary War (1775–1783) the Santee fought on the side of Great Britain. As the 18th century came to a close, the Dakota people's lives had been transformed by European goods (e.g., steel tools, guns, brass cooking pots); however, their core culture remained relatively unchanged. Bands of the Santee maintained seasonal villages and nomadic hunting grounds in what is now Minnesota.

The Dakota people began their formal relationship with the U.S. government when Lieutenant Zebulon Pike arrived in what is now Minnesota in 1805–1806 with an intention to "establish United States sovereignty over the territory where British traders continued to operate much as they had before the Revolution. Recognizing the control over the area would not be achieved without a military presence" (Meyer, 1993, p. 24). As a representative of the U.S. government, Pike approached the Santee people with an offer to purchase a portion of their lands, resulting in the Sioux Treaty of 1805 and the subsequent construction of Fort Snelling, near what is now Minneapolis-St. Paul, Minnesota, in 1819. In the negotiations, Pike promised to pay the Santee $200,000 for about 100,000 acres of land; however, the specific monetary amount was not written into the treaty when it was signed and Pike later filled in the blank with the sum of $2,000. While the identity of the Santee signers of the treaty is not certain, it is likely that they represented only a proportion of the bands of the Santee people. Perhaps it is not surprising, then, that when the War of 1812 occurred, the Santee once again sided with the British.

As the newly formed United States government found stability, increasing numbers of White settlers arrived in Santee lands. This, of course, also increased the number of Christian missionaries seeking to convert the Santee people. One outcome of their proselytization in the region was the development of a written form of the Dakota language. As the Santee people adapted to changes in the region that included scarcity of game and the need to expand hunting grounds, the U.S. government increasingly organized its policy toward American Indians with the 1824 establishment of the Bureau of Indian Affairs, aptly situated in the War Department. By the mid-century mark, the pressure to expand White landownership in the region intensified, and in 1851, the U.S. government "negotiated" a pair of treaties with members of the Dakota people that forever altered the future. As Meyer (1993) points out, White agents "knew—or thought they knew—what was best for the Indians, and the end justified the means. By a remarkable coincidence, what was best for the Indians was invariably also to the advantage of the government, the traders, and, above all, the land-hungry settlers" (pp. 77–78). In this case, the U.S. confiscated the Dakota people's homeland through the Treaties of Traverse des Sioux and Mendota in 1851, ratified by the U.S. Senate in 1852. Immediately settlers arrived, staking claims on land. Thus, by 1854, the majority of the tribe was removed to temporary reservation lands, as no permanent land had been allocated in either treaty.

The Dakota people resisted being resettled, refusing, in many cases, to remain on temporarily assigned lands; they continued to travel, trade, and even farm across the region. Tensions increased as the U.S. government, intent on waging the Civil War, did not fulfill its treaty agreements in making payments or dispensing other benefits. In a final bloody uprising led by Little Crow, which came to be known as the Dakota War of 1862, four Dakota warriors killed four White settlers near Acton township. The killings, according to the affidavit of John Moore, a scout for General Sibley and member of the Medawakantonwan tribe of the Santee people, happened as a result of ongoing frustrations that promised payments from the U.S. government had not come after the treaties of 1851. Santee people were desperate and starving, attempting to hunt to provide food for their people (United States Congress, 1897). The deaths of the four settlers stoked already-tense relations in the region. Between August and September there were multiple skirmishes and casualties before Little Crow was defeated in the Battle of Wood Lake and over 1,200 Santee were captured, 400 of those held for trial. Little Crow and a number of other Dakota people managed to flee to South Dakota and later Canada. Following legal proceedings, the U.S. military commission condemned 303 of those Santee men to death. While President Abraham Lincoln spared the lives of the majority of the men, 38 were hanged near Mankato, Minnesota, the day after Christmas that same year. It remains the largest mass execution in U.S. history. The arrests, imprisonment, and multiple hangings further devastated a people already dislocated from their homelands.

A DAKOTA EDUCATION

Thanks to Charles Eastman, first named *Hakadah* and then later *Ohíye S'a* (sometimes written Ohiyesa), a Santee physician, social activist, and writer born in 1858, we have descriptions of Santee life and a child's education from the turbulent time described above. His writings are some of the earliest published descriptions of the colonization of the Santee people from a Native point of view. His mother died at his birth. During the Dakota War of 1862, he was separated from his father, who was believed to have died in the 1862 mass execution in Mankato. Eastman was adopted by his grandparents and uncle who traveled with a band of Santee people in North Dakota and Canada during his childhood. When he was 15, he was reunited with his father and his brother in South Dakota, both of whom had converted to Christianity. Ohíye S'a later changed his name to Charles Eastman, adopting his father's new last name and Christian faith.

Among his essays on his Santee childhood, *Indian Boyhood* (1902), Eastman included descriptions of a boy's education in his Dakota tribal community. Even at publication in 1902, Eastman acknowledged that colonizers "commonly supposed that there was no systematic education" for American Indian children and he asserted that "nothing could be farther from the truth" (p. 12). He explained that the customs of education were believed to be rooted in the divine and thus "[the customs] in connection with the training of children were scrupulously adhered to and transmitted from one generation to another" (p. 12).

Most of Eastman's narrative focused on his boyhood. He described how a Santee child's education began immediately following birth with the lullabies mothers sang, filled with "wonderful exploits in hunting and war" for male children and images of "the future mother of a noble race" for females (p. 13). In early boyhood, a child learned about "preserving and transmitting the legends of his ancestors and his race," through a practice where the child listened to elders' stories and the following evening would be expected to share a retelling of the story (p. 13). Eastman's grandfather conducted his education until he was 15, challenging the child each morning to observe and notice the world around him, then orienting evening discussions about these observations: "He meant to make me observant and a good student of nature" (p. 13).

Eastman's education also included opportunities to learn how to face hardship and practice endurance. For this learning, Eastman tells of the ways his uncle taught him how to fast and then began to awaken him with "sudden war-whoops over my head in the morning while I was sound asleep. He expected me to leap up with perfect presence of mind, always ready to grasp a weapon of some sort and to give a shrill whoop in reply" (p. 14). Training intensified as a boy began to grow into manhood. Santee warriors challenged new warriors with feats of bravery to test their skills. Children tested their skills alongside peers in play that included "feats with the bow and arrow, foot and pony races, wrestling, swimming and imitation of the customs and habits of our fathers. We had sham fights with mud balls and willow wands; we played lacrosse, made war upon bees, and shot winter arrows (which were only used in that season), and coasted upon the ribs of animals and buffalo robes" (pp. 15–16).

A Santee child's education also included teachings on etiquette and morality. Customs included listening to elders, addressing them with terms of respect. While living in exile in what is presently North Dakota and Canada, children listened to the stories from when people lived in what is now Minnesota—the land, the lakes, the wild rice, and the annual harvest of corn, beans, and squash. "We were taught generosity to the poor and reverence for the 'Great Mystery.' Religion was the basis of all Indian training" (Eastman, 1902, p. 15). Children in mixed gender groups play-acted the medicine-dance with the boys pretending to be medicine men and the girls covering up the "bodies" with blankets, symbolizing burying the dead.

As evidence of the influence of colonization, Eastman also described the occasional playing of "White man," a game where children

> painted two or three of our number with white clay and put on them birchen hats which we sewed up for the occasion; fastened a piece of fur to their chins for a beard and altered their costumes as much as lay within our power. The white of the birch-bark was made to answer for their white shirts. Their merchandise consisted of sand for sugar, wild beans for coffee, dried leaves for tea, pulverized earth for gun-powder, pebbles for bullets and clear water for the dangerous "spirit water." We traded for these goods with skins of squirrels, rabbits and small birds. (p.18)

According to Eastman, this kind of play illustrated that "[my] knowledge of the pale-face was limited" (p. 18) beyond knowing the history of the "'Big Knives,' as we called the white men, when the terrible Minnesota massacre broke up our home and I was carried into exile" (p. 68).

"BIG KNIVES" AND THE "PHYSICAL AND MORAL DEGRADATION" OF RESERVATION LIFE

Following the Dakota War and the forced removal of the Dakota people from their lands in Minnesota, they were first taken to Crow Creek in South Dakota. The 3 years at Crow Creek were devastating. The land was not suitable for agriculture, and within the first year more than 300 Dakota people died of starvation or lack of access to appropriate clothing (Meyer, 1993). In 1865, a peace commission led by Superintendent of Indian Affairs for the Northern region Edward B. Taylor recommended that the Santee people be relocated again—this time to the mouth of the Niobrara River in Nebraska Territory. By May and June 1866, the Santee people arrived at Niobrara township and, ultimately, more permanently settled near Bazile Creek just a few miles to the east of Niobrara, Nebraska (Meyer, 1993).

The permanence of the Nebraska reservation remained uncertain as late as 1868 when Hampton Denman, then Northern Superintendent of Indian Affairs, encouraged the U.S. Office of Indian Affairs to permanently fix reservation lands for the tribe. He asserted that "all treaties with these Indians have been abrogated, their annuities forfeited, their splendid reservation of valuable land in Minnesota confiscated by the government, their numbers sadly reduced by starvation and disease; they have been humiliated to the dust" (United States Office of Indian Affairs, 1868, p. 265). In his report Denman stated that "wisdom and humanity" demanded the government adopt a new policy toward the Santee (United States Office of Indian Affairs, 1868, p. 265). He suggested that future policy "take them [the Santee] once more by the hand," and "restore enough of their former annuities" in such a way that members of the tribe would once more be able to establish a life for themselves and their people in a new home (United States Office of Indian Affairs, 1868, p. 265). If such a policy were put in place, Denman believed that "in a very few years," the Santee Sioux would become "good citizens and entirely self-sustaining" (United States Office of Indian Affairs, 1868, p. 266). Ultimately, the land in northeastern Nebraska that Denman scouted and described as "desirable" in his report became the Santee Reservation in 1869. The reservation lands were fixed as a "rectangular tract of land, twelve miles from east to west and averaging about fifteen miles from north to south, encompassing 115,075.92 acres" (Meyer, 1993, p. 163).

SCHOOL AS A POLICY TOOL

Following the forced removal of American Indians from their lands and the establishment of reservations, federal agents and missionaries accelerated efforts to "civilize," assimilate, and "Americanize" Native peoples (Reyhner & Eder, 2004). Efforts included education policies and practices designed to erase Native culture and ways of being (Adams, 1995; Lomawaima & McCarty, 2006). For the Dakota, before reservation lands had been defined, White missionaries from the American Board of Missionaries established a school in 1866. In 1870–1871, the American Board of Missionaries expanded schooling on the reservation and established a normal school to train teachers, and by 1877 it was the educational hub for the reservation (Meyer, 1993). During this same time, a boarding school run by the Bureau of Indian Affairs also existed on the reservation. The policy intention of these boarding schools (whether located on or off reservation lands) required the removal of Indigenous children from their homes and communities; according to Richard Henry Pratt, the founder of the Carlisle Indian Industrial School, the goal was to "remove the Indian" from each child

(Reyhner & Eder 2004). However, despite efforts to eliminate Native culture, it endured, as "the power of home was so intense . . . few students left that world behind" (Child, 1998, p. 27).

Instruction in schools on the reservation was first conducted in the Dakota language. Over 150 years later, it is impossible to assess the quality or effectiveness of this schooling; however, it is worth noting that the initial curriculum acknowledged the history and background of the enrolled students at least to the extent that it affirmed their language (Deloria, 1998). However, an 1887 order issued by Commissioner of Indian Affairs John D. C. Atkins stated, "The instruction of the Indians in the vernacular [their native language] is not only of no use to them but is detrimental to the cause of their education and civilization, and no school will be permitted on the reservation in which the English language is not exclusively taught" (Meyer, 1993, pp. 188–189). The American Board of Missionaries school director, Alfred L. Riggs, decided to comply in order to maintain government financial support for the normal school (Bonvillain, 1996; Meyer, 1993). He did so, however, under protest, even pointing out in an official report submitted to the Secretary of the Interior that use of Dakota in schools on the Reservation was "indispensable to the best instruction" (U.S. Department of the Interior, 1887, p. 244). Despite this insight, from 1887 English-only instruction continued in Santee. It was not until the late 1990s that state policy acknowledged the Dakota language as meeting high school graduation requirements and added an alternative certification for teachers of Indigenous languages—as a foreign language (Neb. Rev. Stat. § 79–802.01).

The contract between the American Board of Missionaries and the U.S. government ended in 1893. After the Bureau of Indian Affairs closed the boarding school in Santee in 1909, the Santee were incorporated into Nebraska's county-based public school system, or they attended a federal boarding school on the reservation. A representative of the Bureau of Indian Affairs visited schools on or near the reservation in 1916; he found that "since the teachers were not employed by the government, they felt no responsibility toward the Indian children. 'The irregularity of attendance and the natural timidity of the Indian children rather annoy the teacher,' he reported, 'and, in most cases, no doubt, the teachers feel relieved when the Indians drop out'" (Meyer, 1993, p. 304). In the early years of the 20th century the federal government gradually decreased its presence in Santee, closing its agency in 1917 (Meyer, 1993). This also decreased federal oversight over the education of Santee children. In 1936, the Santee Normal Training School also closed its doors.

For decades, as children from the community continued to attend local public schools, members of the Santee community discussed a vision for having their own school, a school that would preserve Dakota culture and language and prepare the next generation of tribal leaders. It was not until 1971 that the Dakota people began to realize this wish with the founding of Santee Public School, a primary school that began with 12 students and one teacher. In the early years, school took place in one building and two double-wide trailers (Santee Community Schools, 2015). With supporting funds from a federal grant, the Santee district built a brick structure and renamed itself Santee Community Schools (SCS), expanding from a K–8 school to a K–12 system. (I will refer to the school as SCS until the point in the timeline when the school's name changed.) The school district, renamed *iSanti* Community School in 2021, is now a PK–12 system located in the village of Santee, which has a population of around 350 people. The school district is governed by a locally elected school board according to the statutes, rules, and regulations for all public school districts in the state of Nebraska.

Certainly, the founding of a school on the Santee reservation governed by a locally elected board organized around the Dakota virtues of *Woksape* (wisdom), *Woohtka* (bravery), *Wowacintanka* (fortitude), and *Wacantognaka* (generosity) is something to celebrate (iSanti Community Schools Staff Handbook, 2019). It also illuminates the complexities of public school governance with tribal sovereignty and right of self-education. Despite efforts in the 1960s and 1970s (like that in Santee) to return schooling control to local tribal communities and to reinvigorate Indigenous languages through bilingual education, assimilationist education policies endured (Castagno et al., 2016; Lomawaima & McCarty, 2006; McCarty, 2012; Reyhner & Eder 2004; Wyman, 2012). The school has experienced external state and federal government oversight almost since its inception in 1971. Most recently, efforts to oversee and improve educational outcomes in Santee have been the result of the standards reform–accountability reform movement in public education, and the school has been the subject of several federal and state school accountability interventions since NCLB.

SOVEREIGNTY, SELF-DETERMINATION, AND SELF-EDUCATION

Tribal Nations' sovereignty in governance and ways of being long preceded the arrival of European colonists and the establishment of what is now called the United States. Tribal sovereignty is acknowledged in the U.S. Constitution, and as I pointed out in the Introduction, there has long been a stated federal recognition of distinct tribal governments with the authority to govern their own people on their own lands (Hopkins, 2020; King, 2018; Wilkins & Lomawaima, 2001). The recognition of tribal sovereignty and the rights of Native peoples to governing, schooling, and determining their own societies has less frequently been acknowledged in the actions of the U.S. government or state governments.

The ongoing dynamics of policy in Santee fit well within a TribalCrit framework (Brayboy, 2005), as illustrated in the brief history of the Dakota people outlined above. Too often, education policy through U.S. federal and state law, regulation, or rule has been done *to* rather than *with* Native peoples, overlooking the right of Native peoples to self-education. TribalCrit emerged from Critical Race Theory (CRT). According to Brayboy (2013) "TribalCrit problematizes the concepts of culture, knowledge, and power and offers alternative ways of understanding them through an Indigenous lens" (p. 94). I hold to TribalCrit as an overarching framework as I interrogate the ways culture, knowledge, and power intersect in Santee.

While schooling in Indian Country, as illustrated in Santee, includes attempts to strike a balance between tribal commitments to self-determination and the preservation of self-governance and self-education, there is inherent conflict when schools in Indian Country are held to often-assimilationist demands placed upon schools by state and federal governments. Throughout the standards-accountability education policy reform era in the United States, particularly since the implementation of NCLB (2001), the focus on educational outcomes as measured by high-stakes testing in particular content areas (e.g., reading and math) has narrowed the curriculum and increased the time allocated to standardized assessment, resulting in a decline in culturally based instruction (Beaulieu et al., 2005; Mette & Stanoch, 2016; Patrick, 2008). Like schools serving students on or near American Indian reservations across the country, *iSanti* Community Schools was consistently listed among low-achieving schools in the state and has endured the accountability gaze of NCLB and more recent state accountability systems. The school received a federal School Improvement Grant (SIG) in 2010–2011 (Welch et al., 2015) and federal and state agency oversight expanded. Scrutiny intensified following the 2014 arrest of the SCS superintendent on charges of embezzlement from the SIG grant. Just a year later, following the completion of the SIG and the indictment of the former superintendent, NDE named SCS as one of three priority schools singled out for state-directed intervention out of 1,130 public schools in the state. At the time of the school's designation as a priority school, the student demographics were 84% Native American and 16% Hispanic students with 100% of students qualifying for free and reduced lunch. The district had experienced a more than 70% teacher turnover in the previous 2 years, and 40% of eligible enrollees living in the village of Santee used the state's option enrollment statute to enroll in the neighboring school district.

As will be described in upcoming chapters, state oversight and intervention in Santee looked remarkably similar to improvement efforts implemented in the other two named priority schools, both non-Native schools that were dramatically different in their student demographics and community context. Even as state or federal policies or mandates have recommended interventions and practices intended to improve test scores, administrators and educators from outside the reservation have come and gone from the school. Santee's local school governance, members of the community, and a number of key educators continually endeavored to mediate the tension between maintaining the mission to be a school of the tribe and for the tribe while also fulfilling the external expectations of what makes a school "good," as determined by the state. Legislators and policymakers pointed to Santee as they debated proposed school accountability legislation on the floor of the Unicameral. They conceptualized the Santee community and its students as a place filled with problems that needed more accountability to improve test scores and graduation rates. As Brayboy et al. (2015) assert, this view of Native peoples as the same as any other minority group ". . . ignores and undermines the totality of history and diving concepts like self-governance, sovereignty, and self-determination" (Brayboy et al. 2015, p. 5). There is a contrasting way to think about and to work to improve learning experiences and outcomes for American Indian children in the United States that begins with viewing Native knowledge and culture as "an ally" (Lomawaima & McCarty, 2006, p. 170) and demonstrates appreciation for tribal sovereignty and the right to self-education.

AGENCY, SURVIVANCE, AND SCHOOLING

Beyond acting within the larger policy context, individuals in Indian Country demonstrate their agency through the daily, ongoing struggle for self-government, self-determination, self-education through resistance and refusal, employing everyday tactics (de Certeau, 1984). There are several examples of the ways that Native peoples have resisted and remade policy spaces (e.g., Gram, 2016; Hopkins, 2020; Sabzalian et al., 2019). Sabzalian (2019) points to the "quieter, subtler" ways schools have been and continue to be "massive instruments of colonization" (p. xiii) and the ways individuals practice survivance as a tactic to resist ongoing colonization or deficit framing of Native culture and ways of knowing in schools. Sabzalian draws upon Vizenor (1999) and Morrill (2017) in defining survivance as something beyond the combination of the basic terms "survival" and "resistance." According to Morril (2017), "Survivance describes 'Indigenous creative approaches to life beyond genocide, beyond the bareness of survival' (Morrill, p. 15). It signifies "a sense of native presence over absence, nihility, and victimry" (Vizenor, 2007, pp. 12–13) (p. xv). Sabzalian offers nuanced examples of the everyday tactics Indigenous students, families, and educators practice through survivance stories in schools and the courage and artfulness demonstrated through the telling of individual and collective storytelling that resists deficit colonial frames and proffers counternarratives to make and remake the learning space for Indigenous children in schools.

WHAT'S A "GOOD" EDUCATION?

A central question in the neoliberal standards-accountability reform era is around what makes a school a "good" school. The federal government and states have quantified student performance and determined that a good school is one where students perform according to the metrics of standardized testing in identified content areas, and have high graduation rates (Carr, 2008; Cowen, 2014; Jaffer, 2010; Jester, 2002; Patrinos et al., 2015). As McNeil (2004) pointed out in a still-apt analysis, narrow numerical indicators and rankings have become the only language for assessing school quality in education policy. As a result, complex and technical accountability systems continue to be lauded and expanded at national and state levels. These policies contrast with comparative applications that allow more nuanced understandings of school quality (e.g., Barnhardt & Kawagley, 2005; Nelson-Barber & Johnson, 2019) and that highlight the importance of studying educational policy and sites of implementation in deeply contextualized ways (e.g., Anderson-Levitt, 2012; Simola & Rinne, 2011; Takayama, 2009) that offer contrasting views of what "good" schooling might look like and according to whom.

In 2014, McCarty and Lee argued that schools serving Native American children should be accountable not only to state and federal policy, but also to tribal nations. What does good schooling look like for schools that are also accountable to their Tribal communities? In a 1988 report, the Bureau of Indian Affairs described an overall lack of culturally relevant or responsive curriculum and pedagogy in schools. Education researchers have since explored Native American schooling environments and terms like *culturally relevant* and *culturally responsive* have been used to describe asset-based approaches that acknowledge tribal sovereignty and Indigenous ways of knowing and being (Beaulieu, 2006; Castagno & Brayboy, 2008; McCarty & Lee, 2014).

Gloria Ladson-Billings, building upon an array of research developed post–*Brown v. Board of Education* (1954), put forward a theoretical approach to teaching and learning in her foundational 1995 article "Toward a Theory of Culturally Relevant Pedagogy," arguing for pedagogical practices and structures in schooling that are inclusive of students' linguistic and cultural assets. In the years since, educational researchers have extended and expanded ideas of culturally relevant pedagogy to include culturally responsive teaching (Gay, 2002) and culturally responsive schooling (Ladson-Billings, 1990, 1995), and deepening what these ideas mean in the context of particular categories of students.

Culturally responsive schooling (CRS) expands culturally responsive practices beyond pedagogical practices in classrooms to thinking about culturally responsive structures and practices in school- and district-wide systems and practices (Castagno & Brayboy, 2008; Pewewardy & Hammer,

2003). It acknowledges the "mismatch in cultures" that contributes to lower academic performance among minoritized students as measured by high-stakes assessments. Addressing the mismatch "requires a shift in teaching methods, curricular materials, teacher dispositions, and school–community relations" (Brayboy & Castagno, 2009, p. 32). Successful CRS implementation in Indigenous contexts reflect common characteristics:

- School leadership and governing structures that are committed to the Indigenous community and to CRS, and that expect and support shifts in structures and practices in the school and in classrooms (Bird et al., 2013; McCarty, 2002; Robinson & Toney, 2021)
- Educators and support staff drawn from the community in the school (Deyhle, 1992; McCarty, 1993; Pewewardy & Hammer, 2003)
- Community support (Agbo, 2004; Alim et al., 2020; Cleary & Peacock, 1998; McCarty, 1993; Swisher & Deyhle, 1989)
- Indigenous epistemologies, pedagogies, and curriculum (Barnhardt & Kawagley, 2005, 2010; Cleary & Peacock, 1998; Demmert, 2001; Deyhle, 1998; Klug & Whitfield, 2003; Lipka, 1990; Lipka et al., 2005; Nelson-Barber & Estrin, 1995; Nelson-Barber & Johnson, 2019)
- Tribal rituals and traditions (Deloria & Wildcat, 2001; Lomawaima & McCarty, 2006; Powers et al., 2003)

In Santee, visions of a good education included culturally sustaining approaches to prepare the next generation of the tribe *and* a commitment to maintaining high academic expectations to ensure that students graduating from high school are equipped to pursue future careers and contribute to communities on or off the reservation.

CULTURALLY SUSTAINING AND RESPONSIVE PEDAGOGY

Django Paris (2012) extended work on culturally relevant/responsive pedagogies and schooling, offering a new framework: *culturally sustaining pedagogy* (Paris, 2012; Paris & Alim, 2014). Culturally sustaining pedagogy (CSP) critically builds on CRP, expecting that educators "support young people in sustaining the cultural and linguistic competence of their communities while simultaneously offering access to dominant cultural competence" (p. 95). It rejects a long history of linguicide, colonization, and deficit framing, and centers multilingualism and multiculturalism.

McCarty and Lee (2014) expanded these ideas, proposing critical culturally sustaining/revitalizing pedagogy (CSRP) as a way "to address the sociohistorical and contemporary contexts of Native American Schooling" (p. 103). According to McCarty and Lee, CSRP has three core features: (a) responding directly to power imbalances in ways that diminishes the legacies of colonization, (b) "reclaiming" and "revitalizing" Native language and ways of knowing and being in the world, and (c) "community-based accountability" that "serves the needs of Indigenous communities as defined by those communities" (p. 103). They go on to describe the structures and practices present at two case schools where CSRP is at the core of the way school is conducted, with educators attending to the languages and rituals and traditions of individual Native communities and to the common values and beliefs among the Tribal peoples served by the school. Evidence demonstrates that practices in schools that center students' cultures, identities, and communities in curriculum aligned to state standards enhances students' academic outcomes (Castagno & Brayboy, 2008; Demmert, 2001; Lee, 2009, 2015; McCarty, 2012; McCarty & Lee, 2014). At the same time, McCarty and Lee (2014) acknowledge the tension that is present when trying to balance state policy and school accountability expectations with CSRP commitments, which surfaces a question about what culturally sustaining and revitalizing policymaking and implementation could look like in practice. In the face of what Paris (2012) describes as the "current policies and practices that have the explicit goal of creating a monocultural and monolingual society," in the "democratic project of schooling," culturally sustaining and revitalizing philosophies need to extend beyond school to the policies that shape the ways we do school (Paris, 2012, p. 93). What would it look like, for example, for a state to be responsive to Tribal nations in the development and implementation of education policy? What would it look like for state-directed school improvement efforts to be rooted in Indigenous knowledges, structures, and practices? What if the state were accountable to Tribal communities just as schools are accountable to the state (Lomawaima & McCarty, 2006)?

CULTURALLY SUSTAINING/REVITALIZING EDUCATION POLICYMAKING

Policymakers and educational institutions need a better understanding of the history and sovereignty of Indigenous peoples and their responsibility toward students and the local tribal community (Austin, 2005). There should be humility and a willingness to listen and to understand the ways that even well-intentioned policies that seek to improve student outcomes or to advance equity through schooling have also homogenized and pathologized certain kinds of students and certain kinds of communities.

Policymaking is a sociocultural process (Sutton & Levinson, 2001) and is implemented not in a lab, but with all kinds of people in all kinds of communities. According to Sandra Stein's (2004) "policy culture" framework, the government often situates itself as a "corrective force" to remediate perceived deficits among individuals or groups (p. 19). The history of education policy toward Indigenous peoples in the United States, and the Santee Sioux more specifically, repeatedly framed individuals as needing guidance and "correction" (Bartlett & Brayboy, 2005; Child, 1998; Kawagley, 1995; Sumida Huaman & Valdiviezo, 2012; Wilkins & Lomawaima 2001). This history implores us to consider culturally responsive and sustaining approaches to policymaking and implementation that are authentic and that resist simplistic ways of incorporating cultural knowledge (Castagno & Brayboy, 2008; Hermes, 2005, 2007).

In the next four chapters I explore the development and implementation of school accountability policy in Nebraska that ultimately led to state intervention at SCS. The narrative ahead gives many examples where policymaking and implementation were not culturally responsive or sustaining; I will point to opportunities or missed entry points where individuals might have acted differently. Also, just as Lomawaima and McCarty (2006) describe finding "footprints of Native presence," or "the unexpected, the overlooked, the seemingly paradoxical results of and responses to domineering policies in institutions" (p. 13), I will point to critical moments of agentic acts and the ongoing pursuit of self-education in schooling spaces in Santee. First, we must go to the legislative floor in the country's only Unicameral where the proposed legislation that became AQuESTT was first imagined.

CHAPTER 4

Policy Crafted on the Legislative Floor

I'm sure children across the United States play a game of "I spy the capitol" when making a pilgrimage to their own state's legislative home. For 4th-graders in Nebraska traveling across a table-top prairie, the monument rising 400 feet into the air is the first landmark on the horizon one can see for miles. Upon the exterior of the Art Deco building completed in 1932 is inscribed each of the state's 93 counties along with the name of each American Indian tribe who first called this land home. Like all Nebraska school children, I made my own journey to this building and was awed by its wide green lawns, burnished woodwork, and the busts of Nebraska heroes like William Jennings Bryan and Willa Cather lining its marble hallways.

The capitol was built when the state still had two legislative bodies. The first single-body legislature (unicameral) took possession of the building's West Chamber in 1937. The larger of the two chambers, it displays images representing westward expansion, the prairie settler, and agriculture. The capitol tour guide ushered our class into the legislative chambers and told each of us to find a senator's seat. I sat up straight, short legs swinging from my perch, looking up at the gallery above and the names of each senator in front alongside the speaker's podium. I rubbed my small hand across the senator's name plaque on the desk before me and imagined being here as a grown-up. We role-played taking a vote, each 4th-grader buzzing in a yea or nay vote and watching the light alongside our senator pseudonym illuminate on the board above.

It was not until 26 years later, as an employee of NDE, that I visited the second legislative chamber. The East Chamber, now the Werner Chamber, is no longer home to a legislative body and is used for various governmental meetings. The room is adorned with symbols and images of Native cultures. Upon entering the room for a meeting, much like my 10-year-old self, I claimed a seat in front of a stately desk polished to a high shine. I leaned back, taking in the mosaic tilework on the ceiling above and the tapestries adorning the walls. Above me, images of harvest, buffalo hunts, and a tribal council made my throat ache and tears surface. On this particular day, while I waited among my colleagues for the Commissioner of Education to introduce a guest speaker, I felt the weight of the work happening in Santee. I thought about current policymaking and implementation and the ways it was reminiscent of the many policies carried out toward Indigenous communities in the United States. I recalled conversations that had happened across the hall in the West Chamber during debates on school accountability legislation, hearing the words of senators discussing schools like Santee. Bringing myself back to the present, I anchored my feet on the floor and rubbed my hand across the wood desktop, tracing the dents and dings on its surface, evidence of its history and the histories carried out in physical legislative spaces.

THE INTRODUCTION OF LB438

What follows here is an account of the development of Nebraska's school accountability bill, LB438, the debate around it, and ultimately, its signing into law in 2014. Evident in the floor debate is (a) an acknowledgment that school performance is related to broader societal structures that perpetuate inequities, as well as (b) an overall trust in the public education system as functioning well, alongside (c) a desire to support schools and communities that might be struggling to ensure an equitable education for all students. Conspicuous throughout LB438's journey through the legislative process, however, is the prescription of neoliberal reforms as remedies for "failing schools" (i.e., vouchers, charter schools) and the effort to align state education policies with what was going on in Washington, DC. For example, elements present in proposed legislation not so coincidentally aligned with national policies that would enable Nebraska to pursue a *Request for ESEA Flexibility*, which would relax some of the mandates under NCLB.

Senator Greg Adams, the Speaker of the Legislature, introduced LB438 at the beginning of the 2013 session. Prior to representing District 24 in the Unicameral, Adams spent his career in a small community of about 8,000, where he taught in a public school for 31 years and then served as mayor for 10. In his time in the Unicameral, Adams spent 4 years chairing the Education Committee. In the session in which he was elected Speaker of the Legislature, he made LB438 his priority bill amending previous (2012) legislation on school accountability.

The proposed bill, LB438 (Nebraska's 103rd Legislature, 2013a), would require the SBOE to develop a new school accountability system. The system would incorporate multiple indicators (e.g., student achievement data from assessments) into a single performance score for schools and districts, and classify them into performance levels. The SBOE also would be responsible for selecting up to five priority schools for intervention from the lowest performance level. An intervention team would be appointed for each priority school as well as a community school operating council to support the school's rapid improvement. The intervention team and community operating council would work in tandem to ensure that a priority school was accountable for improvement and that improvement efforts were aligned to the local community's wants and circumstances. Together, in collaboration with a priority school's staff and administration and the local board of education, they would develop a progress plan to improve the school and submit it for approval by the SBOE.

PUBLIC HEARING: A BETTER WAY TO "FIX" SCHOOLS

LB438 was assigned to the Education Committee for its first public hearing on February 25, 2013. Included among the bills and resolutions to be discussed that day were other school reform bills introduced by Sen. Lautenbaugh, representing District 18 in Northwest Omaha. The state's largest newspaper described Lautenbaugh, a notable politician with a booming voice, as "enjoy[ing] a fine cigar almost as much as baiting Democrats" (Duggan, 2014). In his time in the Unicameral, Lautenbaugh introduced several charter school bills before stepping down in the middle of his term to become a lobbyist in late 2014. In this particular Education Committee hearing, Lautenbaugh worked to advance bills he had introduced that session: one that would allow (but not require) the SBOE to adopt Common Core Standards and a charter school bill that would allow the establishment of five charter schools as a mechanism of school reform for "failing schools."

When Sen. Adams made his introductory remarks on LB438 to the Education Committee he asserted that while the proposed legislation had not been designed or introduced as an alternative to charter schools, the accountability and support in the bill could be perceived as such an alternative. He described how LB438 expanded upon previous school accountability legislation, updating it to authorize the SBOE to assume a new role in intervening in schools that "may be failing, but the fact they're failing means that we need to prioritize them and do something about them" (Nebraska's 103rd Legislature, 2013b).

Adams explained that priority schools support was not intended to be a state takeover, but rather collaborative intervention facilitated through the work of a team. He said that members of the intervention team would come alongside the school and community to "analyze the situation, prepare a report and say you've got to follow this plan and then continue to follow up on that to see to it that the plan is being followed" (Nebraska's 103rd Legislature, 2013b). Adams described the role of proposed community operating councils who would serve in an advisory capacity to ensure "local buy-in from the people that are right there whose kids go to that building or maybe they own the store right down the street, but they're part of that attendance area, and want to see that school improve" (Nebraska's 103rd Legislature, 2013b). These proposed structures, connecting external support and attending to local voice and context, contrasted with Sen.

Lautenbaugh's introduced legislation in the session. It makes sense, then, that Lautenbaugh was one of the first to speak in opposition to LB438 during the comment period. His advocacy for more forceful intervention measures, or, in his words, a "hammer" for "failing schools," ultimately influenced later amendments to the LB438 legislation and the role of a community operating council disappeared as a result.

Concerns among members of the Education Committee about the proposed legislation in the initial public hearing, however, focused primarily on finance. NDE had submitted a "hefty fiscal note" of $4.2 million. Adams agreed that the fiscal note was "dead on arrival," and would need to be addressed. He acknowledged, however, that the legislation would require significant financial support in order to provide intervention for the proposed five priority schools. The design of the intervention, he explained, would not "pump money and resources" into the schools but would focus on identifying the right expertise and local support to help the identified schools. The legislation did not prescribe any particular intervention model and would allow the SBOE to determine the model and expertise necessary to improve each priority school.

The Chief of Staff from NDE testified on behalf of Commissioner of Education Roger Breed in support of the proposed legislation. He stated that LB438 was both "reasonable and restrained" in its approach to "ensure all Nebraska students are afforded a high-quality educational opportunity." He called the bill "learning focused" in its provision of "a level of support and oversight that brings the community, the school, and the Department (NDE) into alignment to improve Nebraska schools" (Nebraska's 103rd Legislature, 2013b). He also addressed the concerns about the fiscal note, stating that "there is a cost to doing the kind of work necessary to accomplish what Sen. Adams proposed in the bill." If the legislature were looking for cost savings, he suggested amending the bill to three priority schools rather than five.

Other testimony on LB438 that day included representatives from educator unions (teacher and administrative) and Nebraska Association of School Boards (NASB). The Nebraska State Educators' Association (NSEA) representative Jay Sears stated that proposed legislation would allow Nebraska to consider how it could support its schools that might need improvement to develop plans to ensure that it happens. According to Sears, charter schools won't solve the problem; the state should take the opportunity to figure out how to coordinate support "and do the right thing for kids in the school districts" (Nebraska's 103rd Legislature, 2013b).

John Bonaiuto, registered lobbyist for the Nebraska Council of School Administrators (NCSA) and the Nebraska Association of School Boards (NASB), provided neutral testimony on the bill, expressing appreciation on behalf of both organizations for Adams's proposed legislation. He encouraged policymakers in the legislature to highlight the benefit of being a priority school. Being named a priority school ought to communicate that "you mean a great deal to your district and to the state, and we really do want to help and help you succeed. I think that's going to be an important part of this, that it's not a bad thing to be designated, but it's a helpful thing" (Nebraska's 103rd Legislature, 2013b).

Bonaiuto's comments regarding the opportunity within the legislation to transform ways of thinking about support for schools and communities through accountability brought the testimony on LB438 to a conclusion. In the days after this Education Committee discussion, Sen. Adams responded to the aggregation of the testimony by filing an amendment to the bill, changing the total number of priority schools that could be designated to three and removing the formation of operating councils for each priority school. The bill was placed on General File and postponed to the next session.

LB438 AND THE SECOND SESSION OF NEBRASKA'S 103RD LEGISLATURE

As LB438 waited on General File for a new session, the state education policy landscape shifted. Commissioner of Education Roger Breed announced that he would retire, effective July 1, 2013 (Dejka, 2013). The resignation shifted the policy landscape in Nebraska as the retired superintendent had been a moderating influence in the SBOE and legislative circles who supported moving forward with state accountability through an implementation model that included voices that represented the different kinds of school districts in the state. Despite the change in leadership, in the beginning of 2014 discussions in the Legislature, the SBOE, and NDE revolved around school accountability as the SBOE worked to identify the state's next Commissioner of Education. Sen. Adams continued his work toward advancing LB438 in collaboration with Chair of the legislative Education Committee, Senator Kate Sullivan (first elected to the Legislature in 2008 and representing the 41st District). The pair met with members of the SBOE and NDE in December 2013, prior to the start of the legislative session. As a result, when the SBOE gathered for their January 2014 work session and business meeting, the full board heard updates on LB438 and NDE's work to prepare for accountability policy implementation in anticipation that the bill would be reintroduced in the new legislative session.

When the Unicameral opened its session on January 8, 2014, Sen. Adams reintroduced LB438 along with a new amendment (AM 1540) put forward by Education Committee Chair Sen. Sullivan. Beyond giving LB438 the title *Quality Education Accountability Act*, the amendment updated the language and timeline so that data determining school and district classification and priority school designation would come from the 2014–2015 school year. In response, Sen. Lautenbaugh introduced another school accountability bill, the *Working to Improve Nebraska Schools Act* (LB952), a stark contrast to LB438. Lautenbaugh's bill included provisions related to retention at 3rd grade for students who did not demonstrate grade-level reading proficiency on statewide assessments, imposition of an A–F grading rating scale for schools and districts based on student performance on assessments, alternative teacher certification routes in the state, and school recognition and performance bonuses to schools for improvement (Nebraska's 103rd Legislature 2nd Session, 2014b).

When it was time for the LB952 Education Committee hearing, new Commissioner of Education Dr. Matthew L. Blomstedt testified in opposition to the bill. Blomstedt outlined how important it was for the SBOE and the commissioner to lead the development of an accountability system to best meet the needs of Nebraska students rather than legislators. Representatives from both the teachers' and administrators' unions spoke in opposition to LB952 as well. Bonaiuto, representing school administrators, indicated that the SBOE "should be involved in these types of [accountability] changes" and pointed to Speaker Adams's bill LB438, which "is trying to find out how do we help districts that are not making the kind of achievement that's necessary" (Education Committee Hearing, 2014). He pointed out that Adams's proposed legislation, unlike Lautenbaugh's, was developed in collaboration with the Commissioner and the SBOE.

Floor Debate: The First Day

Debate on LB438 opened on the floor of the Legislature on February 11, 2014. Sen. Adams and Sen. Sullivan provided introductory testimony. Adams stated that the bill would expand upon the previous accountability legislation (LB870) passed in 2012 and "put the State Board and Legislature in the same place so we're working together, not up against each other" (Nebraska 103rd Legislature 2nd Sess., 2014b). The proposed school accountability system included indicators that the SBOE would determine using data already collected by NDE. This flexibility within the bill allowed the SBOE to design a system to "evaluate school districts and school buildings to determine where we really have issues" (Nebraska 103rd Legislature 2nd Sess., 2014b). The bill also included provisions that authorized the SBOE to intervene in school districts with identified priority schools. Adams concluded his statements highlighting the importance of having an accountability system for Nebraska, not only a system imposed by Washington, DC. He reminded his fellow lawmakers of the larger education policy ramifications in the bill, stating that "We're one of the few states that cannot ask the [U.S] Department of Ed for waivers because we don't have an accountability system" (Nebraska 103rd Legislature 2nd Sess., 2014b). The passage of LB438 would grant the SBOE the authority to move the state toward a *Request for ESEA Flexibility*.

Sen. Sullivan spoke next, detailing how her amendment, AM1240, adjusted the 2013 version of the bill by decreasing the number of priority schools from a maximum of five to three and, as a result, the fiscal note projections decreased from "$4.2 million down to $800,000" (Nebraska 103rd Legislature 2nd Sess., 2014b). Sullivan also detailed how a second amendment, AM1580, updated the timeline from what was originally proposed to a timeline where the SBOE would classify schools and districts and name priority schools by December 2015 and approve priority school plans detailing how schools would improve their student performance in August 2016.

Initial discussion among senators on the first day of debate on the floor included a number rising to speak in support for the bill and others seeking clarification on processes that might be used to classify schools and districts or to designate priority schools. To each, Adams explained that the proposed legislation had intentionally left the decisions about how to accomplish the implementation of the accountability system up to the SBOE.

Floor Debate: The Second Day

The next day of debate on LB438 included broader debate on education reform policy. It began with Sen. Chambers, representing District 11 in North Omaha, expressing his opposition to the amendment that had decreased the number of priority schools from five to three. Chambers, a long-time Civil Rights advocate known for his eloquent, and often fiery, oratory, questioned whether the state was actually committed to improving schools or rather to being able to say they had done something when the proposed legislation would, in his opinion, have little result.

Sen. Larson, representing rural Northeastern Nebraska, including the Santee Sioux Reservation, expressed similar concerns. He described the challenges facing Santee Community Schools, pointing to "underlying issues that continue to hinder or hold it back" (Nebraska 103rd Legislature 2nd Sess., 2014c). Larson worried that three priority schools were not enough when considering the number of communities facing similar challenges. He asked how likely it would be that the three schools selected for "help" would come from outside Omaha or Lincoln. Larson told his fellow senators that "it's very easy to pick the priority schools that are close to home and ignore rural Nebraska" (Nebraska 103rd Legislature 2nd Sess., 2014c).

At the time of this legislative debate, Sen. Larson would have been well aware of some of the more recent turmoil in Santee. A month before, the tribal police had escorted the district's superintendent off the reservation.

The school was in the midst of an external evaluation of their $3.1 million School Improvement Grant (SIG) implementation and reeling from an FBI investigation into whether their superintendent had embezzled federal funds from the grant. Further debate included questions about broader societal constructs in communities that influenced schools and their ability to "perform." Sen. Harms, the former president of Western Nebraska Community College, representing a district in the state's rural panhandle, put forward his response to the bill. He questioned whether holding schools accountable in the current bill ignored the large number of children "coming in [to schools] with 'deficiency.'" According to Harms, "We're going to watch those children go all the way through this system and we are going to see failures all the way along the line" (Nebraska 103rd Legislature 2nd Sess., 2014c). Harms encouraged fellow senators to think about alternate education investments (like early childhood programing) before thinking about school accountability metrics and investments.

Sen. Lautenbaugh shared similar concerns about students' access to quality education. He asserted that Nebraska's education system was a problem and went on to say,

> And you may gasp, and you may say, oh my gosh, that can't be true, our schools do great, my schools do great, my kids go to a good school. Well, your kids might, but too many don't . . . [and] too many parents who wish their kids go to a good school have to put their children on a bus and send them elsewhere. And that's not how our system is supposed to work. (Nebraska 103rd Legislature 2nd Sess. 2014c)

To this, Education Committee Chair Sen. Sullivan responded, stating that the system was far from perfect; legislation like LB438 was necessary to help improve the system, because the state's "most valuable resource is the human capital and the young people that we have." Sullivan exhorted her fellow senators that

> there is no more important job that we have than to educate our young people. And no child should fall behind; no child should fall between the cracks; no child should be disengaged in this process. We want them all to be successful. And I'm proud of the system that we have. (Nebraska 103rd Legislature 2nd Sess., 2014c).

Sullivan described the opportunity inherent in the bill, that through supporting struggling schools the state could learn about interventions that could be applied in other schools.

Sen. Lautenbaugh was undeterred, and later asked Sen. Adams what would happen if a plan to improve a priority school didn't work. As he had done repeatedly, Adams explained that the language of the bill had intentionally been written to provide flexibility to the SBOE. On this, Lautenbaugh made his primary point in opposition of the bill. He asserted that while the state waited to see whether a priority school intervention plan would be successful, "with every year we fail more children" (Nebraska 103rd Legislature 2nd Sess., 2014c).

Lautenbaugh also countered Harms's assertion that the state should invest in early childhood in order to mitigate the effects of poverty. Lautenbaugh declared that outside factors like poverty or other outside neighborhood challenges could not be an excuse for schools and their accountability. He said,

> Well, I'm sorry, but that's the hand you're dealt. Teach them. . . . Some people think of the State Board or State Department of Education as coming in with the green eyeshades on and having a, you know, discussion over coffee about how this should change and how we could do better at these schools that are failing. And I keep using the F word: failing. Failing, failing, failing, because some of these schools are, by any reasonable measure, failing our children. I have a different image in mind of reformers from the State Department of Education in a perfect world swinging in on ropes through the windows and saying we're here to take over; we've assumed control; this ends today. . . . For true accountability to exist, there has to be a hammer; there has to be a sanction; there has to be something that happens if you fail to perform. (Nebraska 103rd Legislature 2nd Sess., 2014c)

In an effort to reinforce these remarks, Lautenbaugh put forward an amendment to LB438. He described the amendment, which he later withdrew, as a "kind of snarky thing," for it would have changed the bill's title from the *Quality Education Accountability Act* to the *Quality Education Postponement Act* (Nebraska 103rd Legislature 2nd Sess., 2014c).

Lautenbaugh's antics drew a new crowd of senators into the chambers. One of them, Sen. Heath Mello, responded to his fellow Omaha senator's statements. Upon taking the floor, Mello told his fellow senators that he had not originally planned to speak on the legislation that day, but that

> anytime I hear my good friend and colleague Senator Lautenbaugh stand up and discuss the perils of trying to blame poverty for why we just don't have the education system that we have and need right now, I get a little nervous and I get a little concerned. Because, unfortunately, that mindset is what is trying to drive a national debate right now when it comes to education policy, that, you know what, there's just poor kids and we've just got to deal with it. . . . I wish, Senator Lautenbaugh, there was simply a silver bullet to deal with poverty. There's not. (Nebraska 103rd Legislature 2nd Sess., 2014c)

Sen. Cook (also from Omaha) echoed Mello's arguments when she had the floor and extended the discussion to include broader education policy investments, citing access to early childhood as an example before pointing to larger systemic issues of race and long histories of oppression. She said:

> Sometimes I do feel, colleagues, that we frame our conversation around those issues, poverty, early childhood, limited English proficiency, because we are uncomfortable talking about the impact of race on the situations that we see in the schools, not only in Omaha but across the state. . . . I hate to say it but it is a fact in the state of Nebraska, people move away from people that they do not relate to racially. (Nebraska 103rd Legislature 2nd Sess., 2014c)

The remainder of the debate after Sen. Cook's remarks included continued commentary related to poverty and early childhood programming. The floor debate highlighted two distinct education policy approaches present in the session, one that embraced privatization and punitive mechanisms to encourage school improvement and one that focused on community input and providing reform efforts that were contextually appropriate to local school districts.

Floor Debate: The Third Day

The final day of debate on LB438 moved from discussions on education reform policies at large to the work of intervention teams in designated priority schools under LB438. Sen. Harms, who the day before had described the challenges some schools in his districts in the Western part of the state faced when children with "deficits" come to kindergarten unprepared, commented that the intent of the bill was to identify schools that needed help and to send a team to help the superintendent, board, and leadership adjust. Harms asserted that "what this bill is all about is to get into those schools that are failing and the children to come along that are not doing well, to intervene with that and put a team together to help them get there" (Nebraska 103rd Legislature 2nd Sess., 2014d).

Sen. Larson, representing the legislative district for Santee, again took the floor, this time inquiring about the makeup of these teams and whether selected individuals might have expertise in "school turnaround." Sen. Adams responded yet again that decisions about intervention models would be the responsibility of the SBOE and NDE to define. He stated, however, "I don't have any reason to believe that the department [NDE] is going to put blinders on to those people who within the state or outside the state . . . that couldn't help us" (Nebraska 103rd Legislature 2nd Sess., 2014d).

Larson disagreed, saying that in his opinion NDE had repeatedly put blinders on regarding other education policy reforms, including charter schools, teacher certification, and Teach for America. He was concerned

Policy Crafted on the Legislative Floor 67

about who might be selected to intervene and what might happen should a school not turn around. Larson took the opportunity to reassert that national charter school chains be considered as possible interventions in priority schools, stating that

> Why don't we say if the priority school has not improved in five years we will convert it to an Achievement First charter school or a KIPP [Knowledge is Power Program] charter school or an Aspire Public School charter school? Because we've made them a priority in LB438, they still can't get their stuff together. We've seen in other states that these charter schools, KIPP schools are some of the best schools in the nation, highest rated public schools in the nation. Why can't we do that in LB 438? . . . We know it works. We know there's been turnarounds, yet we're willing to pass or look at something that's watered down. (Nebraska 103d Legislature 2nd Sess., 2014d)

Larson's frustration was evident when he stated that "there still could be a school that's a priority school for 5 years or 10 years with no conversion." To these criticisms of the legislation Sen. Adams responded that his bill obviously did not address charter schools. (At that time, charter schools were not permitted in Nebraska.) Adams reminded the senator that "[t]hat's a whole other issue, a whole other issue that is currently being dealt with in the Education Committee" (Nebraska 103rd Legislature 2nd Sess., 2014d).

Then, before taking a vote on whether to move LB438 from General File to Select File, Sen. Adams provided his closing statements on the legislation. He told assembled senators that the legislation, while not a "silver bullet," was a start, a start that would give the state "an opportunity to add to the federal accountability system," as well as the "statutory authority to intervene in these schools that don't seem to get it turned around." In response to the most recent debate on the floor, which included repeated references to "failing schools," and the necessity of reforms inclusive of charter schools, Adams reminded his colleagues that, "we get into a discussion like this, [and] all the focus is on the failure and you forget about all the successes out there" (Nebraska 103rd Legislature 2nd Sess., 2014d). On this note, with a vote of 35-0, the bill advanced. Debate on the priority schools illuminated how senators were imaging priority schools, where they might be located, the communities they might serve, and what approached might bring change and improvement in student achievement outcomes.

Nearly 3 weeks later, on March 5, 2014, Sen. Adams filed an additional amendment, AM1934, which granted the SBOE stronger authority should a priority school not demonstrate progress after 5 years. It was referred to as the "hammer" by legislators in floor debate, which included comments from Sen. Lautenbaugh on the proposed amendment expressing his impatience about how long it would be until real change happened in schools that weren't performing as they should. Lautenbaugh said:

> I don't think business as usual is acceptable anymore and it shouldn't have been acceptable for as long as it has been. . . . I'm not sure we have a sledge[hammer] yet . . . more to the point, I don't know that we have anyone willing to swing it." (Nebraska 103rd Legislature 2nd Sess., 2014e)

To this, Education Committee chair Sen. Sullivan asserted that with the proposed legislation the SBOE would develop the tools to identify "low-performing schools" as well as the processes to "help those schools." She reminded her colleagues, "This is a new process. We don't know exactly what it's going to look like," and acknowledged Lautenbaugh's impatience, stating,

> It's going to be a methodical process because they [State Board of Education] want to develop appropriate indicators, appropriate measurements so that they don't just tell a school "You're failing, you're doing a bad job." Well, how are we doing a bad job and how can you help us do a better job? So that does need to be a thoughtful and somewhat methodical process. (Nebraska 103rd Legislature 2nd Sess., 2014e)

She also rejected statements that the education system was broken in Nebraska, pronouncing that she was so proud of the schools across the state.

Sen. Mello offered his appreciation for both Sen. Sullivan's and Sen. Adams's work in bringing LB438 forward and continuing to work with senators to improve it throughout the session. Mello pointed to one particular feature included in the amendment, referring to it as the "hammer" that had been requested in earlier debates, which gave the SBOE the authority to put in an alternate administrative structure if progress was not made in a priority school within 5 years. Mello acknowledged how the bill had been modified in response to the dialogue on the floor requesting more heavy-handed responses to schools not performing well.

> That gives the Department of Education, under this bill, the ability to come to a school district, and if necessary, if they don't meet the ongoing benchmarks that's needed for progress, the Department of Education can come forward and they can close down a school. They can come into a district, to a specific school and completely change the administrative leadership. This, essentially, was part of that hammer that we had discussed. (Nebraska 103rd Legislature 2nd Sess., 2014e)

The Unicameral approved amended changes in a vote of 28–0, and the bill was forwarded to Enrollment and Review for engrossment.

LB438 was placed on Final Reading on March 10, 2014. Fifteen days later, Adams filed another amendment to the final copy, AM2624, adding an emergency clause that would make the bill immediately effective upon being signed into law by the governor. On March 27 the bill was returned to Select File and once again brought to the floor of the Legislature. Following its adoption, the bill advanced once again to engrossment and review. On the last day of March, the bill was placed on Final Reading for a second time.

The Final Reading and vote on LB438 took place on April 3, 2014. Across a wide marble hallway from the Werner Chamber with its mosaic testament to the peoples native to Nebraska, the bill passed, with 48 senators voting affirmative and one senator present but not voting. In the accompanying appropriations bill, 48 voted affirmative, no senator voted against the appropriation, and Sen. Lautenbaugh was present but did not vote. The President/Speaker of the legislative body signed the bill immediately and presented it to the Governor on the same date. With the addition of the emergency clause, it would be made effective the day following the governor's signature.

LB438 BECOMES LAW

On April 9, 2014, Governor Dave Heineman signed LB438 into law. The bill became Nebraska Revised Statute §§79-760.06-07. After 2 years of collaborative work among Sen. Adams and the Education Committee chaired by Sen. Sullivan, the SBOE, and NDE, the state, by statute, had a requirement to develop an accountability system that would include the classification of schools and districts into performance levels, and the authority to identify and intervene in up to three priority schools. Reviewing the crafting of LB438 in this chapter with such detail illuminates the ways legislators imagined failing schools and what might "fix" those schools. Repeatedly, legislators described schools as "failing," using deficit frames that included terms like "poverty" or "urban" as a proxy for racial or ethnic groups. In particular, Sen. Larson raised concerns about the "underlying issues" in Santee that contributed to the school's low achievement present in all the Native schools in the state. While the proposed bill initially included a proposal for a community school operating council intended to work collaboratively with NDE to construct an improvement plan to be submitted to the SBOE for approval, such councils were removed after a number of senators raised concerns that the legislation did not include enough direct state oversight or accountability for priority schools. As one senator asserted, there needed to be a bigger "hammer" for schools that were "failing." Instead, an amendment allowed the SBOE to institute an alternate administrative structure should a school not be released from priority school status after 5 years.

LB438 made it through the legislative process; a block down the wide Centennial Mall from the Capitol, Commissioner Blomstedt, the SBOE, and

NDE employees were just beginning the state's work to develop how the provisions of LB438 would become actualized in practice in the state. The legislative intention of LB438 shifted the role of the SBOE and NDE in responding to certain kinds of schools, which highlights the importance of attending to policy spaces and the way people within policy leverage structures of power and personal agency to recreate or reproduce systems and institutions. Tracing LB438's pathway through the legislature also highlights whose voices are missing and how certain groups of people are framed within policy.

Setha Low (2014), in her work on space in urban anthropology, asserts that theories of space "provide a powerful tool for uncovering material and representational injustice and forms of social exclusion" (p. 34). Taking up an exploration of policy spaces requires interrogating physical spaces (e.g., legislative chambers, board rooms) as well as figurative spaces, or what Lévi-Strauss (1963) described as *unconscious mental structures* like the spaces of legislative or board discussion and decision-making. It is also necessary to consider both official and unofficial policy spaces. Official policy spaces include public-facing spaces where policies are made, like legislative chambers or hearings. Unofficial policy spaces include hallways where conversations among colleagues occur, or in the case of AQuESTT, classrooms where educators made sense of, and acted according to their own interpretations of, official policy.

I will continue to attend to this thread of space in the upcoming chapters. The humans engaged in policymaking and implementation, and those who are the intended recipients of policy, are acted upon by space nested within systems or structures of power (Foucault, 1977). They also employ agentic tactics to reconstitute space or to author a new configuration of space. Low and Lawrence-Zúñiga (2003) refer to these spaces where social actors engage in conflict or resistance to transform space or the distribution of power as "contested spaces" (p. 18). I raise the following questions for consideration in relation to the unfolding implementation of AQuESTT in upcoming chapters: In what ways do policy structures constrain stakeholders' identities and agency? How do educators, families, communities, and students act within policy spaces that constrain? How do social agents contest space in evolving policy cultures that impose marginalization?

CHAPTER 5

Nebraska's AQuESTT
Bolder, Broader, Better

Until 2020, NDE took up nearly all of the sixth floor of the Nebraska State Office Building, which is just a block from the Nebraska State Capitol. A reception desk sat at one end of a landing, and the waiting area just outside the commissioner's office was lined with photographs of former commissioners of education. A side door led into the SBOE meeting room, where a large semicircular table was flanked by high-backed office chairs. There, for at least 2 days a month, the names of eight SBOE members filled placard spaces in front of each chair. Projection screens filled three walls behind the semicircular table; in front, there was a long table where people presenting or providing public comment sat before the gathered board. Behind this table were four rows of chairs, the public gallery. Depending on the items on the board's agenda, this gallery was vacant or overflowing.

Organizationally, NDE was divided into various teams that included Federal Programs; Assessment, Accreditation, and School Improvement; Data, Research, and Evaluation; Teacher Certification; and Teaching and Learning. The area for each department on the sixth floor of the building was demarcated by plastic signs hanging from stained ceiling tiles. On my first visit and tour of the office in 2014, my thought was *Mad Men*, quickly followed by "rat maze," as the space had few permanent walls, was segmented into small cubicles divided by long hallways, and had many dead ends. Take away the cubicles, and the floor plan would indeed be reminiscent of an open-concept office in the 1960s, with wide-open spaces dotted by desks and a constant hum of noise. Even as late as 2017, at times I could hear a typewriter clacking a few cubicles over. Particularly in those moments, I felt transported to what NDE must have been like when it moved into the space several decades before.

I share this because the segment of the school accountability policy implementation I chronicle is a recent history tucked in a much longer history of schooling. In Chapter 2, I introduced Susan Follett Lusi's (1997) work that examined two state education agencies (SDEs) responding to complex education reform in the 1990s. The questions about NDE's role that emerged in Nebraska in 2014 are the same ones that emerged for Lusi in her study of Kentucky's and Vermont's SDEs. Therefore, I echo Lusi when

I ask whether it is possible for states to achieve the alignment necessary to turn plans on paper into an implementation reality that reflects what was envisioned. In order to interrogate what happened, I draw the reader's attention back to the key actors described in Chapter 2 who transformed LB438's legislation into AQuESTT between 2014 and 2017. I ask the reader to also note I am moving backward in the timeline to provide context for what was happening at NDE while LB438 was moving toward becoming state law.

THE SBOE HIRES A NEW COMMISSIONER OF EDUCATION

While discussions were happening about LB438 between legislative sessions in 2013–2014, the SBOE was in the midst of a search to fill the Commissioner of Education position left vacant by Dr. Roger Breed, who had served as commissioner since 2009. During their December 6, 2013, meeting, then-President of the SBOE Pat Timm announced a special session to take place on December 11 and 12 to interview candidates. Also in this meeting, board member Mark Quandahl, in his Legislative Committee report, shared that the sponsor of LB438, Sen. Adams, and chair of the Education Committee, Sen. Sullivan, had visited with the committee to discuss the bill. Quandahl informed fellow SBOE members that in the upcoming January board meeting they would need to discuss and then adopt at least a skeletal framework for the new accountability system. Also during this board meeting, in her Accountability Ad Hoc Committee report to the full board, Molly O'Holleran described NDE's work in framing an accountability system that would align with both LB438 and, potentially, the requirements for ESEA flexibility. O'Holleran pointed out that in any accountability work, "We like to do things the Nebraska way." O'Holleran outlined a vision of accountability that, according to the committee, included revisiting the purpose and role of accountability so as "not just to point fingers and blame, but to get answers and to provide solutions . . . really the carrot of accountability instead of the stick" (NSBOE, 2013a).

On December 12, 2013, the SBOE voted 8–0 to hire Dr. Matthew L. Blomstedt to become the new Commissioner of Education in Nebraska. Most recently serving as the Executive Director of the Educational Service Unit Coordinating Council, Blomstedt acknowledged that his path to the position had not followed the typical trajectory of teacher, administrator, or superintendent. When making their decision public, SBOE members highlighted Blomstedt's leadership and relationship with many of the state's superintendents, as well as his understanding of state education policy and school funding and previous practice in working in the legislature with people with different political affiliation, as some of the reasons he was selected. Blomstedt immediately announced that his first priority would be to "focus on the legislative agenda [and] a measure introduced by State Sen.

Greg Adams of York and the Education Department [that] would create an accountability system to address schools with achievement problems" (Anderson, 2013).

In January 2014, the Director of Statewide Assessment provided an update on NDE's plan for and progress toward developing parameters for a new accountability system aligned with proposed legislation that would be reintroduced in the new legislative session (LB438). Small in stature, with a blunt cut bob of blond hair, she commanded every room she entered. Chin held high and with laser-precise locution, the Director of Statewide Assessment reminded board members of the recent development of the state's current accountability ranking system (NePAS) that was developed in response to Sen. Adam's previous (2012) legislation. She described a plan to design what she called NePAS 1.1, which would use additional indicators that could include student assessment participation, graduation rate (for high schools), and student performance on assessments using status, growth, or improvement. She explained that in order to ensure that students across the traditional subgroups outlined in NCLB met grade level proficiency, the new system design could include a "super-subgroup" of non-proficient students rather than the subgroups used under the federal annual yearly progress (AYP) system. This super-subgroup was the state's approach to addressing equity in the wide range of student demographics present in Nebraska schools. Incorporating a super-subgroup would hold schools accountable for the number of students who were not meeting proficiency on the state's annual assessments.

The Director of Statewide Assessment clarified that what she was presenting was merely an introductory framework for how the state might respond to LB438. She outlined a plan that would establish a task force representative of districts across the state along with national accountability and assessment experts that would further develop an accountability model that could be presented to the SBOE. She reminded board members that in order to meet the ambitious timelines proposed in LB438, it was requisite that NDE begin initial work on the accountability system's structure. In their meeting the next day, the SBOE unanimously approved the initial framework for what was then called NePAS1.1 and would become AQuESTT.

By the time that the SBOE convened for their work session and business meeting in April 2014, LB438 had passed the legislature and awaited the Governor's signature. In this meeting, following the resignation of two members from the SBOE, the newly appointed Commissioner of Education, Dr. Matthew L. Blomstedt, PhD, welcomed two new members: Glen Flint of District 2, representing suburban Omaha, and John Witzel of District 4, representing a significant part of the Omaha metro area. In his opening statements, Commissioner Blomstedt asked that veteran board members provide a brief history and context to support new board members' learning about each discussion and action item on the day's agenda. Much of the conversation focused on LB438, the state's history with accountability, and the work that had moved forward since the board's January approval of an initial accountability framework, NePAS 1.1. In his legislative overview, NDE's Chief Legal Counsel told board members that

> we are certainly hopeful that the Governor will sign 438 and provide the funding to the Department to carry out those provisions. This has been the focus of the Board for the last two years. Senator Adams and Senator Sullivan have been very helpful in working with us. They've met several times with the Board's legislative committee on this bill and everything. Hopefully the Governor will sign this bill yet this week so that we can finally complete Nebraska accountability and do it the way we do things in Nebraska. (NSBOE, 2014a)

With the Governor's signature, the SBOE and department of education assumed a new role related to accountability. For the first time, the state had the authority to intervene in a local school.

The Director of Statewide Assessment provided new board members with a brief history of school accountability in Nebraska. She explained how accountability developed through the state's School-based, Teacher-led Assessment and Reporting System (STARS) system and statewide writing assessment in 2001. STARS was followed by Nebraska Statewide Assessments (NeSA) in reading, math, and science and then, in 2012, the Legislature passed Neb. Rev. Stat. § 79–760.06, which mandated a basic accountability system. NDE, in collaboration with educators from across the state, developed NePAS, the Nebraska Performance Accountability System, to meet the requirements of the 2012 legislation. The Director of Statewide Assessment described the measures and reporting included in the NePAS system along with benefits as well as some of the confusion that had been expressed regarding its multiple rankings. She reminded the board that the rankings in NePAS included status assessment scores from statewide assessment along with measures including growth, improvement, participation, and graduation rates. She explained that when one looked at the State of the Schools Report for Nebraska schools, there "are like 40 rankings there. For some people, it's sort of confusing," she stated. The Director of Statewide Assessment went on to point out the advantage of publishing all the rankings, that all data is available to the public. "While it may look like a complex system," she asserted, "there is a certain simplicity about listing all of it and leaving that to the local district to tell their story, based on those data" (NSBOE, 2014b).

With this context, the Director of Statewide Assessment described how LB438, if signed by the Governor, would change school accountability in Nebraska. The legislation would do away with NePAS's multiple rankings and reports. "The major difference is that it asks us to develop a system to assign schools and districts to a performance level," she specified, "so we need to determine however many performance levels we are going to have, and assign schools to one of those, based on the criteria that are determined to identify the three lowest performing schools in the state" (NSBOE, 2014b). She then outlined how the new legislation required the SBOE to assume an entirely new role, moving beyond analyzing and ranking school performance to providing intervention and school improvement help, particularly for the three priority schools.

The Director of Statewide Assessment reminded board members that in working collaboratively with Sen. Sullivan and Sen. Adams from the Legislature, NDE had been able to begin work in anticipation of LB438's passage. Since the SBOE approval of an initial framework for NePAS 1.1 in January, NDE had created a task force made up of between 50 and 60 members who represented all different roles in education across the state, including superintendents, principals, teachers, district assessment coordinators, NDE experts, and intermediate service agency partners representative of the array of school contexts in the state. Also participating in the work of the task force were national school assessment and accountability experts who provided professional development and support for task force members as they researched accountability models and analyzed the impact of policy decisions on the state's available data. In a 4-day meeting held in February, the task force discussed the number of performance levels that should go into the new accountability system and how the system could consider subgroup performance. They debated what a formula might look like to place schools and districts in performance levels that would also identify the priority schools. She explained that the task force would bring a recommendation to the SBOE soon, acknowledging the shortness of the timeline ahead.

The Director of Statewide Assessment concluded her update with the unique processes Nebraska leveraged in designing its accountability system. She stated that the process "is pretty typical of what we do in Nebraska" (NSBOE, 2014b). Acknowledging NDE's history of engaging stakeholders in the work of policy development, she asserted, "We go to educators, we use state department expertise, we work with our State Board committees, and eventually we move that to a process where we are able to adopt that" (NSBOE, 2014b). She contended that this kind of approach to policy was unusual and pointed out that "I go to the federal meetings, and I can tell you not every state has their legislature, their state board, their schools, and their state education department working on the same page. I think that really speaks well for Nebraska" (NSBOE, 2014b). It is important to note here that while there was a diverse representation of roles and district contexts on the task force, the only person representing Native voices was the Multicultural Education Coordinator from NDE; there were no other representatives from tribes in the state. There was, however, one non-Native curriculum and assessment director who represented the school district located on the *UMÓⁿHOⁿ* Nation reservation.

Following the Director of Statewide Assessment's presentation, Accountability Committee chair O'Holleran commented that while NCLB was a "failed law," it had forced schools to look at their at-risk student population performance. She vowed that the SBOE would continue to focus on "ameliorating those achievement gaps that exist between our at-risk groups; it still matters that we're addressing the needs of some of our lowest-performing groups" (NSBOE, 2014b). O'Holleran also described the long-term vision for the new system that would incorporate broader measures beyond statewide assessment, possibly including dual-credit and Advanced Placement course offerings as a way to incentivize practices in schools that could provide greater access to students across the state.

Commissioner Blomstedt outlined his broad vision for assessment that might think about pulling in student performance data differently. He told SBOE members that from a policy perspective he wanted to "dip our toe into the water" of accountability to see how districts were doing while also using the data to engage and support schools in their improvement processes (NSBOE, 2014c). Blomstedt acknowledged the collaborative work among the Legislature, the SBOE, and NDE. He thanked both Sen. Sullivan and Sen. Adams for moving LB438 forward. He informed SBOE members that collaboration with the Legislature would be necessary if Nebraska were going to design an "education system for the future" (NSBOE, 2014c). What he, O'Holleran, and the Director of Statewide Assessment described pointed to a Nebraska Way of engaging in policy development and implementation. Up to this point, the process of moving school accountability forward had been a collaborative one. For the future, Blomstedt committed to pushing for a conception of accountability that would be "bolder and broader" (NSBOE, 2014c).

FROM VISION TO PLANS ON PAPER

In August 2014 Commissioner Blomstedt gave his keynote address to education leaders gathered for the annual Administrators' Days Conference. He told the group he was there to talk about "building support systems for every student every day" (NDE, 2014a). He acknowledged the significant work ahead in developing an accountability system that met the requirements of LB438 and that would support schools' improvement. Blomstedt explained that each public school and district in the state would be placed in a performance classification. He assured administrators that he did not want accountability to feel punitive. "These are schools that are in most need of assistance to improve," he explained, and it was his moral obligation as Commissioner to provide them support (NDE, 2014a). Blomstedt informed gathered administrators that the following week the State Board of Education (SBOE) would release a "high-level model" of what the system might include and concluded his remarks by encouraging audience members to provide feedback and to continue to dialogue to develop the system together (NDE, 2014a).

A week later, the SBOE, in their August 2014 meetings, unveiled a draft document outlining components of the state's new accountability system: AQuESTT. Accountability Committee Chair O'Holleran opened the discussion, pointing SBOE members to a document with the image of a light bulb on its cover and saying, "It's a system to support every student, every day and we're calling this Accountability for a Quality Education System Today and Tomorrow: AQuESTT for Nebraska" (NSBOE, 2014c). She explained that LB438

> put a new onus on the State Board of Education to really talk about a type of classification system where we can look at school districts and provide support for those lower performing school districts and also highlight best practices for our high performing districts. (NSBOE, 2014c)

Commissioner Blomstedt said AQuESTT would categorize schools and districts in one of four performance levels: Excellent, Great, Good, and Needs Improvement. The three priority schools would be chosen from schools in the Needs Improvement classification. He also unveiled SBOE work to develop six tenets to be included in the accountability system that could point to best practices. The tenets, or "key investment areas," were Positive Partnerships, Relationships, and Student Success; Transitions; Educational Opportunities and Access; Assessment; College- and Career-Ready; and Educator Effectiveness.

A special presentation on accountability during the SBOE's September 5, 2014, business meeting illuminated how the work of the NePAS 1.1 task force and the AQuESTT accountability framework might fit together. Accountability Committee Chair O'Holleran explained that AQuESTT would focus on continuous improvement and move from ranking schools to classifying them into the four performance levels. She made it clear that Nebraska would continue its commitment to a collaborative process that would include local boards of education, districts, schools, policy partners, and other stakeholders.

It was against this backdrop that Commissioner Blomstedt and SBOE President Rachel Wise welcomed representatives of the NePAS 1.1 task force that had been working since February 2014 on models that could help the state move forward in meeting the requirements of LB438. Representatives of the task force present for the meeting included a curriculum and assessment director at a school for *UMÓⁿHOⁿ* Nation, a national psychometrician and assessment and accountability consultant, a superintendent of a midsized district, and an evaluation director for the second-largest district in the state. NDE personnel who had worked with the task force included the newly hired Accountability Coordinator and the former federal programs director contracted to work on AQuESTT.

The national assessment and accountability consultant explained that the task force's work on accountability had progressed from examining national and some international models of accountability to looking at what Nebraska needed its system to be able to do in order to meet the state's statutory requirements. He explained that the group had also received direction from Commissioner Blomstedt that they were to be "aware of, but not driven by whatever the federal policy might be" (NSBOE, 2014c). The task force developed policy descriptors for each performance level and explored methodologies that would also allow for a range of indicators to be folded in together to create a single score. They analyzed the application of methodologies for all sizes and school contexts and developed draft business rules that could be considered using authentic data throughout the modeling process. This overall work, task force members described, was built around the culture of Nebraska and Nebraska schools. One superintendent commented, "I think that in this case it's a real credit to Nebraska culture that we've taken our time and we've analyzed what else is out there and we haven't made a rushed judgment or a rush to judge schools" (NSBOE, 2014d). Task force representatives seemed to be in agreement that while the work was challenging, they felt it was important to have Nebraska educators as a part of that work. Commissioner Blomstedt commented on the task force's presentation:

> I view it, this is truly a Nebraska thing and in a powerful and good way. Because we are engaging our schools and our stakeholders across the state in pretty complex issues. I think it is amazing as we start to lay out a vision for what this looks like and what we're trying to do is essentially bring that together into a very solid accountability system for the state of Nebraska. (NSBOE, 2014d)

Beyond the presentation and the attached executive summary, the models referenced in the meeting were not made available to the public. There were descriptions about the process used by the task force and references to multiple indicators that could include status scores, growth, and improvement, but the models themselves would be presented at a future meeting.

The apparent alignment among the parties (e.g., legislators, SBOE, NDE, educator unions, school districts) looked hopeful, but the transition from vision to implementation reality on the ground would be a testing point. It was near the beginning of this significant state education policy reform that I found myself in the middle of AQuESTT's development and implementation at NDE.

It was at this point of the development of AQuESTT, in September 2014, that I began working as the Student Achievement Coordinator at NDE. As my position was a newly legislatively created role, there was no way for me to know how much of my job description might include AQuESTT. I met the Commissioner of Education on my second day on the job, and only a week later I sat in a hotel ballroom in a Western Nebraska town made famous by Buffalo Bill Cody and his Wild West Show for the first AQuESTT policy forum intended to gather input on the nascent accountability system from stakeholders across the state. Throughout October 2014, NDE staff and SBOE members met with stakeholders by region to discuss AQuESTT and the SBOE's vision for school accountability. In total, there were 252 participants. Themes that emerged from those conversations included recommendations to include a broader set of indicators such as student mobility, attendance, or teacher effectiveness. Within that first month it was clear that much of my time at NDE would be focused on AQuESTT.

Stakeholder input from the policy forums was a central part of the discussion in November 2014 SBOE meetings. Commissioner Blomstedt commented that he learned a lot in the process of listening. He asked board members to consider how they might authentically involve stakeholders throughout the development of the new accountability system. He wondered aloud in the meeting, "Just how do we engage more community members? How do we really listen to our schools? How do we really share the message?" (NSBOE, 2014e). Finally, he thanked the board for their continued support and their leadership in building AQuESTT and for the discourse they had shared with constituents and among themselves in the process.

CODIFYING AQuESTT

Just as the Unicameral passed LB438 into law under the authority of the Nebraska Constitution, the legislative body authorized NDE under the leadership of the Commissioner of Education, and the authority of the SBOE, to adopt or promulgate regulation "in order to clarify and define processes and requirements outlined in state law" (Nebraska Secretary of State, 2016). Rules and regulations have the same "force of law" and comprise the Nebraska Administrative Code (N.A.C.). There is a mandatory regulation adoption process whether a rule is being created, amended, or repealed that includes a rule drafting period, a 30-day notice of public hearing, a public hearing, submission of proposed rule to the attorney general and governor's offices for review and approval, and finally being sent to the secretary of state, where rule becomes law after 5 days. Just as the public has a role in the lawmaking process, the central purpose of a rule hearing and adoption process is to ensure that the public is able to participate in rulemaking.

At this point in the AQuESTT development and implementation process, the Commissioner and the SBOE needed to determine how to codify the new accountability system in rule and regulation. They debated on whether to create a new regulatory rule or to amend *Rule 10: Regulations and Procedures for the Accreditation of Schools*. Decisions needed to be made quickly in light of the overall implementation timeline outlined in Neb. Rev. Stat. §§ 79–760.06-.07 and the necessity of providing a 30-day notice to the public prior to a hearing on a rule. Discussions in the board's December 2014 work session and business meeting centered on the inclusion of AQuESTT into the standing rule for school accreditation, known in short as *Rule 10*.

SBOE Board President Rachel Wise opened the discussion of revisions saying, "We are excited to discuss *Rule 10* today," and the Director of Accreditation and School Improvement quipped back with a grin, "Aren't we all!" (NSBOE, 2014e). The Director of Accreditation and School Improvement referred board members to their *Rule 10* drafts and documents that outlined revisions related to AQuESTT. The Accountability Coordinator, a calm and quiet contrast to the Director of Accreditation and School Improvement's energy and charisma, guided the SBOE page by page through the draft rule and explained, in her typical even cadence, each proposed change. These included incorporating definitions into the first pages; fitting the six tenets of AQuESTT into sections of the rule related to them; and, where appropriate, adding language taken directly from the statute related to the classification of schools, the designation of priority schools, the development of a progress plan in each priority school, the implementation of progress plans, and the annual reporting on progress to the SBOE.

Following this presentation, Commissioner Blomstedt outlined a timeline should the board grant him the authority to approve a hearing draft of proposed revisions to *Rule 10*. Following any final revisions, the Commissioner would approve a hearing draft, appoint a hearing official, and announce the hearing at least 30 days in advance of a scheduled hearing. The hearing would provide opportunity for public input on the draft for the SBOE to review by their February meeting. Blomstedt explained, "By March we would have to have the framework pretty well laid out so that we could actually run, do the numbers so that we can prepare to actually start to share that information with schools" (NSBOE, 2014f).

SKETCHING OUT AQuESTT'S IMPLEMENTATION

In their first meeting of the 2015 calendar year, the SBOE approved the *Rule 10* hearing draft. Thus, the Commissioner was able to provide 30 days' notice and schedule a public hearing for January 27, 2015, at six different sites spread out across the state. Blomstedt explained that following final approval, the rule would move forward "for the Governor at his level and the Attorney General's side of the equation" (NSBOE, 2015a). Blomstedt also reminded the board that their work would soon shift to specifics related to accountability indicators and measures for classification.

In February 2015, the SBOE reviewed the public hearing comments and discussed nonsubstantive additional changes that had been made before being asked to approve revisions to *Rule 10: Regulations for the Accreditation of Schools* in order to move the rule forward to the State Attorney General's office. They also heard expert testimony from a consultant from the National Center on Assessment and members of the task force on their work in developing a classification model for AQuESTT.

The assessment and accountability consultant opened his remarks to the SBOE by describing how important purpose is to the development of accountability systems. "You have to know why you are doing—what you want to achieve and why you are doing them" (NSBOE, 2015b). He complimented board members on their stated values in AQuESTT and on those values being "comprehensive and not merely about labeling schools or looking at minimum outcomes" (NSBOE, 2015b). He reassured the board that the model collaboratively developed by the task force was conceptually and empirically sound. He explained that the task force would likely return to the SBOE in March with specific recommendations for classification.

Accountability Committee Chair O'Holleran commended the consultant and task force's commitment to collaboration and shared her hope that in shifting accountability from ranking schools to a system where "we can all move up in a classification by sharing best practices. And where schools don't feel like Big Brother's going to come in and punch some heads. We are coming in to provide support and intervention that can be sustainable after the Department leaves" (NSBOE, 2015b). The work on school and district accountability in Nebraska at this point had been a dance between a commitment to the Nebraska Way, in which local input and stakeholder engagement had historically influenced local policy implementation; a disposition to try to understand local context in "showing up to help before showing up to criticize"; and pressures in the state to stake a more aggressive and intrusive stance on accountability and intervention (NSBOE, 2015b).

BOLDER, BROADER, BETTER

Nine months ahead of the AQuESTT classification statutory deadline, in the March 2015 SBOE meetings, representatives from the task force introduced a classification model for the SBOE for discussion and a vote. The Director of Statewide Assessment referenced a two-page handout that outlined the key indicators in the proposed system. She explained that schools have many facets and "a system that assigns a classification system bears a heavy burden to be accurate, reliable, valid, and equitable" (NSBOE 2015c). According to the proposed model, all schools and districts in the state would be classified according to students who were enrolled in a full-academic year. An initial performance level would be assigned based on students' results on statewide assessments. Adjustments to that classification could be made based on improved student performance (comparing current year data to previous year data), growth (student result compared to the assessment cut-score), change in the nonproficient supergroup, the rate of assessment participation in the school, and graduation rate (for high schools only). Following adjustments up or down the classification system, schools and districts would then be assigned a final classification as either Excellent, Great, Good, or Needs Improvement.

In April 2015, NDE personnel shared the draft model at the first AQuESTT Conference with attendees representing school districts from across the state. The presentation on classification included a timeline for implementation of AQuESTT with an upcoming prototype classification and draft business rules that would be released once "all indicators were complete" (NSBOE, 2015d). This was particularly of interest to superintendents and education leaders of schools and districts trying to anticipate their classification and how to communicate that with their local boards and communities.

Then in June 2015, Commissioner Blomstedt unveiled a new component of AQuESTT Classification, a special website for the accountability system, and a tagline: "AQuESTT Bolder, broader, better" (NSBOE, 2015e). He described a system "led by the state of Nebraska" and issued an invitation for stakeholders to be "a part of something, something much bigger than we've done in the past around accountability" (NSBOE, 2015e). Eventually, he explained, the system would include data not currently collected by NDE or for any federal purposes in order to provide "a more holistic picture [of schools]" (NSBOE, 2015e). He also introduced a first new data collection tool, the Evidence-based Analysis (EBA), a survey that would ask schools to self-report on items aligned with "best practices in schools." The EBA, once fully developed, would not only provide data to be incorporated into the classification system, Blomstedt explained, but would serve as a tool of communication that would offer "an opportunity to ask them what other supports they need from us" (NSBOE, 2015e).

Blomstedt warned the SBOE that he anticipated pushback on the EBA from school district personnel who had not been engaged in its development, a significant departure from the collaborative approach that had been in place to this point. However, he encouraged members: "I think you're bolder as a board to actually take this on because doing something more, would also require doing things differently across the system and particularly at NDE" (NSBOE, 2015e). He reminded the board that the public release of classification for all public schools and districts and the identification of three priority schools would happen in 6 months. In the meantime, however, NDE would release a "prototype of their classification using the previous year's data and without data from the EBA," which was being called "Raw Classification" (NSBOE, 2015e). Districts and schools would submit EBAs by November 1, 2015, and that data would be incorporated into a Final Classification that would be released in December 2015. Blomstedt also explained that the three priority schools would be designated "based on the same indicators as AQuESTT" (NBOE, 2015e).

Just days before the beginning of the 2015–2016 school year, Blomstedt presented to over a thousand school leaders at his second Administrators' Days keynote. Blomstedt described AQuESTT as "next generation accountability" that would "help us figure out how to get better" (NDE, 2015a). He asserted that the SBOE was "trying to tell the whole story of what's happening in schools, instead of just a name, a title, or a score" (NDE, 2015a). He assured administrators that the new EBA data collection allowed them "to provide a bigger picture of what's happening in a school," and could only improve a school/district classification level. He requested that administrators "pay attention" to the conversations happening at SBOE meetings, because "our role as policy leaders is more critical now at the State Board level than it has ever been in the past" (NDE, 2015a).

INCHING CLOSER TO CLASSIFICATION/DESIGNATION

Just over a week later, in the August 2015 SBOE work session, the Commissioner introduced Dr. Deb Frison, whom he had hired as the Deputy Commissioner of School Improvement and Support. Her work, he explained, would focus on working "with schools as the state implements a new accountability system" (Duffy, 2015). Frison, an experienced building administrator from the Omaha Public Schools, quickly took the lead on the day-to-day management of AQuESTT's implementation efforts.

Beyond its general requirement to classify all schools and districts in the state class, Neb. Rev. Stat. §79-760.06-.07 also required the designation of up to three priority schools for state support and intervention. Blomstedt briefly described this process, which would happen alongside classification throughout the fall. Priority school designation would include a review of additional data for each school in the lowest classification. Representatives from each NDE department would review schools and districts to identify schools most in need of assistance to improve for recommendation to the SBOE. Following designation as a priority school, a school would have an intervention that would be "customized for each school" (NSBOE, 2015f).

Beginning in January 2016, priority schools, in collaboration with the identified intervention team, would develop progress plans to be approved by the SBOE in August 2016. Blomstedt acknowledged that there was a great deal of work that would be necessary between August and December for the members of the Board and NDE in order to implement the plan he had outlined. From my cubicle I watched the Commissioner's presentation on the livestream and feverishly took notes. I had been tasked with leading the development of a methodology to identify three priority schools. Colleagues from the Data, Research, and Evaluation team at NDE estimated that 3–5% of schools in Nebraska (approximately 100 schools) would be identified as "Needs Improvement." It felt like the clock had started to tick a little faster as December approached.

In September 2015, Commissioner Blomstedt described to the SBOE that a "Raw Classification" would be made available to all public schools and districts in October as an indicator of what final classification might be. This, however, would not include the EBA survey tool (NSBOE, 2015g). Blomstedt highlighted that beyond receiving a classification, schools and districts would also see a unique profile that would synthesize data from classification and the results of the EBA. Blomstedt discussed the future decisions he imagined the board would need to make before classification could be made final in December, which would include rules for how the EBA would be incorporated into classification. The SBOE would also review the process to designate up to three priority schools.

When November 2015 arrived, the SBOE was 1 month away from AQuESTT's first classification of schools/districts and designation of three priority schools. Blomstedt put forward recommendations for the classification of schools and districts that included "a symmetrical distribution" (bell curve) among the classification levels of Needs Improvement, Good, Great, and Excellent. The SBOE unanimously approved the business rules, granting the Commissioner the authority to determine AQuESTT distribution percentages for accountability classification levels, how the EBA would factor into classification, and the process for designating priority schools. Even with classification and designation only a month away, there was very limited information regarding the classification or designation processes available outside board committee structures to allow the full board to engage in dialogue in the full board work session or business meeting, and no supporting materials. It was evident that there was quite a bit of work left to do in order to meet legislative deadlines for the new accountability system's first classification.

December 2015 had the potential to be a significant education policy window in Nebraska, with rumors of a long-overdue ESEA reauthorization happening around the same time as the state's first AQuESTT accountability classification and designation of priority schools. Behind the scenes, I was meeting with staff from across NDE, exploring quantitative and qualitative data on the schools with a high likelihood of being classified in Needs Improvement. Our team developed profile pages for each Needs Improvement school in the prototype data. Profiles represented trends found in the quantitative data collections and summaries of the qualitative data available in written reports in state and federal data collections (e.g., School Improvement Grant applications, accreditation reports) and data submitted in the EBA survey tool. Each week, we presented to an internal larger AQuESTT Team for critical feedback on our progress and narrowed the pool of potential priority schools through a ratio of school performance in AQuESTT Classification in comparison to evidence of strategies and capacity to improve. With only days to the December SBOE meeting, the team narrowed its list to 10 potential schools. And in the 48 hours before the classification and priority school designation announcement, we explored patterns among the data for schools classified in Needs Improvement. Not surprisingly, we found patterns that reflected the types of schools often identified as "failing" in accountability systems, those schools that serve students for whom the education system was not designed. For example, all schools on American Indian reservation lands and a high proportion of schools serving historically marginalized students would be labeled as needing improvement. In sharing this information with the NDE leadership team, I had no idea how the data would be taken up or how they would be used in determining priority schools and, ultimately, policy decisions for how priority schools would be served.

THE FIRST AQuESTT CLASSIFICATION AND DESIGNATION

The night before AQuESTT's classification of districts and schools and designation of the three priority schools, I sat at my dining room table, eyes blurred from staring at the laptop screen. I glanced at my mobile phone and saw a text from the Commissioner. He was trying to make a final decision on the third priority school he would announce the next morning and had a question on a piece of data. A few hours later, I arrived at NDE's offices before dawn. I pondered the day ahead. I wondered what it would be like to be teaching on a Friday only to find out that your school was one of three in the state named as a priority school. I wondered how the Commissioner's conversations had gone with each superintendent and how information would be shared with teachers, parents, students, and the community. In many conversations on designating priority schools, there had been conversations about how the label of priority school and its associated stigma might affect a community's trust in its local public school. Would school staff or members of the community feel shamed, or hopeful that they schools might receive additional resources?

By the 9:00 a.m. start of the SBOE meeting, the gallery was so full that a few members of the media spilled into the adjoining hallway. Down in my cubicle, I watched the livestream. The announcement of priority schools would be no surprise for me. The Commissioner unveiled a range of resources about AQuESTT on the AQuESTT website. He assured SBOE members that there was much to be proud about in Nebraska's education system. One of those things, he asserted, was "that we're honest with ourselves about where we need to do our work." He went on to say that "if there is one Needs Improvement school, then the entire system needed to respond to improve" (NSBOE, 2015h). When discussing the schools identified as "Needs Improvement," Blomstedt challenged the SBOE: "If you walk around the state of Nebraska and walk into any school, I would dare you to say that school isn't a good place" (NSBOE, 2015h). He shared that when he looked through the schools in "Needs Improvement," he recalled that he had visited some of these schools as Commissioner and "you go, this is a 'Needs Improvement' school? They're doing remarkable work, and I do not want to undermine that work in an accountability system" (NSBOE, 2015h).

Among those Needs Improvement schools, Blomstedt explained, "we have to identify three priority schools" (NSBOE, 2015h). The designation was weighty because it was the SBOE and NDE's opportunity to really think about "building capacity for the future for all of our students" (NSBOE, 2015h). He asserted that the role of the SBOE and NDE included understanding the dynamics in the Needs Improvement schools because "I really think it's those places that need support for improvement ultimately" (NSBOE, 2015h). Blomstedt explained that among the schools listed in "Needs Improvement," four primary themes had emerged: schools in Native American communities, demographically transitioning communities, small communities with declining populations, and urban or metro school communities. The identified priority schools would become the first schools in which NDE and the SBOE would have state authority to intervene.

Discussions around the SBOE's new role and the way that NDE would intervene in priority schools included rhetoric around school accountability as a function of ensuring equity, and thus equitable entrée into democratic society. Thus, rapidly improving or turning around priority schools had policy implications that were greater than simply identifying three schools and providing resources allocated by the legislature to those schools. The Commissioner had a vision for the way the state would intervene. Support for the priority schools, he explained, would provide knowledge as to how the system of education in Nebraska might be able to support all struggling schools according to the kinds of schools in the Needs Improvement classification. And at last, Blomstedt named the three priority schools: Loup County Elementary in Taylor, Nebraska; Druid Hill Elementary in Omaha Public Schools; and Santee Middle School in Santee, Nebraska, on the Santee Sioux Reservation. Figure 5.1 includes Blomstedt's comments as he introduced each priority school.

Following this announcement, the SBOE President, Rachel Wise, asked if there was a motion to adopt the recommendations the Commissioner had

Figure 5.1. Priority School Descriptions

Loup County Elementary, Loup County Public Schools	Druid Hill Elementary, Omaha Public Schools	Santee Middle School, Santee Community School
"When you go to Loup County, I will tell you, they're during wonderful things. Many of our small communities across the state trying to do the best by their students, but the reality is they're a school that's in a situation where we saw an increase in their non-proficiency, that this has been kind of a year-over-year. . . . We want to actually be able to designate them a priority school, not just for Loup County itself, but the fact of the matter is we have lots of schools that are similar to Loup County that are rural and otherwise probably not getting the type of support that I believe we ultimately ought to provide as a state, and working with our ESUs, working with others, and so that's one of the stories in our priority school designation."	"I had the opportunity to walk through Druid Hill with Dr. Frison here just the other day as well. The reality is you walk in, you go, 'This is also a good school,' but we know what their assessment results look like; we know that we're facing challenges in these places and we know that there's a level of support that needs to be generated and we need to play our role in working with a school district like Omaha Public Schools, like our larger districts."	"I truly believe there we have the dynamics of the historical challenges that we see in communities such as Santee. I feel as if we must actually be able to step in and help provide a level of support and think about a level support for Santee, but for all of our Native American schools, quite frankly. If in some way this designation of Santee helps me with all of the remainder, I feel like we are doing our job and so we will look at that and we will work with Santee in the sense of making sure that this priority school designation actually assists in our efforts."

made for the three named priority schools. The SBOE voted unanimously to approve the schools.

Blomstedt touted the design of his first major policy implementation as Nebraska's Commissioner of Education as he briefed the gathered media after the meeting. He introduced AQuESTT as a "broader" way of thinking about accountability with the "systems of support" that would undergird intervention processes. The question-and-answer portion of the press conference hinted at the ways low performance had become expected in some schools. No one raised larger questions about how, in a process that singled out 87 of the state's 1,130 schools as "Needs Improvement," every single school on American Indian Reservation lands was classified in the lowest classification. No one asked what a state-led intervention might look like or how it might "provide a level of support" through an accountability system that leaned primarily on student performance on statewide assessments as its measuring stick for quality (NSBOE, 2015h).

Back in my cubicle watching the press conference, my eyes felt gritty; I was exhausted. I looked forward to catching up on some sleep and perhaps some shorter days at the office. My relief was short-lived. Two days following the priority school announcements, Deputy Commissioner Frison summoned me to her office and asked me to shut the door. She asked if I would act as the NDE liaison to Santee Community School. The state's intervention, while officially named for the middle school would take a system-wide PK–12 approach to address the entire school. In the silence that followed, she joked that she was not really asking. She assured me that the work in Santee would be done through authentic relationships and partnership. Ultimately, I said yes.

A RETROSPECTIVE VIEW

In hindsight, when I review the months of school accountability system development, the classification of schools, and the designation of priority schools, knowing that eventually policy would be enacted in Santee, I cannot help thinking about the ways that education governance in the state was not designed to respond effectively in a sovereign Indian nation. More broadly, I also see the ways policy spaces, both official and unofficial, were sites of both constraint and exclusion as well as sites of agency, and how critical moments shaped AQuESTT's emerging policy culture. The metrics that were incorporated into AQuESTT accountability structures and the patterns that emerged among Needs Improvement schools in the 2015 classification demonstrate the systemic ways that dominant European American thought and knowledge were centered.

First, the decision to identify SCS as a priority school requires an interrogation of school governance in the very particular context of a sovereign nation with rights to self-education. SCS is governed by a locally elected board and all board members are members of the tribe. When LB438 became law, priority schools, their district, and their local boards were expected to cooperate to ensure their continued state accreditation to operate in the state of Nebraska (Neb. Rev. Stat. §§ 79–760.06-.07). Thus, the SBOE had expanded legislative authority to oversee the development and implementation of an intervention in designated priority schools. What state intervention should look like in Indian Country was never a part of the SBOE's conversation. Perhaps this is because SCS was not new to labels or external oversight.

SCS, having been identified as a Persistently Low Achieving School (PLAS) in previous years according to federal accountability metrics (under NCLB), was not unfamiliar with external oversight for improvement efforts. SCS, with the approval of the local school board, had made the decision to pursue, and was awarded, sizable 3-year Title I School Improvement Grants (SIG) for both the elementary school ($1,527,551) and high school ($1,616,492) in 2010 (Holman et al., 2014). A formal evaluation of the SIG's impact at SCS highlighted "little change" that occurred over the course of the 3-year implementation and said that future investments intended to improve student outcomes in the school needed to take into account the contextual factors present in each unique site (Holman et al., 2014, p. 16).

Just a year after the SIG finished and the evaluation was filed, SCS was once again identified as low achieving, but this time, improvement efforts would come through direct state intervention. This was not popular news in a district whose boundaries encompass a single community with a population of about 500 people, and where nearly 40% of eligible students opted to attend school in the adjacent district the year of designation because of its reputation for being the "better school." Santee's designation came just weeks after their third superintendent in 3 years was put on indefinite administrative leave. At the time SCS was named a priority school, the only school administrator employed by the district was a first-year principal with a provisional administrative license. SCS informed stakeholders about their priority school designation in their December 2015 newsletter, stating that

> This [priority school designation] is something that is to be looked at as a positive for our district and shared accordingly with students, parents and members of the community. We all want what is best for the students and will look at this as an opportunity to do just that. (Santee Community Schools, 2015)

At the same time, SCS's local school board, principal, and staff had questions about how the state would approach intervention, what kinds of consultation with local educators and members of the community might be included in the process, and how the unique context of the Santee community might be considered.

The stated intention of SBOE members chronicled above was to pursue approaches that would be collaborative, consultative, and tailored to the contexts of each priority school community. Categorizing schools as "Needs Improvement" and identifying priority schools that represented different contexts of schools and communities in the state signaled intention to differentiate state intervention responses and resources to the particular needs present in each kind of school. This leads us to questions I will explore in the next two chapters around stated policy intention vs. the enactment of policy on the ground and the intended and unintended consequences that come from the alignment or misalignment of intention vs. practice.

Finally, I cannot leave this chapter without revisiting ideas of space, power, and agency I raised at the end of Chapter 4 and considering the shifting policy culture that was beginning to emerge in the early days of AQuESTT development described above. As the SBOE made decisions related to how to classify schools and districts in performance levels, there was no discussion in official policy spaces (e.g., board meetings, publicly available documents) on the ways identified quantitative metrics from high stakes assessments would likely disproportionately affect schools and districts with higher levels of poverty, English learners, and racial/ethnic groups. Nor was there Native representation from tribal communities on the assessment task force making recommendations for accountability formula modeling to the SBOE. Despite the stated intention to attend to equity as one function of school accountability in the state, the lack of attention to the impacts of policy on the kinds of schools that are often stigmatized with labels of failure, and the absence of representation of particular minoritized communities, are examples of the ways policy spaces reproduce structures that can further marginalize and constrain.

At the same time, there was a policy culture shift from a culture that once reflected a measure of resistance to federal policy aims and a dedication to a Nebraska Way of engaging multiple voices in the coconstruction of policy. Instead, policy was evolving toward a more directive approach to decision-making concentrated among NDE leadership and the SBOE, with dialogue about policy decisions more frequently occurring in nonpublic committee meetings with brief reporting on discussions in full board work sessions or meetings. One prominent example of this shift was the contrast between the construction and work of the assessment task force with representation from a number of districts and stakeholders in the state and the efforts to consult with a broader range of stakeholders through AQuESTT policy forums, and the rather late decision by the SBOE to include the EBA in the school and district classification business rules. While the EBA was well-intended, to broaden the metrics used to classify schools, it was developed late in the legislative timeline and internally at NDE without transparency or consultation. Thus, with the benefit of hindsight, we can see that at some early critical moments that shaped a school accountability policy culture, opportunities were missed for policy spaces to include broader representation of perspectives more meaningfully. One significant constraint was the ever-ticking timeline for the SBOE and NDE to develop a classification and priority school designation system by the end of 2015, a monumental task that certainly contributed to rigidifying of accountability policy space and policy culture in the state.

CHAPTER 6

Run by Outsiders

On January 4, 2016, I took my first trip to Santee in my role as liaison from NDE. The landscape was a frosted winter wonderland, glowing pink in the morning sunrise. The horizon opened before me as I drove into the village of Santee, the center of life on the Santee Sioux Reservation. I drove slowly through town, stopping my car near the playground as a student ran to retrieve a ball. I parked in front of the single-story brick building that housed Santee Community School and checked my phone for any last-minute messages from NDE. Once inside, I waited in the school's atrium, feeling the weight of the responsibility of my role as I stood before a large mural chronicling the resistance, hangings, forced migration, and resettlement of the Dakota people upon the land where I stood. The principal, in his first year at the school, greeted me. He led me to a conference room where he introduced me to the school's steering committee members. As I was sitting down and shedding my coat, a veteran teacher leader in the district asked, "So, what's this *really* going to look like?" We sat in silence for a couple beats. I repeated what I had heard Commissioner Blomstedt say, that progress plans would be tailored to the needs of each of the three schools, so that lessons might be learned to better support other similar schools. "Whatever the process," I said, "it will vary according to school." I did not yet know what state implementation might look like, but believed that a progress plan would follow a collaborative process to identify key areas to improve academic achievement. I told the group that as much as I wished I could describe step by step the structure of what was to come, it was not yet defined; it would be built in the coming months. I left the school with more questions than answers and made my way back to Lincoln to report to Dr. Blomstedt and Dr. Frison.

A month later in February 2016, board conversations were centered on how provisions of ESSA might align with the state's accountability system, and particularly how the state would design its efforts to intervene in each of the priority schools. Board member O'Holleran described the board's vision and intention for priority school intervention. "It is not there to punish, or to say, 'you're doing it all wrong, or you put this on the shelf,' but that we're there to work with them and listen to them" (NSBOE, 2016a). She acknowledged that "other schools that are in the Needs Improvement category are going to be watching how we treat and how we intervene. . . . I just hope that we go in with the respect for what they are doing" (NSBOE, 2016a). Commissioner Blomstedt asserted that an overarching goal of priority school intervention was to create models that could be scalable in other Nebraska schools with similar demographics and contexts. Blomstedt once again referenced the "kinds of schools" found among Needs Improvement schools and how the work in each of the priority schools representing one of those types of schools would create models for supporting other schools, including schools on or near the state's other American Indian reservations. While vision and intention were discussed, the logistics of who might be engaged in an intervention team or in developing a progress plan was not. Nor were the unique characteristics of each of the three priority schools or intentions around how to engage members of the community in responding to the contexts of each place.

INITIAL THOUGHTS ABOUT IMPROVEMENT IN SANTEE

I made two trips to Santee in February 2016, once on my own for a staff professional development day and the other time with a delegation from NDE. Similar to my first visit to the school, I waited in the atrium until a newly hired NDE contractor who spent 2 days a week acting as superintendent to support the district's principal came to greet me. Together we walked to a staff meeting area, where I set down my bag and greeted staff members as they arrived for the professional learning day.

The school's steering committee divided the staff into groups of about 6–8 across grade levels. Groups spent time brainstorming and writing ideas about where they believed improvement efforts should be focused in the following year on large sheets of poster paper. When groups completed the task, they brought their posters to the front of the room for all to see. Themes that emerged included the staff's desire for consistency—through policies and procedures, with behavior management, and an induction program for new staff. Staff pointed to a need for curriculum vertical alignment and an understanding of what textbooks and materials teachers were using in different grade levels. They asked for more collaboration time to plan and implement projects and for stronger communication and parent and community engagement. Later, when debriefing with the principal, he said he was nervous going into the activity and encouraged by the staff's openness. "We named the problems and we agree about what they are," he said, "and hopefully now we can do something about it." This seemed like a productive place to start building a plan for progress. Before I left for the day, I took photos of the posters and shared them with NDE leadership.

In the 2 weeks between this professional learning day and a visit from the priority school team, Deputy Commissioner Frison and the Accountability Coordinator called another meeting of the priority school liaisons, announcing that a contract would be issued to an external consultant who would complete a diagnostic review to assess improvement needs in each priority school. As a result, I had company on my next visit to Santee. The delegation from NDE on February 24, 2016, included the Deputy Commissioner, Accountability Coordinator, and an external consultant, who had flown in from North Carolina. The purpose of the trip, according to Deputy Commissioner Frison, was to establish a positive working relationship that would support the development and implementation of a progress plan at SCS. Our physical placement at tables was striking enough to me at the time that I sketched our seating arrangement: the NDE delegation, including me, on one side, and the Santee principal, director of student services, contractor who had served in a part-time superintendent role in the past month, and two representatives from the educational service agency on the other side of the table. From the very beginning, physical positioning marked the team from the state and the team from Santee. While I did not know it yet, the demarcation of two separate teams on two sides of a table would come to reflect two opposing beliefs in what would improve SCS.

The Deputy Commissioner skipped introductions, immediately asking the principal to describe his experiences in the school. He talked about the range of programs and grants in the school and that his biggest fear would be not having a good superintendent to hire the next year. He outlined some of the toxic culture challenges, which included a lack of trust among teachers in the administration and a lack of trust among the community in the school. The principal talked about how essential it would be to put the "Santee DNA—the school and community" into whatever the progress plan might be. Following this, the external consultant shifted the conversation to curriculum and instruction, asking the principal how often he was in classrooms observing instruction, what professional learning staff had been provided throughout the school year, and what his vision for the school would look like in the next couple of years. The principal did not respond directly to the questions about his frequency of classroom observation or the professional development, again pointing to the challenge of being the only administrator in the PK–12 building. He did address her question about his vision, describing higher test scores, higher graduation rates, no teachers leaving, and an increase in community involvement. No other questions were addressed to Santee staff in the room.

The principal then divided the NDE delegation into three groups, introducing each group to a pair of high school students who provided a tour of the building. The students with whom I walked admitted they were nervous; however, when asked about some of the student artwork in display cases in the hallway, they seemed to relax. They said that the installations were examples of student artwork developed when a Native artist visited each year to work with students in art class. Moving into the secondary wing of the building, the quieter of the pair became animated when we arrived at the science classroom. He told us about planting some hydroponic tomato plants and that the students were hoping to get to the appropriate pH balance in order to have fish in the bottom of the tanks. He described a plan for a garden that might provide food for the cafeteria and a grant the science teacher was working on that he hoped might get funded. We made other stops in the band room, where we heard about the new music teacher who was reviving a band program, and the preschool program, where students were learning words in Dakota. Tour complete, the Santee principal encouraged us to stay for lunch, but the Deputy Commissioner declined. She reminded the principal that priority school next steps would include the external consultant's return visit in March to complete her diagnostic review, along with two priority school liaisons.

With the time and hindsight I have now, I hear what the principal, as the representative of the school, was asking for from the state. I hear what the students described as engaging them in their schooling as connected to place and what it meant to be Dakota. The principal described the "Santee DNA" and students described representations of themselves through stories of identity through art and food, while the NDE delegation was more focused on the alignment of curriculum and instruction to state standards, professional learning, and teacher supervision of instruction. Maybe the implications of this contrast should have been clear to me at the time. I did not yet see how state-directed improvement efforts focused on better assessment scores might become so narrowed as to constrain the Santee DNA inside the school.

In March 2016, the Commissioner updated the board on this priority school progress. Initial visits, he explained, were for teams to "begin identifying and working with and building necessary relationships with the school district, the administration, and the board" (NSBOE, 2016b). The Commissioner shared that he had been in communication with the local school boards for each priority school. He reiterated to the SBOE that "our intent is to very much be there to begin looking and to be honest about the opportunities for us to work together to improve the education for those students" (NSBOE 2016b). Once again, O'Holleran asserted that NDE's approach should be providing support, not telling schools "the way it is" (NSBOE, 2016b). She described a balance of humility that should be present, while not ignoring the problems that might exist. The work in the schools would take bravery, she said, but it was the right work for the board to do. Following this brief update, the board approved a month-long contract of $18,000 for the external consultant to complete a diagnostic review of each priority school and submit findings to the SBOE.

A DIAGNOSTIC REVIEW

On March 10, 2016, a priority school liaison for one of the other named schools and I met the external consultant at the airport in Omaha. The external consultant, a retired assistant superintendent from a district in North Carolina, described her process, which included classroom observations, conversations with the administrative team, and a group facilitation to gather input from a cross-section of teachers, community members, and students. She explained that following the data collection she would compile her findings into a report for each school that would be submitted to the Deputy Commissioner. Her findings would include recommendations for each school's priority school progress plan.

For the next 2 days, my priority school liaison counterpart and I acted as scribes for the consultant, documenting responses from key stakeholders and participating in classroom observations. Following each 5–10 minute classroom visit, the consultant facilitated a brief conversation with building administrators. She asked what coaching feedback might be offered to the teacher to improve instruction. She inquired about the curriculum materials each school employed in their instruction and about the last 3 years of statewide assessment data. As we logged miles between the priority schools and on our return to Omaha, the consultant previewed some initial findings on the phone with the Deputy Commissioner and confirmed that she would submit her reports before the end of the month.

In the April 2016 SBOE meetings, however, there was only one reference to the work in the priority schools: another contract, this time for a retired superintendent who would act as a consultant in Santee through the end of the year, supporting the local principal and the local board in their superintendent search. During this time the Commissioner maintained communication with each local school board. A "Commissioner's Report of Priority School Activities for the Santee Community Schools: Preliminary Efforts, Findings, and Next Steps" was presented to the SCS local school board and discussed at their April 28, 2016, meeting. The Commissioner shared that since the time the school was designated as a priority school he had assigned an initial team to support the district in developing their progress plan that would ensure improved educational outcomes for students in Santee. He explained that the team assigned to work with Santee had worked to understand the challenges the district faced.

> There have been multiple visits, meetings, and conversations to establish a base of information important to establishing the next steps. The process has included opportunities to observe and interview staff and students in the school as well as opportunities to interact with the school board. All of these have provided valuable insights. Additionally, [the external consultant] provided a thorough summary as part of a diagnostic review process. (NDE, 2016a, p. 1)

He explained that reports submitted by the external consultant would be organized around her categories of improvement: Clear and Compelling Direction, School Culture, and Instructional Capacity. Next steps would include establishing priorities for an improvement plan "with a special focus on immediate efforts to be accomplished over summer and before the beginning of the next school year" (NSBOE, 2016c). While he did not describe specific next steps for ongoing collaboration in the development of a priority school progess plan, the Commissioner's communications highlighted the intended role of the intervention team as one of support and collaboration.

As the academic year was coming to an end, the principal and staff in Santee were moving forward with planning for the following school year. On April 8th, the staff gathered after school for a school improvement meeting session. They reviewed previous discussions on areas for improvement and identified some key action items they could make progress on before the end of the school year. They discussed the school's relationship with the Santee community and ways to better support teacher retention in the district to slow the churn of educators coming and going from the district each year. Teachers and staff met in smaller school improvement committees and then came back together in the elementary wing's multi-purpose space. By the end of the session, staff had identified the following actions: Expand community nights to cultivate greater community/school engagement, develop a morning routine that includes the Dakota Flag Song, communicate the assessment schedule with families, develop a framework for new teacher mentorship, and develop a process for collecting and organizing artifacts for school improvement. I point out here that without having seen the external consultant's diagnostic review report, staff prioritized improvements aimed at connecting the school with the Santee community and Dakota culture, history, and elders. I took these recommendations back to NDE. Again, a contrast emerged between locally identified areas for improvement and areas of improvement that would be prescribed by the state.

On April 18–19, 2016, over 1,000 educators represented school districts from across the state convened in Kearney, Nebraska, for the first AQuESTT Conference organized around the state's new accountability system. Sessions aligned to AQuESTT tenets were available for teams from each school district team to attend. Santee brought a team that included the high school principal, preschool director, interim superintendent recently contracted by NDE, the front office administrator, librarian, and special education director. When I was not presenting, I attended sessions with various team members. At the end of the day, the high school principal and I met the commissioner, deputy commissioner, accountability coordinator, and external consultant. The purpose of this meeting was to provide a draft of the consultant's diagnostic review findings to the SCS school administration. The consultant provided an overview of the findings, highlighting the need for work in instructional leadership and support for standards/

curriculum alignment and instructional strategies. The principal paged through the report while the consultant talked. When there was a pause for questions, he asked about the work that he and the staff had done to set priorities throughout the spring; the deputy commissioner interjected that the consultant was skilled in helping schools turnaround and that her findings would carry weight along with the work the staff had been doing when drafting progress plans in the coming month. As the meeting came to close, I noted that the bulk of the consultant's recommendations had a standards-reform academic focus and when she referred to "culture" she was describing the network of relationships and ways of working together and being among the adults in the building, rather than the connection between the school and community or addressing the role of Native culture in the teaching and learning and ways of knowing and being in the school. The commissioner made final comments, reminding everyone in the circle that the following week, the Santee board members would also receive access to the diagnostic review in a meeting in Omaha.

A week later, on April 23, 2016, that same circle of individuals, along with members of the Santee school board and the legal representatives for both SCS and the NDE, gathered around a larger table at a conference room in Omaha. The atmosphere felt like a cocktail hour mixer as individuals circulated and made informal introductions, trading handshakes while the hotel staff set out boxed lunches. The Commissioner directed everyone to find their seats. He and the Santee board president sat at the head of the long conference room table, taking turns introducing the individuals from Santee and those from NDE. The meeting then followed an agenda that included an overview of the state's accountability system and how SCS was identified as a priority school and a discussion of the ongoing communication and collaboration between NDE and SCS, with the diagnostic review and planning for an upcoming retreat for the principal and a couple of teachers, where they would work on a draft of the progress plan that would go to the SBOE in August.

Following these NDE presentations, the SCS board president asked the district's legal counsel to outline SCS's recent history. He mentioned the leadership churn and the distrust between the school and community and teachers and administration following a former superintendent's embezzlement of thousands of dollars in federal school improvement grant (SIG) funds 2 years before. The board president prompted board members to share their hopes for what the state's intervention might look like moving forward. They described the community's lack of trust in the school as "the biggest hurdle to improvement" and expressed a desire that SCS once again "be something the community can be proud about." The board president then described how the school district's name and the use of *community* had been an intentional choice, one anchored in a vision that the school would be for the community, a tribal community on reservation lands; it was a school *for Santee*. Board members asserted that they wanted to see a greater presence of Dakota history, beadwork, powwows, drum groups, and star quilt ceremonies as a part of the school culture. The board president mentioned a grant collaboration with the tribal council to have a garden-to-school program and highlighted the partnership with the tribe to provide buffalo meat for school lunches. For the Santee board members, the priority for improvement was centered on cultural knowledge and identity.

When the NDE leadership and the consultant shared their vision for improvement, based on the diagnostic review, they described hiring an additional principal and instructional coach to support better special education programming and instruction in classrooms. They mentioned shifts in the organizational structures to engage more teachers in decision-making and implementing changes like a schoolwide behavior system and new reading and math curricula in the elementary grades. Improvement would be measured by assessment performance and graduation rates. SCS administration and NDE efforts appeared focused on what Dr. Frison described as the most "efficient way to move the needle" to demonstrate improvement and to be released from priority school status.

Following the meeting, the Commissioner composed a letter for the Santee school board that could be shared with the community. He expressed his appreciation for the school's welcome of "my team and our efforts" and reasserted the state's commitment that "our collaborative work will result in the proper investment in your wonderful students, families, and community as a whole" (Santee Community School Board, 2016a). He then explained that in an effort to better understand the context in Santee, the state had created a team led by the consultant with members from NDE and the regional service unit that would work to develop and support the implementation of a priority plan. While a stated intention for collaboration and learning remained, the communication clearly positioned the consultant as the key driver in determining the direction of a progress plan for Santee.

STATE PLAN DEVELOPMENT

The SBOE's May work session included an update on priority school intervention. The Commissioner informed the board that the diagnostic review had identified what was working and not working in each site. The review, he explained, supported the larger state accountability work, enabling each priority school to work toward improvement with progress plans aligned to the state's accountability system. Even though there would be common alignment, each school's progress plan would be tailored to the "unique circumstances" in each of the three schools (NSBOE, 2016d). The Commissioner outlined next steps in crafting improvement plans and promised an update on improvement plans in June before the SBOE would be asked to approve each plan in August. He reiterated the importance of the work in the priority schools and the lessons learned that could inform how NDE might support schools with similar contexts across the state.

The Commissioner asked the Accountability Coordinator to explain how intervention teams would develop plans for each priority school. She shared an improvement plan template that included goal areas for improvement, strategies, resources, and timelines intended to keep improvements moving forward. The draft templates, she explained, had also been designed to align with the tenets of the state's accountability system to track how the improvement activities were moving each school forward according to AQuESTT. The board president asked for a sample plan to review prior to August. Another board member asked whether plan timelines would be limited to a single year. This initiated a discussion on whether plans would need to reflect more than a single year in the timelines as some of the improvements would likely, according to NDE's Accreditation and School Improvement Administrator, take longer than 1 year to accomplish. In some ways, board member O'Holleran explained, the timelines and the plans represented a "hypothesis of improvement and [with] that feedback, they'll [priority schools will] do an update" (NSBOE, 2016d). O'Holleran's comments indicate the intention of the SBOE to consider priority school implementation as an adaptable process as feedback and data emerged from the early interactions with each school. Following this dialogue, discussion on priority schools concluded and the SBOE moved to the next item on their agenda.

The following week, on May 10, 2016, I made a trip to Santee to be present for SCS's local board meeting. The board met in the school's library at 5:00 p.m., directly after school. As board members gathered, I reintroduced myself to each arriving board member and to the board's hired attorney, who was present to continue to consult the board through the ongoing litigation from the termination of the previous superintendent's contract. Following the principal's report I moved to address the board. I reminded board members that they had received communication from the Commissioner at the end of April that included an update of the ongoing work to develop progress plans, and a recommendation to broaden the leadership team by hiring an elementary principal. I also reminded the board of NDE's contracted consultant's visit and introduced her plans for improvement. I believed at the time that Dakota culture would be woven into the school's improvement plan. "Dakota culture in the building and in the community will be essential," I said, but in the immediate future there would be a focus on stability in staffing and on developing a plan that will support "a multi-year commitment and create some urgency to do the work necessary to better support students" (Santee Community School Board, 2016b). I wrapped up my comments to the board with an assurance that the Commissioner would make a return visit to Santee soon. The board did not have questions for me. In this same meeting, the immediate concerns of the local board included finalizing the school district's school calendar for the following year, hiring a new superintendent and elementary principal, filling teacher vacancies, and making decisions on new or proposed programs. No final decisions were made, as the board and administration expressed uncertainty about what decisions were theirs and what decisions were now the state's to make. I was asked to bring these inquiries back to the Deputy Commissioner and Commissioner for their guidance in decision-making.

PRIORITY SCHOOLS: DEVELOPING PROGRESS PLANS

Upon my return to Lincoln, I shared the immediate concerns raised by SCS's local board with NDE leadership. Throughout the next week, the Accountability Coordinator worked with the Deputy Commissioner and the external consultant, contacting priority school administrators and informing them about the process and dates for each priority school intervention team to develop draft progress plans. Prior to that work, however, the Accountability Coordinator and priority school liaisons were directed to make a trip to meet with each priority school's staff with the purpose of sharing a summary of the consultant's diagnostic review. In Santee, the visit would also include passing along a directive from the Commissioner to halt any local planning or personnel hires for the following year until the progress plan was drafted and leadership hires had been made in Santee.

The Accountability Coordinator and I immediately made plans to return to Santee for a meeting with staff. As staff gathered in the library after school on May 18, 2016, it was clear that word had already spread about the halt NDE had placed on the school's planning for the next year. There was little eye contact, faces were set, and gazes were narrowed as the Accountability Coordinator began her presentation, sharing the consultant's key findings and her recommendations. In an attempt to bridge the gap of trust caused by the state's oversight and control of local decision making, I tried to make connections between the consultant's recommendations and what the staff themselves had identified in their planning for the coming year. My efforts felt hollow when looking out on the faces of educators I had come to know and appreciate over the previous months. While I did not state it, I shared their sense of disappointment; it felt like the state's intervention was moving forward without focusing on the areas for improvement staff had identified.

Questions following the presentation were not related to the summary of the diagnostic review but directed toward NDE's decision to halt local planning. Frustrations ranged from not having a school calendar to know when classes would resume in August to not having a superintendent hired for the following year. Staff members left the room in silence. One teacher whom I had come to know well since January stopped on her way out the door saying, "I know you were just the messenger, but this is hard to swallow." I drove the 3 and a half hours home in silence, feeling apprehensive and every bit an agent of the state.

A week later, on May 24, 2016, the consultant, who was often referred to as the "Lady from North Carolina" in Santee, returned to NDE. The consultant reviewed her findings from each school with priority school liaisons to each building. The Accountability Coordinator shared an improvement plan template. We sat in a conference room all day, a draft progress plan projected on a screen, as the consultant directed us in writing mock goals, actions, and strategies that aligned with her levers for improvement. She discussed the goals that should be included in each school's plan and directed the Accountability Coordinator on how she ought to facilitate the processes at each school to ensure that teams identified aligned goals with the writing teams, which included at least two teachers and school administrators at each site. Drafts of plans would be shared with the full staff for review, but significant changes would not be made. As the day went on, I felt my unease grow. I recalled my reassurances to staff in January and to the local board in May that the state's intervention work would be coconstructed, and that local Dakota knowledge would be forefronted. My understanding was based on the Commissioner and SBOE members' stated intentions throughout the spring. But the draft goals and actions outlined before me were not reflective of that intention. Two days later, it was time to return to Santee. The Accountability Coordinator and I met the principal, two representatives from the ESU, and three Santee teachers in the school. I had sat in this same conference room on my first visit to Santee and 6 months later, I looked around the table at the faces of people who had become colleagues and friends. I hoped that we would somehow represent Santee in whatever we wrote. I also knew that our directive was to maintain the focus on the consultant's pre-identified goals.

The June 2016 SBOE work session included an update on the work in the priority schools. The Commissioner, after making a couple of remarks about the need to support improvement in the priority schools, asked the Lady from North Carolina to provide information about the work that had gone on to develop progress plans. I was surprised to see that the consultant, who had not been present in Santee during the progress planning, was the only one sitting before the board, going into detail about an experience drafting plans. She explained that she began her work with a diagnostic review using a model focused on three areas: clear and compelling direction, staff and student culture, and instructional leadership capacity.

The area of clear and compelling direction, the Lady from North Carolina explained, "really focuses on the vision of the school—the core values, the mission, and not just having a sense of mission" (NSBOE, 2016e). The sense of the school's purpose, she explained, should be present across all stakeholders from the local board of education, to students and families, and teachers and administrators. "It's beyond just test scores," she told the board. "It's really looking at the overall direction of how the school prepares the students for the world of work, to pursue college education, or serve in the military" (NSBOE, 2016e).

The second area in her diagnostic review model, staff and student culture, was an examination "to determine if the schools were places where students wanted to attend" (NSBOE, 2016e). She looked at whether or not "the staff wanted to be there to teach the students and have that sense of urgency around educating students and meeting the needs of the children there." An element of the culture in the building was also related to whether the school "is a place where parents want to send their students to learn and they feel safe in doing so," she explained (NSBOE, 2016e).

The Lady from North Carolina then described the third and final component of her diagnostic review: instructional leadership capacity. Citing longtime education leader Kati Heycock's work on teacher efficacy, the consultant stated that "if teachers feel good about their role in the school and what they're doing in the school . . . student achievement soars." The support that would be provided in each of the schools would be focused on

> developing the talents of teachers . . . providing support to them with curriculum alignment to the Nebraska state standards, also their lesson planning processes [and] are they adding rigor to the curriculum and differentiating instruction for students who need it most on both ends of the spectrum . . . most importantly getting students ready for the next level of learning. (NSBOE, 2016e)

Following the Lady from North Carolina's overview, the Accountability Coordinator described next steps for each school and what the board could expect in August. She explained that each school was in the early stages of drafting their progress plans. The consultant and NDE staff would continue to communicate and work with each school to finalize their plans, "so that they feel they are informed and still have their voice around the table as we are working out the best plans for each of those schools" (NSBOE, 2016e). Watching the live feed, I felt a familiar tension. The consultant's process and levers did not seem to take into consideration the voices or the long sociohistorical and sociocultural contexts present in Santee. It was finally clear to me that despite stated intentions, local educators and community members were not viewed as co-decision-makers in the development of Santee's progress plan. While they had symbolic seats at the table and gave voice to their visions and intentions, in the end they were the objects of mandates crafted by a consultant hired by the state whose model for improvement was built upon an amalgamation of neoliberal standards and accountability approaches that largely ignored the contextual factors in any of the three priority schools.

In mid-June 2016 I received the news that the Commissioner and Deputy Commissioner had recommended a superintendent hire for Santee, the Multicultural Education Director at NDE. Within days, the Accountability Coordinator and I met with the new superintendent to share the draft progress plan and summer schedule for the Santee staff. The new superintendent, herself Native, had a long history at the NDE and thus a long history working with SCS. It was only days following her hire that Santee, with help from the Commissioner's office and the consultant, hired an elementary principal and part-time instructional coach. These actions illustrate the way the state exercised its authority to intervene in Santee, directing day-to-day decisions. While there were many moments that provided evidence of this shifting state role, the turning point and recognition among educators in the building seemed to occur at that meeting in the library after school, when the Accountability Coordinator and I shared the consultant's diagnostic review findings. Officially, that was our purpose in making the trip to Santee. Unofficially, our role was to make it clear that any decision-making regarding Santee's future planning and improvement would be approved or guided by the state. There was a divergence between stated intention of the Commissioner and board members in their official policy spaces and policy enactment in Santee. Efforts that had been facilitated by the principal and school improvement team throughout the spring to identify areas for improvement and to begin mapping out some initial plans for the following academic year were put on hold. This was when state-level policy, directed by a state agency, intersected with local knowledge and practice, and the incongruity was palpable in the blankness of the gazes and in that final comment from a teacher leader on her way out the door. SCS being run by outsiders, a clear demonstration of the local dissonance that can occur when policy is enacted, was indeed hard to swallow.

In the last week of June 2016 I made yet another trip to Santee. Staff were gathered for 3 days of classroom management training. As was usual, the principal met me in the atrium and together we walked to the staff meeting area in the elementary school wing of the building. Despite tensions from NDE's oversight, it seemed as if leadership and staff viewed me as a messenger of the state, but somehow not an embodiment of the state. Staff articulated their disagreement with the state's decisions I delivered, while also commenting that they appreciated that I took the time to listen to their concerns. One teacher commented that she noticed my efforts to learn about the school and to build relationships among staff members and members of the community. The strange in-between space was uncomfortable to inhabit, particularly in the cases when I did not agree with the decisions from the state I came to deliver. On the last day of training, the Accountability Coordinator joined me in Santee to share the draft of the progress plan that would be presented to the SBOE in August. Again, we stood before the assembled staff, this time passing around paper copies of draft progress plans.

The Accountability Coordinator explained the format and the process for developing plans, asking the teachers who had been part of the writing team to make comments about the rationale for each goal. Staff had few questions; whether this was the result of the plan being presented after 3 long days of training or a general acceptance that the state was in control now was not clear. Following the end of the meeting, however, a 16-year veteran of the teaching staff sat down next to me. I asked her what she was thinking after her initial review of the plan. There was a pause. "It remains to be seen," she began. "We've been through this before, you know." That comment hung with me for the drive home. I could not help but think about how many times outsiders had made plans for what education should look like in Indian Country.

SCS Board Reviews Progress Plan

On July 8, 2016, the Accountability Coordinator and I were together again, this time in Lincoln with the Commissioner, members of the Santee school board, and the Santee leadership team (which now included the new superintendent, two principals, and the instructional facilitator). The purpose of this meeting was to examine the progress plan goals, as the Consultant had drafted aligned goals for both the superintendent and the local school board. We sat around a U-shaped conference table with binders in front of us. I thumbed down the tabs of the progress plan's "draft" watermarked pages as we waited for the Commissioner to begin the meeting. Following introductions, the Commissioner asked the Santee Board President to share his hopes as we moved forward with progress plan implementation at SCS. The board president described, with great pride and emotion, what it was like to attend SCS in the 1980s. He acknowledged the challenges facing the students in his community and expressed a desire for stability in the school. His vision was a Santee where students would stop getting on a bus to attend the neighboring district and all children would feel the same pride he felt about being a graduate of a public school governed by members of the tribe. He described a place that would celebrate the Santee people and also to prepare the future leaders of the tribe and community for greater opportunities. When I saw the tears in his eyes, I blinked back on my own.

In the afternoon, the Commissioner and the Accountability Coordinator met with the board while I worked alongside the Santee leadership team, reviewing the strategies and outcomes for each goal, discussing the calendar and schedule for the upcoming year, and starting a long list of "to-dos" that needed to be accomplished before the beginning of school, which was only 6 weeks away. Before new teachers showed up or the staff participated in a teacher evaluation training during their back-to-school workdays, the leadership team was to attend a 2-day training with the consultant on how to implement the progress plan. Despite the short timeline and long list of things to accomplish, the team demonstrated excitement and determination as they began to learn about one another's strengths and philosophies about working with students. The retreat ended with final reminders about all that needed to be accomplished before the SBOE approval and the start of the school year. One of the items on the list of reminders was a training the consultant would provide for all priority school administrators to equip them to supervise teachers' instruction according to a specific model aligned with the progress plan.

Training Begins

In July 2016 I met the Santee administrative team in Omaha for the 2-day training facilitated by the Lady from North Carolina and a subcontractor she had hired to work with her. In the morning, over chewy bagels, the consultant lectured on each of her "high-leverage areas" for improvement. Following training on observing instruction and providing feedback to teachers, the consultant wanted to hear an update from the Santee leadership team on their progress since the last meeting with the Santee local board. This included changes to the staff handbook and the schedule for each of the staff days prior to the start of school. The consultant shared a calendar of which 3 days in each month she or the subcontractor planned to be in Santee in the upcoming school year. She planned to spend 1 day a month in the building, and her subcontractor would be there 2 days to walk the staff through their instructional coaching model as well as to check on the work in the progress plan. The plan seemed promising in part, as the consultant would be making consistent trips to SCS. It was perceived as a let-down in other ways, as school leaders and members of the community stated that it felt like someone was swooping in from the outside to make orders and then departing without truly taking the time to understand the school or community.

Before departing from the training, the SCS leadership team met, with progress plan binders before them, talking through the next 3 weeks. In those 21 days, they would attend the statewide annual Administrators' Days conference, welcome staff back for beginning of the year professional learning, and start the school year. As I listened to their conversation, I found myself making parallel checklists. I listed many of the to-dos under an "NDE" column, signifying priority progress plan requirements, while the other list I put under the other, "SCS" column. Those latter items were more relationship-oriented and described the need to support new teachers and staff, actions intended to cultivate a positive culture for the start of the year, and the need to reach out to the community for a beginning of the year smudging and to have conversations about collaborating with Tribal leaders to improve student attendance in the building. Once again, with hindsight, I see the way building leaders were negotiating official school improvement efforts as mandated by the state in the school's progress plan and their own unauthorized school improvement efforts. They held the tension of complying while also resisting compliance through their own planning.

At the end of July 2016, all but the Consultant and the subcontractor attended Administrators' Days, a statewide conference hosted by the state's school administrator professional organization. On the second night of the conference, the SCS team met for dinner. I sat near the middle of the long table in the loud restaurant and looked around at each person around the table. There were colleagues from the ESU who had been there each step of the way since Santee's designation, the new administrative team, and some steering committee members. Over heaps of barbeque, we talked about a teacher's new engagement and wedding plans, cattle sales, fishing, the new fence around the basketball court at the school, and summer graduate classes. I realized that in a very real sense, the implementation journey had not even begun. We intentionally avoided conversations about consultants, progress plans, or trainings. We all knew that the SBOE meeting and the beginning of SCS's first year progress plan would happen the following week, but none of us talked about what was ahead.

PROGRESS PLAN APPROVAL AND INITIAL IMPLEMENTATION

The August 2016 SBOE work session and business meeting agendas contained discussion and action items related to priority school progress plans and contracts to support the intervention work. In priority school discussion at Thursday's work session, the board president expressed her appreciation to the guests representing the three schools who were assembled in the public gallery. The Commissioner asked the Accountability Coordinator and the Lady from North Carolina to guide the discussion regarding the work in the priority schools and the progress plans that the board would act upon the next day in their work session. The Commissioner told board members that it was "a monumental point in time for us to look at priority schools [and how] our role as an agency is changing" (NSBOE, 2016f). He clarified that unlike in the past, school-level intervention would be directly planned and implemented by the state.

Board members had been briefed on each of the three progress plans in committee that morning. The Accountability Coordinator introduced the consultant to present the progress plans. Just as she had in June, the consultant described the levers of her process, in addition to the tenets of the state accountability system, that provided the framework for the goals in each school's progress plan: clear, compelling direction, staff and student culture, and instructional leadership. In each progress plan, she explained, the voices of a range of stakeholder groups came together with a small team working together. Each of the three school's plans were unique, "based on the needs that they have within their community and within their school district. The teams spent "many hours, many, many hours creating the plans that they have submitted for your approval" (NSBOE, 2016f). She described the ways each school would be held accountable for making progress implementing their plans. "We intend to report back to you as well as their local boards, as well as their superintendent and teachers how we're doing with these particular strategies within each one of these goals" (NSBOE, 2016f).

The Lady from North Carolina then outlined key components of each school's progress plan goals. Each plan contained three sections containing aligned goals for the school, the superintendent, and the local board of education. As a result of the administrative instability and teacher turnover in Santee in recent years, one of the primary goals of the school's plan was to "establish, implement, and communicate a climate of high expectations for everybody in their building and outside of their building that supports the school" (NSBOE, 2016f). The consultant did acknowledge the need to incorporate the Dakota language and Santee Sioux culture with the SBOE. She mentioned that the intervention in Santee had included significant investment from the Commissioner and Deputy Commissioner who had "done a lot of work creating a leadership team that's going to be collaborative to ensure that this plan is carried out and successful" (NSBOE, 2016f). The consultant concluded her presentation by telling the board, "I think they're [the schools are] ready for it. They're excited about it. They see it as an opportunity to provide an exceptional education for the students that they serve" (NSBOE, 2016f). With no other comments or questions, the board went into a break, allowing members to briefly greet and converse with representatives of each of the schools.

After the break, and with the priority school representatives no longer in the public gallery, the Commissioner and Deputy Commissioner expressed appreciation for the Accountability Coordinator's work and the intention to contract for her continued work in the state. "We have come so very far," Deputy Commissioner Frison said, before going on to say,

> The whole term of relationships needs to be reiterated because in the beginning the priority schools thought of themselves with a designation of Needs Improvement, which was synonymous in their minds to failing, and just to work through relationships to get to a point of support, collaboration, took some convincing, took some time, took some work, and took some beliefs after continuing and continuing and continuing to work with. Just appreciating the process to get to today, to see the excitement of everybody to continue with what's being done, so that would be what I would bring to the process. (NSBOE, 2016f)

Board members' discussion focused on the absence of exit criteria in the plan, and the Deputy Commissioner again requested that the Lady from North

Carolina come up to the table to respond to questions. At that moment, my phone vibrated. It was one of the Santee team members. "We are going for drinks. Can you join?" I held my phone thinking about how to respond. As I typed and retyped a response on my phone, I listened as board member McPherson expressed dissatisfaction with the Deputy Commissioner's explanation that "[progress] plans would be fluid." He asked, "Wouldn't it make sense, though, to have some kind of tangible exit criteria goals for these schools so that, you know . . . they know what they've got to achieve in order to get off the list?" The Commissioner replied that each school is "a priority school until this body says that they're not." The progress plans would last for 1 year; that time "gives us a chance to kind of dissect that, and by next year . . . we make judgment about where they're at in those plans" (NSBOE, 2016f). I texted back, "Wish I could. Could use a drink about now, but I have to stay here 'til the meeting's over." I longed for the camaraderie and time to reflect on the day with the Santee team, however, I recognized the responsibility I had to remain at NDE while the SBOE was in session.

Without any more comments or questions about the plans, the Board President opened discussion on the contracts for the Lady from North Carolina to assist priority schools. The Commissioner outlined the plan to ensure consistency in the implementation of progress plans in each priority school with the larger purpose of informing future work with schools needing help to improve. He asserted that the consultant's work would help the state "in the long run build capacity to do that work—whether at the department, whether ESUs, or sometimes even specifically at the school district level. She brings a special level of expertise to get that work accomplished. We learned a lot, in the, you know, time since engaging her and feeling like she's the right person to carry out that work over the next year" (NSBOE, 2016f).

Looking at the papers in front of him, board member Flint posed the first question regarding the Consultant's contract. "I was just wondering, it is quite a chunk of money, it's like $256,000. Is she bidding hours? Does she have a bio or what other schools she's helped out or something?" (NSBOE, 2016f). The Commissioner asked the Deputy Commissioner to provide details for the Consultant's scope of work for each school. The Board President interjected, "I would just like to say, it's not just her. . . . I don't know how many associates or who all works with her." The Deputy Commissioner stated that the Lady from North Carolina had provided a schedule for the days she would work in the three priority schools. "At a minimum, 3 days a month she [or her associate] would be there [in each school] just coaching the staff in classrooms . . . [t]here's so many things foundationally that had to be addressed with each of the districts in different kinds of ways, so it's kind of an all-inclusive kind of thing to get these schools where we want them to be" (NSBOE, 2016f).

Upon conclusion of discussion on the consultant's contract, the SBOE President moved on to the next discussion item, a proposed contract with the ESU near Santee to provide an instructional coach for the school. Before discussing the proposed contract, the Commissioner described the administrative churn Santee had experienced in recent years and the decision to ask an NDE employee to serve as Santee's new superintendent. With the hire of the superintendent and new principal, the work of the consultant, and an instructional coach, the state was making a significant commitment to stabilize the leadership at SCS. "We really have to look at a way to ensure that we put the staff on the right page," he said. Referring to the consultant's emphasis on staff and student culture, the Commissioner explained that while working with Santee's local board, he learned that

> there's a perception that the teachers don't somehow care about what is happening to students, like the teachers that come from outside [the reservation]. I don't believe that's the case at all, but in the absence of leadership for a period of years . . . we knew that we could not leave them without the capacity to be successful in getting that done [making sure instruction really matters]. (NSBOE, 2016f)

As a result, he had asked the ESU to contract with an instructional coach. The Commissioner commented, "Santee's been through a lot, just unstable from an administrative level. I've watched that really, I mean, unfortunately my first, not even, it was the first day after I was selected, not even on the job yet here and I was in a meeting about Santee. There had been a level of discord there and problems for some time" (NSBOE, 2016f). The Commissioner commented that he believed that the new leadership, the instructional coach, and the work of the external consultant would be pivotal in developing the capacity to truly help Santee.

Board member McPherson inquired about the community-wide needs in Santee. "When you talk about Santee, you've got some very special issues. You got fetal alcoholism that affects a lot of the children. You got diabetes that is rampant, you know? As we go through this process, are we dealing with those issues as well in what we're doing in our plan? I mean, those are serious issues that you know, they're impacting the learning of those children in a great way" (NSBOE, 2016f). The Deputy Commissioner responded, "Yes, those issues are there, but I think I have no doubt that they couldn't be addressed as much as they will be able to be addressed with a larger capacity of a leadership team" (NSBOE, 2016f). The Board President added that the work of the regional ESU in Northeast Nebraska, with all four of Nebraska's Native American school districts in their service area, were also working to address special education services and the unique needs of students, including those with fetal alcohol syndrome. "They're [the

ESU staff] the unsung heroes, already . . . I think there's some real positive possibilities here" (NSBOE, 2016f).

The Commissioner prompted the board to conclude their discussion, summing up with a comment about the important work ahead and the relationships that had already been forged. He encouraged board members, stating that, "When the school community isn't functioning, other things are at a detriment there as well, and so if we can get that to be a really solid base, I think you'll also see other things come along that is really remarkable" (NSBOE, 2016f). The board wrapped up their discussions on priority school-related items they would face as action items on their business meeting agenda the following day.

These final interchanges during the SBOE's work session revealed board member and NDE leadership perceptions of the community of Santee. The deficit framing of the challenges present on the reservation (without any grounding in the sociohistorical or sociocultural context) also framed their understanding of what was happening in the local public school (e.g., administrator/teacher churn, student mobility out of the district to adjacent attendance zone). These understandings undergirded proposed state responses to improve school and community circumstances: a consultant who would hold the school accountable to meeting the outlined goals in the progress plan with the same fidelity as the other identified priority schools and an expanded administrative team that would be able to make great change in the school and possibly beyond in the community.

Approval

The following day the SBOE approved all three priority schools' progress plans without discussion. With a motion for the contracts for the Lady from North Carolina on the table, board member O'Holleran commented,

> I just wanted to say that [the Consultant] seems really pretty amazing, and I was very reassured yesterday that those plans that are being presented for our three priority schools will be set as models for other school districts with similar situations. And I just wanted to reassure people across the state that these are going to be models for future excellence . . . And I think Nebraska's really done it right. (NSBOE, 2016g)

Board member Witzel agreed, saying, "These plans will also be templates for the future, to be used for other schools and other situations around the state." Board member Nickel added, "This sets the model which can provide a guideline for how other schools can improve" (NSBOE, 2016g). McPherson clarified that the money used to pay the consultant would come from the accountability funds allocated by the legislature. "It's a lot of money we're spending here," but the work would be a template, "not just for the future priority schools I think, but for the other 85 or whatever schools are Needs Improvement, so with that said, I'm sure going to vote for this" (NSBOE, 2016g). The board voted unanimously to approve the contract.

That night, I again sat at my dining room table late into the evening. I emailed the Santee leadership team, expressing my appreciation for each of them making the trip to Lincoln for the board meeting. I emailed our ESU partners, thanking them as well. I knew the events of the day were indeed a milestone in the priority school implementation that would continue to unfold in the coming months. In less than a week, new teachers would show up for their orientation, and in just a couple weeks, the doors would open, and another year of school would begin, far away from the chambers of the Legislature or the SBOE meeting room.

Between January 2016 and August 2016, throughout the development of progress plans for priority schools, policymakers repeatedly expressed their desire to improve outcomes through the state's intervention at SCS. They did not ignore the academic achievement of American Indian students in the state. However, Santee was consistently referred to as "broken." Intentions were posed within an accountability reform policy culture pointing toward deficits to be corrected (Stein, 2004). More than a century after the American Board of Missionaries established a school for the Santee Sioux, the dynamics of a policy culture that invokes an external expertise (whether a mission board, state department of education, or an out-of-state consultant) to intervene, to do for, and to "fix" a school, and by extension a community, seems eerily familiar to the policies carried out in Santee that were described in Chapter 3.

Hampton Denman (the Northern Superintendent of Indian Affairs in 1867) claimed that the U.S. government should take the Santee people "once more by the hand" in order to "make them "good citizens and entirely self-sustaining" (United States Office of Indian Affairs, 1868, p. 265). Policymakers in Nebraska in 2016 did much the same. They proposed to aid Santee by bringing in "good" leadership to "stabilize" the school, along with other recommendations for policy fixes external to Santee.

The state incorporated little local voice in the final progress plan submitted to the SBOE for any of the three schools (Phillips, 2019). With time constraints in statute for completing a progress plan to be approved by the SBOE, authentic relationship-building efforts or partnerships to collaboratively develop a progress plan with richer participation among tribal members were set aside. Regardless of the unique "challenges" or "barriers to student achievement" in each priority school, the state determined that the most efficient path to move schools out of priority school status was to contract with the Lady from North Carolina and trust her "levers of improvement." Three days a month, the consultant or her subcontractor would meet with superintendents and coach principals to lead tighter alignment between instruction and the most tested state standards, using posted learning targets, curriculum scope and sequence, or new instructional materials. This largely ignored identified areas for improvement raised by educators in the building and local board members who consistently highlighted a need for greater school and community connections and greater presence of Santee cultural, linguistic, and historic knowledge to be embedded in school practices and instruction.

While the Lady from North Carolina acknowledged the importance of including Dakota language and culture into improvement efforts, resource allocation and strategies outlined in SCS's progress plan were directed toward greater alignment of instruction to statewide assessment and the supervision of curriculum and instruction within the school. The SBOE's external solutions reflected national policy trends far removed from Indigenous knowledge, history, or culture. The approved progress plan focused on what Brayboy (2013) describes as "academic knowledge," or "book knowing," and largely ignored Native "cultural knowledge" or the constructs of power present when the state works with tribal people who are constantly adapting to external requirements while maintaining survival, "the thriving (educationally, politically, spiritually, and many other ways), both as individuals and as a group" (p. 95).

The very structure of the accountability system and the structures of power within accountability constrained the state in responding to Santee in ways that were culturally responsive or sustaining. AQuESTT, despite efforts to include additional inputs through the EBA survey, relied primarily on metrics from statewide assessment and graduation rates. Thus, what counted as a demonstration of improvement were Santee students' assessment scores and graduation rates, despite evidence of the impact of culturally responsive and sustaining practices on school outcomes (e.g., Barnhardt and Kawagley 2005; Castagno & Brayboy, 2008; Demmert, 2001; Lee, 2009, 2015; Nelson-Barber & Johnson 2019; McCarty, 2012; McCarty & Lee, 2014). The structure of power written into the state school accountability law situated the SBOE and NDE with power over priority schools. As a result, the goals and strategies for improvement determined by the state for Santee usurped those in Santee, which held consequential relevance for a school created by and for a tribe with the right to self-education. Improvement efforts in Santee, as has been demonstrated in other Native American communities, have been impeded and community trust undermined when external expertise has been privileged above local knowledge (e.g., Balter & Grossman, 2009; Beaulieu, 2000; Mette & Stanoch, 2016).

The progress plan that was ultimately developed for SCS reflects much of the "policy culture" framework Sandra Stein (2004) wrote about, where the government situates itself as a "corrective force." There were certainly ways the state and the school and community could have worked together to develop a progress plan that met the requirements set forth by that state's accountability statute while also attending to the contextual nuances present in each of the priority schools. There were missed opportunities to implement culturally responsive/sustaining interventions in the progress plan even with the many examples of its effectiveness (e.g., Barnhardt & Kawagley, 2005; Cleary & Peacock, 1998; Demmert, 2001; Deyhle, 1998; Klug & Whitfield, 2003; Lipka, 1990; Lipka et al., 2005; Nelson-Barber & Estrin, 1995; Nelson-Barber & Johnson, 2019). What was possible in Nebraska as the state assumed its new accountability role in Santee was not realized. Policymakers did not demonstrate an understanding of the history or sovereignty of tthe Santee peoples and their responsibility toward students and the local tribal community (Austin, 2005). Well-intentioned policies and plans for enacting those policies fell short in what was actually included in the progress plan.

Throughout the process there were glimpses into what culturally responsive policymaking *could* look like. While the presence of local educators and school board members who were also members of the tribe at the table for numerous meetings with NDE resulted in more symbolic than substantive input into Santee's progress plan, the transcripts and fieldnotes demonstrate concrete suggestions that could have been realized through collaboration (e.g., expansion of Dakota history, culture, and language in the school). In their 2006 book, Lomawaima and McCarty describe "footprints of Native presence," or the evidence of "the overlooked, the seemingly paradoxical results of and responses to domineering policies in institutions" (p. 13). Throughout the development of SCS's priority plan, educators, and representatives of the community on the local school board stated consistent visions for what they believed improvement would look like, visions that were not included in the official progress plan approved by the SBOE. In the next chapter, I will point to the ways that people in Santee acted to bring their own improvement visions to reality outside of the official turnaround efforts directed by the state.

CHAPTER 7

Compliance, Kind Of

As the start of the school year neared, there were nearly daily emails, phone calls, and Zoom sessions with the SCS leadership team, the Lady from North Carolina, and NDE support staff (including myself). As the new leadership made changes to the staff and student handbooks and planned for the first few teachers' contract days in typical preparation for the start of a new school year, they were required to seek NDE approval before finalizing any decisions. It was immediately clear that part of the state's intervention would require ongoing consultation on day-to-day decisions in the school with the Lady from North Carolina before school leadership would be allowed to make any significant decisions. The structure of state oversight put the Lady from North Carolina working directly with Deputy Commissioner Frison who was responsible for overseeing school improvement. This new dynamic shifted my role as liaison from one of relationship bridge between SCS and NDE to that of responding to the consultant's directives and interacting with SCS administrators and staff at her request.

The Lady from North Carolina distributed revised dates that either she or her hired subcontractor planned to be in Santee. On average, she spent 1 day each month, and the subcontractor was on site 2 additional days to reinforce the Lady from North Carolina's work and hold leadership, staff, and NDE staff accountable for follow-through on action items. I was on site for all those days. The consultant outlined her objectives for the fall, which included having principals in classrooms monitoring instruction. The Lady from North Carolina provided a rough outline of what to expect for each day she or the subcontractor were in Santee. Each day's agenda included time to discuss the ongoing book study, classroom observations, and feedback sessions with teachers that included principal coaching from the Lady from North Carolina and updates on the progress plan.

The state's intervention officially began when teachers arrived back in the building for their initial contract days starting on August 4, 2016. Each time I was on site, I recorded field notes that I compared to the official reporting on the Lady from North Carolina's work that was presented by the SCS leadership team at local school board meetings and by the Lady from North Carolina to the SBOE. The first meeting in August included an overview of the approved progress plan. The teachers who participated in drafting the plan back in May led the presentation to staff under the direction of the Lady from North Carolina. Following the presentation of the 16-page plan aligned to the consultant's levers of improvement, no one asked any questions. The elementary and secondary principals described their commitment to making frequent appearances in classrooms as a part of the progress plan. They explained that when the Lady from North Carolina was in the building she would coach them and help the superintendent monitor progress on the actions outlined in the progress plan. They also set the expectation that teachers would submit their first 2 weeks of standards-aligned lesson plans before the first day with students. The practice would then continue in 2-week increments throughout the remainder of the school year. Teachers were released to work in their classrooms and on lesson plans until lunch.

I sat at a table with teachers and paraprofessionals from the community in the school cafeteria for lunch. By this time, I had spent many days in the school. While the table was quiet as people ate, conversation picked up toward the end of the meal. There were comments expressing frustration that the work the staff completed in the spring to identify priority areas for improvement seemingly did not appear in the progress plan, and others pointing to the lack of Dakota culture or of efforts to rebuild trust with the community visible in the plan. There seemed to be no expectation that I would respond, so I just listened. I shared their frustrations. Throughout the previous spring, I had shared the local improvement priorities with NDE leadership. I had also described state intervention as a partnership that would include culturally responsive approaches more than once, echoing SBOE members' intentions stated throughout 2015–2016. In my intermediary role, I had believed that implementation intentions would eventually align with practice, only to sit in that gym turned cafeteria barely able to eat my food. That the state's intervention would largely emphasize instructional leadership, standards-curriculum alignment, pacing guides, and school-wide behavior systems and improvement measured by standardized, high-stakes state assessment was becoming clearer and clearer. In serving as the state's liaison, I wrestled with the knowledge of how I was complicit. It was a constraining space of realization for everyone at the table.

By the end of September 2016, the Santee leadership, intermediate service agency representative, and I began to settle into a pattern for our days with the Lady from North Carolina or her contractor. We began with conversation on immediate school decisions or challenges, followed by an update provided by the superintendent on her activities in the previous month. This introductory session was then followed by about an hour of book study before the leadership team made visits to classrooms. Throughout the fall, classroom walkthroughs with the consultant focused on 15-minute classroom observations with short feedback reinforcing a positive strategy or approach left on sticky notes for the classroom teacher. The team reconvened in a conference room to debrief on what had been observed and discussed and then practice for longer post-observation conferences according to the Lady from North Carolina's model of feedback. Her central tool was the use of a piece of large poster paper where the principal documented instructional actions in the categories of teaching, learning, and naming specific strategies and their impact on student learning outcomes. The tool was used for conversation, and then the Lady from North Carolina would take a photograph of the principal with the poster for future reference when working with that teacher.

In late October 2016, the Lady from North Carolina conducted professional development with the school staff on a *gradual release of instruction* model, where teachers would gradually move from teacher-directed modes of instruction to having students demonstrate greater ownership in the learning process. She also instructed teachers to practice writing daily lesson objectives that would be posted in their classrooms. Throughout the remainder of the school year, examples of gradual release of instruction and posted objectives were elements the leadership team was expected to track. Expectations around post-observation conferences shifted to include critical feedback, or suggestions for the teacher. The Lady from North Carolina referred to these as a "value add." During October and November, the consultant expressed her dissatisfaction with SCS's textbook series in math and informed the superintendent and administrators that they would need to begin vetting new instructional materials for the following year. In the November SCS local board meeting, the superintendent updated board members on the work with the Lady from North Carolina and her subcontractor, sharing that a shift in curriculum material adoption in math was likely, even though it was not in the typical purchasing timeline, and that some professional development in the spring semester would also likely need to be adjusted according to the consultant's recommendations. This had budgetary consequences, as an elementary-wide mathematics instructional material adoption was falling outside of the cycle; however, it was expected that the school district would reallocate funding to meet the state's expectation.

In December 2016, the Lady from North Carolina conducted a conference call with SCS leadership team in lieu of making the trip to Nebraska, citing the unpredictability of winter weather. Walking the school's hallways with the leadership team without the consultant present, and marking the halfway point of the first year of state intervention, there was a sense of performative compliance among teachers and the administrative team. In side conversations on site, representatives of the teaching staff and members of the administrative team made comments about needing to comply with the state while also attempting to respond to what they perceived as the real needs in the school. Priority action plans set out due dates and directives from the consultant around new math instructional material selection and to check that teachers had posted objectives for each lesson. The leadership team and teachers complied, providing evidence in their reporting to the Lady from North Carolina on their progress. But this narrow focus on posted lesson objectives and on following a prescribed format for framing conversations with teachers in a post-observation conference seemed disconnected with the daily reality in the school. Many school staff and community members blamed the state for the current turmoil in the school, where the superintendent, who had been recommended by the Commissioner, was frequently absent and, as a result, tensions with the local board were on the rise. Educators in the building felt that their professionalism was constrained by a consultant who flew in once a month and then flew out, leaving directives in her wake. I received nearly daily text messages from people in Santee to report on the superintendent's absence, confusion about some financial reporting due to the state, and requests to amplify local concerns about teacher morale and dissatisfaction with the consultant's efforts. One teacher called to report that she didn't know "how much longer I can keep doing this if it going to be like this."

In contrast to the more discouraging reports were other improvement efforts happening in the building not among the Lady from North Carolina's directives. These efforts included a music teacher's endeavor to revive a band program in the same tradition as John F. Lenger, who organized an all-brass band on the reservation in 1884. While the aspiration of the small group of students practicing their instruments on the cordoned-off gymnasium stage was a long way away from ancestors who had played at the Chicago World's Fair in 1893, this group looked forward to playing as a real pep band at basketball games in the winter. The vision for what the music program could become drew upon a rich history, and students displayed great pride and vulnerability as they made their way through a new piece of music, starting and stopping, and starting again. Improvement efforts looked like preschool students learning Dakota sight-words and counting and identifying colors in Dakota. It looked like 4th-grade students highly engaged in a small-group math lesson grounded in Dakota culture designed by a teacher from the community. It also looked like a new series of foods and consumer science courses and the development of a culinary program led by another teacher from the community who had visions for partnerships with the tribe's casino and farm-to-school grants that would integrate Dakota culture and promote healthy eating throughout the year. These were all examples of the other work happening at SCS where educators, community members, and the local board collaborated in a space outside the direct work of the state's intervention.

Following the holidays, things in Santee destabilized as the local board placed the superintendent on administrative leave. She resigned, and the local board named the two principals as the school district's designees until an interim superintendent could be named with the direction of the Commissioner and Deputy Commissioner. This turn of events was particularly significant in the ways it eroded the tenuous trust between the state and the school district. The superintendent had been hired at the direction of NDE leadership. On February 3, 2017, SCS's local board met with NDE representatives, including the Deputy Commissioner and the Lady from North Carolina, in Omaha for an emergency session. The first priority was to identify and contract with an interim superintendent prior to the consultant's March update to the SBOE.

By the March 2, 2017, SBOE work session, Santee had an interim superintendent in place. The Commissioner and Deputy Commissioner recommended a former superintendent of a mid-sized district, and the Santee local board hired him immediately. The Lady from North Carolina assured the SBOE that with this interim superintendent in place, there would be tremendous support that would ensure that the staff would fully implement the progress plan moving forward. She reported on her progress in Santee, highlighting the coaching opportunities she and her sub-contractor had on a monthly basis with the leadership team in the school. According to the Lady from North Carolina,

> The staff wasn't used to having visitors in their classroom ever. Nor were there conversations about their instruction by the former principal. They weren't used to that so we started off by writing what we call 30-second feedback notes for the teachers where we would reinforce the things they are doing well and they're much more open in those situations where we talk to them about things they need to work on. (NSBOE, 2017a)

According to the consultant's narrative with the SBOE, efforts at improvement did not exist prior to the arrival of state actors, and once again, improvement was defined within the consultant's framework. Her framing ignored ongoing local improvement attempts at SCS that were well documented in the public record, but were outside of the official progress plan strategies aligned with her levers of improvement.

The Lady from North Carolina's focus remained clear when she returned to Santee on March 15, 2017. In the first meeting of the day she discussed the necessity of adding curriculum mapping work and emphasized a balanced literacy shift in the elementary school as priorities for the remainder of the school year and summer, on top of the ongoing work in gradual release of instruction and a new math instructional materials adoption. We sat around the conference room table with calendars and to-do lists before us as she outlined her plan for implementing these components. She would lead professional learning sessions after school on her days in the building, and she framed how teacher workdays would be allocated for teachers to begin their work in May and June. She also directed the interim superintendent and leadership team to continue documenting their work to meet progress plan expectations, collecting artifacts as evidence of their work on each action-step in the plan (work that had paused with the superintendent change).

The Lady from North Carolina and the interim superintendent also introduced a new school improvement structure, which she called the Warrior Improvement Team (WIT). The implementation of the WIT was a key element of the interim superintendent's 60-day contract that would be evaluated by the local board, the Lady from North Carolina, Deputy Commissioner, and Commissioner. The consultant detailed which staff in the building would be involved and the way that three teams aligned to her levers of improvement would function with meeting schedules in subgroups and in a full group. She listed the next steps and responsibilities for the interim superintendent and principals to roll out the WIT before her May visit to the school, as the team would need to be ready by the end of the school year to work with the consultant to revise the school's progress plan for the second year of state intervention. The introduction of the WIT and its associated rollout was a surprise to the building principals and to the staff who had been meeting monthly in school improvement committees organized according to areas that aligned with the school's external, regional accreditation body.

By the end of April 2017, the tension between the state moving forward with its improvement agenda, directed by the Lady from North Carolina and facilitated by the interim superintendent working directly with the Commissioner and Deputy Commissioner, and the principals and educators working in the school and community every day, was evident. Educators described feeling hopeless, as if decisions were happening to them, and not feeling sure they would be able to endure another year working in an environment "the state has dumped on us." Once again, conversations circled back to the efforts the staff made the year before to identify areas for improvement. Even though those plans were also incomplete, staff pointed to the rejection of their ideas as evidence that what was happening now was being done to them rather than with them. Eight teachers resigned by the May SCS board meeting.

In the day-to-day operations in the school, performative compliance continued as principals and teachers fulfilled their roles and duties on the WIT and collected and organized evidence on their priority plan progress to be submitted at the June SBOE meeting. Principals completed their classroom visits and documented what the Lady from North Carolina required from their observations. Teachers submitted weekly lesson plans aligned to standards, and administrators facilitated post-observations according to the consultant's framework. These activities were documented in preparation for a June presentation on the school's progress to the SBOE. They continued to check the boxes on the progress plan. The staff and community felt hounded into compliance to reforms according to the state's mandated timelines, which led to their compliance-oriented resistance more than the actual nature of the reforms themselves.

On May 24, 2017, the Lady from North Carolina made her final visit to the school for the academic year and reviewed the school's draft report for the SBOE. She pointed to areas where she believed there were gaps in documentation and directed principals to add evidence. She coached the superintendent and principals on what they might expect when they presented to a SBOE board committee and represented the school in the SBOE meeting gallery while she made her report to the full board. She also outlined a plan for revising the progress plan for the following year that would continue to leverage the work of the WIT team. The ongoing work would build upon the initial efforts at aligning curriculum, focusing instruction around the table of specifications of what was tested on the annual statewide assessment, clarity of objectives aligned to standards, and ongoing monitoring of instruction in classrooms. While she did not dissuade the leadership team from additional projects or efforts to improve the school, she noted that getting out of priority school status was contingent on improving state assessment scores and graduation rates and that it was her job to make sure measurable progress occurred as quickly as possible.

And yet, unofficial, or as I came to think of them, incognito improvement efforts continued in the school outside of the Lady from North Carolina's framework. Principals collaborated with the tribe to pursue a grant for a cultural specialist to work in the school. If funded, the position would serve as a connection between the school and the community and would also find ways to bring Dakota culture into the teaching, learning, and ways of being in the building. A group of teachers from the community and the building principals reestablished a morning routine for all students in the school that included the Dakota Flag Song, a tribal anthem that honors warriors, their good deeds, and calls the next generation to a Dakota way of life (South Dakota Board of Education, 2018). The inclusion of the song in the school's morning routine was a clear signal to students and to the community that the school's leadership was striving to incorporate Dakota values into school routines and procedures. The FCS (family and consumer sciences) teacher applied for and was awarded a farm-to-school grant from the Center for Rural Affairs in collaboration with the secondary administrator and kitchen staff. These activities were initiated locally, supported by the building administration, celebrated by the local school board. Incognito improvement activities were reported in the progress plan update submitted to the state at the end of the school year. While not discouraged by the Lady from North Carolina or members of the SBOE, neither were these activities acknowledged or counted as evidence of measurable progress for the state's progress plan. Locally, the school celebrated such efforts on social media, as they had greater meaning in the local community than what would be shared in Lincoln at the SBOE meeting.

REPORTING FIRST-YEAR PROGRESS

All three priority schools presented updates on their progress in the June 2017 SBOE meeting. One of the schools, located in the largest district in the state, requested to be removed from priority school oversight, citing their trending progress in reading and math on the statewide assessment. When approving plans, the SBOE had not included exit criteria for any school; however, the Commissioner supported the school's request to be released from priority school status with the SBOE. He stated that he would bring a recommendation for priority school release in August. It was once again clear to the SCS leadership team as they waited to present their own process that the path to being released from priority school designation and state oversight was directly tied to better performance on statewide assessment. The rules of the game, as the Lady from North Carolina had described them, were clear. What remained absent were any discussions about improvement efforts tailored to local context that embraced culturally responsive/sustaining approaches (NSBOE, 2017b).

Following the return to Santee that week, the interim superintendent and principals shared an update on the SBOE meeting with the local board at SCS. In this meeting the local board also extended a contract to the interim superintendent to continue his service for the 2017–2018 academic year. The SCS board included an expectation in the contract that the interim superintendent should "serve as a buffer" between the school district and the Lady from North Carolina, who had been offered another large contract by the SBOE to continue her work for the second year of state oversight (Santee Community School Board, 2017). While the discussion of this particular point was not extensive, board members expressed their desire that the interim superintendent manage some of the directives coming from the state and particularly the consultant so that principals and teachers might be able to focus on their work in the building and in classrooms. They were concerned that—while turnover was a consistent challenge in the school district—the teacher resignations at the end of the school year were directly related to the state's approach to intervention.

The Lady from North Carolina returned to SCS toward the end of June for a series of teacher workdays on standards alignment and curriculum mapping in English, math, and science (tested areas) in the elementary grades and across content areas in the secondary grades. Previous curriculum maps were discarded, and instructional materials and laptops carried out from classrooms to the multipurpose space in the elementary wing of the building. Grade level pairs spread materials across table tops and began mapping the following year's sequence of instruction in accordance with the state assessment table of specifications according to "priority standards," or those standards most likely to be assessed. There were no discussions about ways to include Dakota culture, language, history, or ways of knowing. Just as Jester (2002) found in the implementation of standards-based reforms in Alaska, improving outcomes for Native students was devoid of culturally responsive approaches. As I looked over the shoulder of a teacher working through the sequence for science, I observed her careful handwriting filling up a grid she had created for herself. She noticed me and sat back, commenting on how easy it would be to produce lesson plans for the administration next year, as she knew what she planned to teach the entire first quarter.

At the end of the day, an elementary teacher, the consultant, and the elementary principal were the last people remaining. The Lady from North Carolina took a photograph of us for her social media, and in that moment I realized that this would likely be my last trip to Santee in an official state capacity. I felt a sense of relief at thinking about leaving NDE and my official state role in Santee even while dreading saying goodbye to the principals and staff. Between January 2016 and June 2017, I had spent more than 200 hours on-site in Santee and innumerable more in communication with leadership and staff via email, phone, and text. I could not have imagined on that first trip 18 months before, peering over the final ridge and seeing the village appear before me, that the SBOE and NDE's stated intentions would fail to reflect the collaborative and place-responsive vision touted in the early public discussions of AQuESTT. In leaving NDE and my official role in Santee, I did not leave my connection to the place and the people who had become valued friends and colleagues. I shared their persistent hope that the agentic stories and acts of survivance would continue to grow and reshape the state's intervention at SCS.

At the end of the first year of state-directed improvement in SCS, the school continued to experience leadership churn with yet another mid-year firing of a superintendent. Several long-time staff with deep ties to the Santee community and tribe, including the school's only Dakota language and culture teacher, resigned. The emphasis on teaching the "necessary skills at the appropriate depth of knowledge" rarely incorporated local cultural knowledge, educator expertise, or improvement efforts. The Lady from North Carolina's prescription for improvement for SCS was largely the same as for the other two priority schools, ignoring each site's local culture, history, knowledge, and resources. Instead, state standards were considered the most apt measure for what students brought to school or needed to learn. Over time and with reflection I can see how the constraint I felt in my official state role illuminated this approach's was problems. First, the state viewed academic performance in Santee as the same as "underrepresented minority" groups (like those attending other priority schools in Nebraska). This kind of approach, as Brayboy et al. (2015) point out, "ignores and undermines the totality of history and driving concepts like self-governance, sovereignty, and self-determination" (p. 5) that should have been at the forefront of the work in Santee. Second, though the local board and educators repeatedly requested that Dakota history and culture be included as a central part of the state's progress plan implementation at SCS, they were not included. Local educators and the community were not viewed as co-decision makers in the plan's development; instead, they were objects of mandates they had limited voice in developing and yet were expected to carry out (Foucault, 1977). In the push to see quick improvement in Santee, state policymakers and hired contractors defaulted to understandings of knowledge and what "good" looks like in education in the same way other "Eurocentric ideology has been used to establish hierarchies wherein the philosophies, worldviews, and languages of Indigenous people(s) have been stripped of value and relegated to the periphery as archaic or irrelevant" (Brayboy, 2013, p. 92). The Lady from North Carolina's levers of improvement remained the focus of state-supported improvement efforts in SCS for year 2 of intervention.

CONTINUED COMPLIANCE, KIND OF . . . AND INCOGNITO IMPROVEMENT EFFORTS

In June 2018, following the SBOE review of the second year of state intervention at SCS, local board members asked then-Superintendent Daniels what they had to do "to get off the priority plan" (NSBOE, 2018). The superintendent shared that she initially tried to fight some of the plan developed by the Lady from North Carolina for the 2018–2019 year, but then decided that it was best for the district to just "go along with everything," in the hope that the school would be able to request a release from priority school progress the following year, as Santee was the only school initially named as a priority school that remained under state oversight after the SBOE released Loup County from state oversight during the June 2018 meeting. Daniels also informed the SCS board that the Lady from North Carolina would continue directing the state's work in Santee for a third year.

A year later, however, instead of a recommendation for a release from priority status and state intervention, NDE representatives recommended significant revisions to the school's progress plan that included officially adding the elementary and high school to the middle school as designated priority schools. The SBOE's official designation formalized the state's approach, which had focused on the entire PK–12 system since the initial priority school designation. NDE also ended the state's contract with the Lady from North Carolina for work in Santee, issuing an RFP to search for new consultants to work with the school district. The newly revised priority school plan, presented in October 2019 to the SBOE, included work to be directed by two new consultants described in Santee as the Big City Professor and Big City Board Consultant. The SBOE hired the Big City Professor to work in the school, collaborating with the superintendent and principals, and the Big City Board Consultant to work with the local school board.

The state's two-consultant approach remained in place in the 2019–2020, 2020–2021, and 2021–2022 academic years. During these 3 years emphasis remained on improved academic outcomes as measured by statewide assessment with formative indicators of progress each year through MAP (Measures of Academic Progress), an adaptive achievement growth assessment from the Northwest Evaluation Association (NWEA) widely used in the state. The schools' progress plan now focused on the implementation of professional learning communities (PLCs) and the school-wide implementation of Multi-Tiered Systems of Support. Expectations for teachers' instruction and administrators' supervision processes in classrooms shifted from standards-aligned instructional materials and posted objectives to fidelity to textbook series and formalized interventions for students falling short of grade-level proficiency as measured by MAP.

Again, absent in the state's approach was any kind of explicit attention to culturally responsive/sustaining pedagogies, content, or Indigenous ways of knowing and being as learners. Locally driven and culturally responsive improvement efforts still "did not count" or carry any influence toward demonstrating improvement to be released from priority school status. And yet, local incognito improvement efforts continued, some of which were encouraged by the Big City Professor. Acts of improvement included inviting Dakota artists and authors to have more guest instructor opportunities in the school. In one case, a guest author who visited the school in the spring of 2018 joined the staff in 2019 and then became the high school Dakota culture teacher in 2019.

In a meeting with the local school board in March of 2020, just before the COVID-19 pandemic temporarily shifted the school's instruction online, the new Dakota culture teacher explained the way that culture should be deeply rooted in the curriculum. "Culture," he asserted, "it's a lifestyle. . . . Culture will help students with behavior, identity, confidence, respect, and pride" (Santee Community School Board, 2020). He thanked the local board for their ongoing support of Dakota language and culture classes in the secondary schools and said that those courses and the culture program "need to be bigger" in the school. They did grow.

Local efforts to cultivate Dakota culture in the school became influential enough that the state acknowledged it with the SBOE in 2019. That summer NDE was represented at the annual Santee Powwow for the first time. The NDE liaison to SCS highlighted the ways that the school had "infused and validated" Dakota culture in the school. "You go throughout the building and they're [students are] seeing their language, their history, and their, you know, resistance and survival being very present in the school" (NSBOE, 2019). Part of this shift was in response to then-superintendent Hayes's efforts to cultivate stronger relationships among school and tribal entities.

While local efforts were lauded, the SBOE continued to emphasize growth in proficiency according to formative assessments and annual statewide testing. In the spring of 2020, NDE's liaison to SCS reiterated the major goals for the school, which included supporting literacy across all content areas; improving attendance; and strengthening readiness from Pre-K to kindergarten, elementary to middle school, and middle school to high school. The liaison acknowledged that proficiency scores averaged below 25% in the school and suggested that the school needed to continue to ramp up social–emotional support, particularly at the secondary level, and to continue to strengthen practices around data in the school's PLC structure. She also acknowledged that school personnel were experiencing yet another transition in the superintendency and secondary principal roles. She cited that the state's desire was "to make sure that we have the most appropriate, best person for the job in the position to be able to lead the school in the right direction" (NSBOE, 2019). In response to ongoing leadership churn, she explained, the state's consultants would direct book studies with the administrative teams "to build their collective capacity and efficacy" (NSBOE, 2019).

The emergence of COVID-19 required SCS to shift its mode of instructional delivery between March and May of 2020. The state's support also shifted, primarily to supporting the leadership in accessing COVID-19 funds and resources. The Big City Professor consultant worked with the leadership team in designing one-on-one tutoring schedules with students and teachers. Schedules allowed small numbers of students in the building for instruction before a COVID-19 outbreak occurred and the school transitioned to completely remote instruction. Santee Warrior Improvement Team committees met remotely until August of 2020 when school personnel prepared to welcome students back into the building with COVID-19 protocols (desk spacing, masking, contact tracing) in place.

As the 2020–2021 school year began, the state maintained its two-consultant approach. The Big City Professor worked with district and building leadership to reset their improvement work to the priorities established pre-COVID with an additional emphasis on social emotional learning. Before there could be very much traction, however, the superintendent was put on administrative leave by the local board. Concerns about financial management in the school led to the termination of the superintendent's contract in a special session in early December. Once again, the school faced mid-year turmoil. The Big City Board Consultant immediately began working with the local SCS board to initiate an interim superintendent search. In January, the SCS board hired an interim superintendent for the spring with a condition that should the semester go favorably, the contract would be extended to the 2021–2022 academic year.

Throughout the spring of 2021, fallout among the teaching staff with those frustrated by the ongoing turbulence in the district grew. In February three teachers submitted their resignations, one of whom was an influential teacher from the community who had revived the FCS program in the early years of the state's intervention in Santee. Despite these challenges, state consultants worked to revive pre-pandemic improvement efforts with the new superintendent, principals, and local board. Incognito efforts for improvement in the school also persisted. The Dakota culture teacher facilitated conversations with students early in the semester to discuss the possibility of changing the name of the school from Santee to *iSanti* Community School, a renaming through a new spelling that acknowledges the history of the land and the forcible removal of the Dakota people from lands near Knife Lake in what is currently Minnesota. The renaming served as a symbolic act to restore the school's identity as belonging to the Dakota people. According to the secondary principal, the student body "embraced the change" and educators from the community envisioned the name change as a way to regain momentum and reclaim Dakota culture as a part of the school's ongoing improvement efforts. The local board discussed the proposal in their January meeting, indicating their support for the name change, and the state's hired board consultant stated that the state also fully supported the idea. The district moved forward with the official name change.

Acknowledging the challenge to demonstrating improvement during the crisis management response of COVID-19, the SBOE voted in May 2021 to exempt the 2019–2020 school year in the priority school timeline, particularly because the state had also suspended statewide assessment, a key benchmark indicator of progress in the SCS improvement plan, in the spring of 2020. Then, in June, six additional teachers resigned. Their resignations were not directly related to what was happening in the school district, but instead a reaction to a COVID-19 vaccine mandate put in place by the tribe. According to the mandate, all employees within the boundaries of the reservation would need to be vaccinated by July 2021, which these six teachers were not willing to do. As a result, the superintendent, building administrators, and local board had to shift from directing improvement efforts to filling open positions throughout the summer. They looked for support from NDE in pursuing provisional teaching certifications in some cases to have teachers in classrooms for fall.

In early fall, the interim superintendent and local board revisited conversations about a full-time superintendent contract for the 2021–2022 school year. In October, the board, with advice from the Big City Board Consultant, offered a full-time contract for October 2021–June 2023, hoping to encourage leadership stability in the district. With this commitment to stability in the district and the ongoing efforts of the same state-hired contractors, it appeared as if the school was well-situated to make gains. However, once again, by January things had fallen apart. The superintendent submitted his resignation effective at the end of the school year, and the secondary principal also resigned, effective immediately. The *iSanti* local board began to explore options for an alternate organizational structure that might help with the ongoing instability in leadership. With input from the Big City Professor, the board proposed that instead of having a superintendent the school transition to a model with three parallel executive directors—a director of business operations, director of curriculum and instruction/elementary principal, and a director of special education/secondary principal. In March 2022 the state encouraged the local board to continue to explore this option and recommended that they develop potential job descriptions. In the meantime, the *iSanti* board and school administration moved the director of special education to the secondary principal role in anticipation of this new structure. Late in May, though, the NDE liaison to the priority schools informed the district that NDE and the SBOE would not approve an alternate leadership structure. The *iSanti* board quickly hired a superintendent search firm, and in June they hired yet another superintendent, the sixth superintendent since the school's designation in 2015.

As of April 2022, NDE also released a new request for proposals (RFP) intent to contract with new consultants who would replace the Big City Professor and the Big City Board Consultant to direct the work in Santee. The RFP's scope of work included supplementing the state's intervention work in priority schools, which would include "intensive, consistent interactions with Priority School teachers, principals, district administrators, board members, and the community (parents, family, and community at large)" (Nebraska Department of Education, 2022). The state put an emphasis on leading "equity-driven improvement efforts," which according to their definition included "instructional and leadership coaching, implementing high quality instructional materials and teacher professional learning, culturally inclusive teaching and learning, resource allocation reviews, and effective leader and local board relationship building and coaching" (Nebraska Department of Education, 2022). The RFP language made it clear that the state no longer ascribed to the Lady from North Carolina's levers of improvement and instead had adopted the Four Domains for Rapid School Improvement from the Center for School Turnaround and Improvement at WestEd. In the fall of 2022, NDE contracted with the New Teacher Project (TNTP) to direct the next phase of state-directed intervention work in Santee. TNTP began their direct work in the school in early 2023.

As authors like Ball (2009) and Mills (2015) have pointed out, the strategy of bringing in outside expertise to implement "best practices" can be an alluring approach, particularly for a state department of education looking for rapid improvement in order to declare a policy success. However, it is worth examining the perils in standardizing and privatizing efforts to improve schools. Renting expertise, as the state has continued to do in Santee, demonstrates a short-term way of thinking about capacity and the potential of the state in supporting local improvement in schools. The decision to rent consultant expertise also stands in sad contrast to the initial rhetoric behind AQuESTT, which promised permanent capacity building and lessons that might be applied to similar kinds of school contexts. Also disappointing is the lack of prior experience or knowledge, among these hired contractors, in working with schools or communities located on or near tribal lands. State-directed improvement efforts have not aligned well with Santee's context. At the same time, local efforts to improve teaching and learning in the school outside of the state's official progress plan continued, and remain very much present in the day-to-day work in the school. However, what I have called "incognito" efforts were consistently absent from the state's public narrative about Santee, at SBOE work sessions, meetings, and NDE presentations, until 2019, and they have not been incorporated as indicators of improvement in the district's state progress plan at the time of this writing (2023).

INCOGNITO IMPROVEMENT ACTS ENDURE

While state consultant and leadership capacity focused on the immediate leadership crisis and ongoing teacher churn, incognito improvement efforts endured. The school principals and the culture director organized a Culture Curriculum Committee in March 2022, scheduling meeting dates for the remainder of the 2021–2022 academic year and the 2022–2023 year. The purpose of the committee was to organize, support, and maintain a number of Dakota culture-building activities that had been initiated in the school. Signaling their support for this work, the local board voted to approve the expansion of the Dakota culture program in their August 2022 board meeting. Then in December 2022, one of the state's news outlets, *Flatwater Free Press*, published a feature article on the progress happening in *iSanti* Community School. The article described the 100% graduation rate in the school and improving attendance rates for the past 2 years that school leaders and educators attributed to the Dakota culture program (Trudell, 2022). The culture program, which was once only for secondary students, is now offered from preschool through graduation and includes language, culture, history (oral and written), and customs. One parent interviewed for the article described how her 4th-grade son "comes home and tells me what he learned in culture class . . . He doesn't tell me about what he learned in math" (Trudell, 2022). Beyond pointing to the graduation or attendance rates, the metrics that "count" outside of Santee, in the article the Dakota Cultural Director described the emerging pride among students and the deeper connection to tribal leaders in the community that has been absent in the community for many years. He explained the importance of knowing Dakota history and the ongoing embodiment of living a Dakota story for students. Pointing back to the same mural where I often used to stand and consider while waiting for a school administrator to greet me in the school atrium, the Dakota Culture Director told Trudell, "We've survived so much. This is our story of how we persevere." In reading those words, I could not help but think about the long arc of education policy and government intervention and the stories of survivance and perseverance in Santee that focus on a Dakota education for children and a school for the tribe.

Evident throughout the state's designation and intervention in Santee are the agentic acts among students, educators, and community members to alternately comply with and resist state-led efforts in iSanti Community School. In Chapter 1, I wondered whether AQuESTT was truly about advancing equity and favorably changing the educational trajectories of students in Santee. I asked whether the political technology at work caused individuals (irrespective of noble intentions and dedication to do the right work) to direct policy implementation in ways that undermined rather than advanced equity, democracy, or sovereignty. I noted that by their very premise, efforts to turn around troubled or "failing" schools were intended to challenge structures of power. Studying the policy implementation space of state oversight in Santee, where state and sovereign tribal powers came into contact, illuminates the structure and functions of power and also the persistent expressions of agency fighting to reimagine the implementation on the ground.

Between the academic years of 2016–2017 and 2022–2023, the school district had six different superintendents and five high school principals. On average, the school district experienced about 25% teaching staff turnover each year. The only consistent leadership presence was the elementary principal who first came to the school in 2016. Even with ongoing changes in district leadership and classroom teachers, educators worked toward the objectives outlined by the state in each year's priority school progress plan, collaborating with a rotation of external consultants and representatives from NDE. Each year, school leadership and the local school board documented their activities in alignment with the state's plan and presented their progress to the SBOE. Each year, they continued to hold a priority school label. Despite the rise and fall of state assessment scores, the school has documented improved graduation rates, attendance rates, and grade-level growth as measured by formative MAP assessments.

Local agentic improvement efforts are examples of ongoing resistance in Santee. Tactics among local educators and community members have included a *yes, and* approach, or "both/and," as Castagno and Brayboy (2008) call it. They point out, "None of the research suggests that Indigenous youth should learn tribal cultures and languages at the expense of learning mainstream culture, English, and the typical 'academic' subjects generally taught in schools" (p. 37). Educators and local board members have complied or demonstrated their "yes" to the state and its emphasis on narrowed academic outcomes, while also funneling resources and capacity toward the "and" strategies they believed would help the school better reflect their vision. From the beginning of the state's priority school intervention, personnel in the school and members of the school board advocated for Dakota culture and ways of knowing in the school. From the principal requesting that the "Santee DNA" be present in the first progress plan, to the school board president describing the vision of students' warrior pride returning to the school so that it could realize its purpose in being a public school of and for the tribe in 2016, to the expansion of the Dakota Culture program in the school in 2022–2023, people in Santee have acted according to an incognito and sometimes patchworked plan for improving the school. As the state applied an array of policy solutions with each consultant that included a narrowed curriculum focus and fidelity to instructional materials that did not include Dakota ways of knowing and being, individuals acted to meet external demands while also charting a course that aligned with what they believed would improve the school.

Through their agentic acts of improvement, school personnel and community members have begun to reshape policy spaces and shift systems of power within the state's intervention in the school. Culturally responsive/sustaining approaches that were once set aside as worthy, but not as immediately important as raising test scores, have become part of the conversations around *iSanti* Community School's improvement. It has yet to be seen whether emerging shifts will result in the incorporation of what have been incognito improvement efforts into the next official progress plan for *i*CS or how the third hired consultant group will carry out that plan. However, the perseverance among a number of key actors both inside and outside the school in the community demonstrate a deeper understanding of what was and is needed in Santee. This kind of action is essential to remaking education policy spaces that better reflect the kind of "serious democracy" that Freire (1998) described, which invites and includes diverse voices in the conversation while challenging structures of power (see Chapter 1).

The agentic acts of incognito improvement reflect the "footprints of Native presence" that Lomawaima and McCarty (2006) described, the "unexpected, the overlooked, the seeming paradoxical results and responses to domineering policies and institutions" (p. 13). They demonstrate the "artfulness" of reframing and resisting deficit approaches that Sabzalian (2019) found in her study of children's survivance in public schools in the Pacific Northwest. Acts of incognito improvement in Santee testify to the ongoing conviction that knowledge of how to improve a school of and for the tribe is rooted in the community and that the community maintains its right to self-determination and self-education. Cultivating culturally responsive policymaking and implementation in Indian Country requires approaches that reflect "serious democracy" with commitments to justice that reject linguicide, colonization, and deficit framing, and instead center multilingualism and multiculturalism. State oversight at *iSanti* CS has not, up to now, reflected a kind of sustaining/revitalizing policymaking that is humble and willing to listen. It has not considered how even well-intended policies, backed by research and sincere lobbyists, may (as I showed in Chapter 3) pathologize students and flatten community distinctiveness. And yet, there are glimpses of progress to highlight. NDE has taken a more active role in showing up to tribal events outside of the school since 2019, and it has begun to acknowledge incognito acts of improvement and their impact on positive trends in student graduation outcomes and attendance rates. Whether that acknowledgment grows into truly centering Indigenous knowledge in the next iteration of the state progress plan in *iSanti* Community School remains to be seen.

CHAPTER 8

Wait, What Just Happened?

It remains to be seen. For 7 years I have continued to observe, document, and analyze the state's ongoing oversight in Santee hoping that there might be a point that would allow me to write a neat and tidy final chapter. On so many drives to and from Santee, sitting at my desk after Zoom sessions, or observing board meetings I imagined what it would be like to write a conclusion that reflected the hopes and vision among students, educators, and community members, and even some policymakers, of a school for the tribe. I wanted to write about a collaborative, culturally responsive/sustaining approach to state oversight in Santee rather than what it *could* have looked like.

In the Introduction I asserted that the telling of Nebraska's most recent education policy reform effort and the state's intervention in Santee mattered because the lessons learned might have application elsewhere. Nebraska has historically been reluctant to embrace national education policy trends, and thus, it was slow to adopt state-directed rapid improvement efforts in local schools until it was legislated in 2014. Until recently, it has also been a place that has pushed against "failing public school" narratives, which allowed for a level of trust that supported collaboration across the system of education and the public it serves. As I stated in Chapter 2, if external, state-directed local school improvement were going to work in any place like Santee, they would work in a place like Nebraska that has a can-do, let's sit around the table and work out solutions that make sense on the ground policy history. And yet, it didn't work—or at least, it hasn't worked yet. After 7 years, three rounds of state-hired external consultants, and a carousel of superintendents and teaching staff, *iSanti* Community School is still a priority school and the state is still intervening with a new progress plan in development at the time of this writing (early 2023).

It is in this context that I synthesize a number of lessons that can be gleaned from state-led intervention at *iSanti* Community School and offer glimpses into what is possible for education policy done *with* rather than *to* Native communities and schools. At a high level, these lessons include (a) the inadequacy of the "consultocracy," (b) that tensions over the definition of a "good" education, and whose definition is adopted, lie behind any struggle over improving education; (c) that policy space can be remade through on-the-ground, modest acts of improvement; and (d) that policymaking can be turned toward being culturally sustaining.

THE "CONSULTOCRACY"

Long before *iSanti* Community School was named a priority school, throughout the debate on the floor of the legislature in 2014, policymakers pointed to solutions to "failing" schools that included using private charter school companies or externally contracted consultants. Since iCS's priority designation in 2015, the state's quest to turn around—rapidly improve—the school has relied on contracted external expertise to guide and direct improvement efforts in the school, which is now enduring its third round of outside consultant expertise. The pattern in Santee has been that progress plans are more indicative of the strengths of the hired consultants and what they can offer than the context of the school and community itself. Unfortunately, privileging external expertise over local knowledge and ways of knowing is not unique to Nebraska (e.g., Courtney, 2015; Mills, 2015; Sturges, 2015). It is Gunter et al. (2015) who first coined the term "consultocracy" to describe "the increasing role of private consultants or consultancy groups and the power they have been given by government organizations" (p. 518). Others, like Mahony, Hextall, and Menter (2004) have used the term "edu-business" to describe the practice that is based on an ideology that privileges private, market approaches and borrows from corporate business models not concerned with notions of the greater good or democratic aims within education, but which instead prioritize efficiency and standardization (Apple, 2013). Datnow et al. (2002) found, in their study of external school reform models, that there is little evidence to support the rationale that what works to improve one school can be replicated, in a standardized fashion, to improve another school. And yet as my co-author Edmund Hamann and I pointed out in 2021 when analyzing the state's work with the first consultant, "the political pressure for system accountability and rapid reform continues to drive policymakers (legislators, state and local board members) toward systemic reforms that often embed 'one size fits all' strategies for reform (even as some rhetoric may acknowledge local differences)" (Phillips & Hamann, 2021, p. 239). The hiring of the first consultant, the Lady from North Carolina, in 2016–2020, followed by the Big City Professor and the Big City Board Consultant in 2020–2022, and then The New Teacher Project in the fall of 2022 largely ignored local knowledge or state expertise. It reduced the role of SDE employees, making them support staff for contracted consultants. This approach also ignored considerations of how the consultants' findings might support NDE's development of capacity to work with struggling schools or to build models for how to serve schools with similar contexts. The prospects of scaling up a model that could be replicated in other Needs Improvement schools, touted by the Commissioner and members of the SBOE throughout 2015–2017, seemed to matter more as rhetoric than as plan or action.

When the Commissioner of Education first designated *i*CS as a priority school in 2015, he described patterns among schools classified in the lowest AQuESTT accountability classification, Needs Improvement. Patterns included schools serving Black students in cities, schools on or near American Indian reservations like Santee, schools in depressed, depopulated counties, or a mix of students in areas where demographics were changing. The schools in this lowest range tended to have minoritized student populations, populations undergoing unusual community stress, and high levels of poverty. An analysis of schools classified in Needs Improvement illustrates the way AQuESTT narrowly defined and measured school quality and ended up pathologizing certain kinds of schools. There was an opportunity to inquire into how very different kinds of schools can struggle and to learn from those schools and communities.

In those early days of priority school designation and oversight the state did not incorporate local knowledge or interrogate the problematic nature of an accountability system that labeled certain kinds of schools as failing. Instead, the SBOE determined that the solutions to "fix" priority schools were similar. The hired consultants did not have experience working with Native communities or schools. The common "problem" to be solved was to raise test scores and graduation rates as quickly as possible, which has been the aim of every consultant hired to work in Santee. AQuESTT's implementation was built on the neoliberal premise, introduced by NCLB, that schools do not have the knowledge or expertise on their own to "close the achievement gaps across social class and racial fissures and that they are in need of outside, often businesslike, intervention" (Koyama, 2011, p. 20). Policymakers' assumptions about what went into the implementation of policies were simplistic and did not consider the histories and current unique realities present in each priority school context (e.g., staff and leadership turnover, poverty, history, culture). System improvement is contextual and complicated, and standardized solutions proposed by an external contractor hired for 2–3 years cannot solve the intractable challenges present in Santee. These realities problematize the roles external consultants or the "consultocracy" are playing in policy implementation efforts to improve schools.

While renting consultant expertise may appear to be less costly than hiring a full-time employee, which requires additional investments in health insurance and retirement benefits, in the long term, the cost of losing capacity is greater than any short-term saving. For example, in January 2019, the state's largest newspaper, the *Omaha World Herald,* published a piece pointing to the $965,000 that had been paid out to the Lady from North Carolina. The journalist asserted that she, "perhaps more than any other person, outside of government officials, has put her fingerprints on school improvement in Nebraska" (Dejka, 2019, pp. 2–3). Alternatives, like including tribal representation in the development of the progress plan in Santee or creating a community council could easily have been imagined that would have leveraged current state capacity to co-construct long-term, sustainable solutions responsive to local context. Certainly, the state's goal of building long-term solutions has not yet been realized after 7 years of investment, a phenomenon with implications far beyond Nebraska's state borders. Schools exposed to the "consultocracy" and relying on these operators and privileging external expertise has not been a success.

A systems policy perspective on the consultocracy where a hired operator answers to a state-level contract and timelines while being expected to enact sustainable change in a local school reveals the conflict inherent in school accountability turnaround reforms that include short timelines to accomplish systemic change. This reflects Noble and Smith's (2000) reform clock metaphor from their study of reforms implemented by SDEs in Delaware and Arizona. The state's oversight and intervention in Santee continues to be driven by the political clock, which "runs fast" and "rarely provides sustained support for any initiative" (Noble & Smith, 2000, p. 182). That lack of sustained support over time remains a challenge with each new consultant hired to work in the school. The tempo and change in turnaround approaches stands in conflict with the tempo of change and improvement on-site in *iSanti* Community School, a contrast that illuminates the political powers and pressures at play. The consultants answer to their funders (the SBOE) rather than to the community or school leadership and staff in Santee. Thus, consultants are incentivized to match the tempo of the political clock rather than responding to the local knowledge, assets, or needs. A constructivist, collaborative approach, Noble and Smith (2000) point out, would require time and sustained efforts. State-directed intervention in Santee can also be seen as a new version of a longstanding story. The reliance on the consultocracy privileged external expertise above local knowledge, repeating the pattern of outsiders acting with power and unexamined assumptions that "they know best" in Indian Country (e.g., Bird et al., 2013; Hopkins, 2020; Williams & Tracz, 2016).

SOVEREIGNTY AND WHO GETS TO DEFINE EDUCATIONAL QUALITY

According to Brayboy and Maaka (2015), the academic achievement of American Indian students has been largely ignored in state education policy. The state senator whose district included Santee spoke, in the 2014 floor debate in DB 438, of concerns that state intervention in priority schools would ignore rural places. Nebraska's SBOE, however, designated *iSanti* Community School as one of three priority schools out of the entire state. Throughout 2014–2016, policymakers touted tailoring solutions and support for priority schools' unique contexts in communities rather than prescribing a "one size fits all" solution or blaming and shaming schools for student academic outcome performance as measured by state assessment.

SBOE members' early stated intentions included plans to develop models of improvement for the kinds of schools most frequently classified in the lowest performance classification. This intention could have resulted in culturally responsive support extended to all schools serving Native students and families in the state. The gap between policy intention and implementation widened. When it came to the development of approaches to state intervention in Indian Country, there were critical moments when Native voices were not present and other moments when voices were present, but not heard or incorporated. I cannot help wondering about the role that the community operating councils envisioned in early versions of LB438 might have played. Structuring priority school intervention with community operating council input as a required part of progress plan development and implementation might have situated local voice as central to the process, reflecting community assets and support and balancing the power of a state-identified intervention team. What ultimately happened in practice raises questions around who gets to define the elements that comprise a quality education, how schools ought to be evaluated, and to whom a school is ultimately accountable for its quality.

The hegemonic construct embedded in the AQuESTT system and its enactment of state intervention are evident in both the labels and the interventions that were imposed by those furthest away from Santee. From the very first meeting between *iSanti* Community School staff and representatives of the state in 2016 following the school's priority school designation, local voices asserted the importance of incorporating local knowledge and ways of being, or the "Santee DNA" as the principal called it. The state's hired consultants focused efforts on standardizing the curriculum and aligning instruction to priority academic standards that had greater likelihood of being assessed, with the intention of rapidly improving scores in assessed content areas (e.g., reading, math). Each round of reclassifying *i*CS as a priority school, each new round of consultants dropping in to direct work in school, and each new progress plan were confirmations for faculty and staff in the school that the state held the power to define and measure school quality. This was yet again an all too familiar reminder of the ways education policy through U.S. federal and state law, regulation, or rule has defined what education should look like for Native peoples, overlooking their sovereign right to self-education. Throughout the development of policy and implementation of priority school intervention in Santee, policymakers and intermediaries missed opportunities to listen, learn, and act *with* the Santee community in designing improvement approaches.

Whatever noble intentions there were, deciding to pursue higher scores as a benchmark of improvement led to narrowed curricula and less culturally responsive education, which is short-sighted, considering the Dakota people's right to self-education (Brayboy et al., 2015; Manuelito, 2005) and the growing body of empirical literature that points to the effectiveness of culturally responsive models in improving academic outcomes for American Indian students (Brayboy & Castagno, 2009; Castagno & Brayboy, 2008; Cleary, 2008). Numerous examples illustrate the ways that incorporating culturally responsive/sustaining approaches to pedagogy and curricular materials transforms educational experiences and outcomes for Indigenous students and their families (e.g., Barnhardt & Kawagley, 2005; Nelson-Barber & Estrin, 1995; Lipka et al., 2005; McCarty & Lee, 2014). Other examples highlight the importance of professional learning that supports the implementation of culturally responsive shifts in teacher practice (e.g., Demmert, 2001; Hill et al., 2012; Pewewardy & Hammer, 2003; Swisher & Deyhle, 1989), and the need for schools in Native communities to cultivate relationships and accountability within the community (e.g., Castagno & Brayboy, 2008; McCarty & Lee, 2014).

I said in the Introduction that the pursuit of balancing the vision for self-education that exists among tribal members with external state and federal schooling statute and rule is complex and is addressed in unique and context-specific ways depending on the tribe and community. In the very first few months of state-directed intervention, the local board for iSanti Community School outlined the freighted history and ongoing tensions between the community and the school for NDE staff and the SBOE's first consultant. They emphasized the need for a shared vision that ensured a future for the tribe and opportunities for its children. Their goal was and remains to be access to a high-quality education rooted in culturally responsive/sustaining schooling experiences (Anthony-Stevens, 2017; Brayboy et al., 2015; Castagno et al., 2016). And the opportunity remains for state policy to respond in ways that acknowledge the Dakota people's right to self-education and to embrace culturally responsive/sustaining approaches to policy implementation.

EVERYDAY TACTICS AND INCOGNITO ACTS OF IMPROVEMENT

In Chapter 4, I wondered how the state's intervention might constrain *i*CS and how social agents might act to resist or even transform policy in what Low and Lawrence-Zúñiga (2003) refer to as "contested spaces" (p. 18). When it became clear that the state's definition of school quality would be defined by outcome measures from statewide assessment and graduation rates and prescribed turnaround efforts would not purposefully include culturally responsive/sustaining approaches, local educators, school board members, and community members in Santee nonetheless maintained individual and collective visions for a quality education and actions for improvement. Priorities for improvement that surfaced in the school and among *iSanti* local board members reflected the kind of culturally responsive schooling Brayboy and Castagno (2009) describe. It included stronger collaborative structures through professional learning communities among educators in the building and a greater presence of Dakota history, language, beadwork, powwows, drum groups, and star quilt ceremonies as a part of life in the school. Even though locally driven and culturally responsive/sustaining improvement efforts did not "count" toward official progress in meeting the state's improvement plan, individuals in Santee demonstrated agency, employing everyday tactics (de Certeau, 1984) through incognito acts of improvement throughout the 6 years of state-directed intervention in Santee. They worked toward their own improvement aims and their efforts reflected beliefs rooted in tribal sovereignty and the right to self-education. Efforts also reflected a desire to pursue better academic outcomes, but better outcomes for the sake of the future of the tribe rather than better outcomes for short-term gains reflected in statewide assessment. Their tactics reflected a *yes, and* approach that I described in Chapter 7, one of compliance to state mandates while investing resources and local capacity toward the strategies they believed would help the school better reflect their vision of a quality education. Their vision included renaming the school to *iSanti* Community School as an assertion of tribal survivance. It reaffirmed what the local board president had told the Commissioner in 2016, that the naming of the school and the use of the word "community" had been intentional and rooted in a school for and of the tribe.

As discussed in Chapter 7, local agentic acts of improvement have begun to be recognized in official policy spaces. With each acknowledgment of the impact of local improvement efforts in official policy spaces (e.g., SBOE meetings, documents published by NDE), school personnel and community members are remaking policy spaces and shifting constructs of power in small, but notable, ways. Native knowledge and culture in Santee is slowly gaining recognition as "an ally" (Lomawaima & McCarty, 2006, p. 170) in improvement efforts among more policymakers and intermediaries at NDE. But it did not have to be this difficult. And it is not enough. A culturally responsive and sustaining approach to policymaking and implementation in Nebraska could have existed from AQuESTT's inception, when SBOE members' rhetoric described listening to local efforts and building authentic relationships to support collaborative efforts.

THE DECOLONIZING WORK OF CULTURALLY SUSTAINING POLICYMAKING

Serious democratic policymaking and implementation requires both participatory and deliberative democratic opportunities that include a wide range of ideas, an authentic disposition of listening with mutual respect, and a shared aim of understanding (Greene, 1985; Noddings, 2013). Democracy that is "serious" in Freire's (1998) sense, or democracy committed to social justice, must not only include but heed the voices of those who have historically not been served well by schools. It must embody a commitment to equity that challenges structures of power. Philosopher and democratic theorist Amy Gutmann (1999) stated that a democracy is "not deliberative" to the extent that "it treats people as objects of legislation, as passive subjects to be ruled, rather than as citizens who take part in governance" (p. xii). If equity is going to be advanced through AQuESTT, through state-directed intervention in places like Santee, it is necessary that the policy culture evolve to reflect culturally responsive/sustaining policymaking. It requires commitment to equity through intentional attention to the sociocultural aspects of schooling and the unique contexts present in each community. Rather than applying deficit frames or invoking SDE interventions as the corrective fix where "deficiencies will be corrected, and policy subjects will acquire the skills and tools, thus enabling them to partake in the promise of freedom and prosperity" (Stein, 2004, p. 19), let's consider the possibilities of a culturally responsive/sustaining policymaking approach and what it could look like in Indian Country.

First, culturally responsive/sustaining policymaking centers local ways of knowing and being for the sake of decolonizing educational spaces. Education policymaking and implementation (and in this case state-led intervention) in schools serving Native students and communities ought to support culturally responsive practices according to local context and voice (Beaulieu, 2006; Castagno & Brayboy, 2008; Jester, 2002; Lipka & McCarty, 1994). Crafting culturally responsive/sustaining policy requires policymakers and educational institutions to see differently, with a clearer understanding of the history and sovereignty of Indigenous peoples and the mutual responsibility of serving students and the local tribal community (Austin, 2005). Montana's Indian Education for All (Carjuzaa et al., 2010; Hopkins, 2020; Ngai & Koehn, 2016) and Nevada's recent Native Youth Community Project grant funded by the U.S. Department of Education (Nevada Department of Education, 2017) are both examples of culturally responsive shifts in education policy implemented in collaboration with local tribes intended to support student success.

Second, culturally responsive/sustaining policymaking should attend to the unique languages, histories, and customs present in each tribal community. It should not be surprising that external, one-size-fits all interventions do not help schools improve students' (or educators') educational experiences, which was once again found to be true in the initial state-directed intervention at *i*CS. Local board members, school leaders, and educators expressed frustration at the consultants' narrow focus on standards-aligned instruction and assessment gains and the setting aside of Dakota ways of being and knowing. These findings reaffirm Demmert's (2001) conclusion that "congruency between the school environment and the language and culture of the community is critical to the success of formal learning" (p. 9), which seems like common sense, but was not common practice.

Finally, culturally responsive/sustaining policymaking requires a commitment among policymakers and intermediaries to self-education and change. Deficit-laden assumptions were made and publicly stated about Santee both on the legislative floor during the debate on school accountability legislation and in SBOE meetings. Policymakers invoking stereotypes or making broad generalizations that apply deficit frames to Native peoples is unacceptable. Despite repeated statements of good intention and hope for accountability outcomes that might advance equity in places like Santee, policymakers' ways of thinking certainly informed the decisions they made in designing school accountability legislation and implementing it on the reservation. Listening and learning, and an understanding of the impacts of colonization and power through the lens of critical theory, and particularly TribalCrit (Brayboy, 2005) ought to be prerequisites to policymakers codifying policy or enacting that policy with intended impacts in Indian Country. Tuck and Yang (2012) point out that decolonizing approaches require changing minds, changing frameworks for understanding the world, and changing actions. As Mignolo & Walsh (2018) assert,

> Decoloniality denotes ways of thinking, knowing, being, and doing that began with, but also precede, the colonial enterprise and invasion. It implies the recognition and undoing of the hierarchical structures of race, gender, heteropatriarchy, and class that continue to control life, knowledge, spirituality, and thought, structures that are clearly intertwined. (p. 17)

Accountability to culturally responsive/sustaining policymaking in flyover country states like Nebraska will likely require greater grassroots efforts and broader calls to action, as there is little political leverage through sheer numbers of Native peoples or lobbying power. Shifts will likely begin through individual and collective grassroots efforts evident in the incognito improvement efforts happening in Santee and the artful way that members of the community and school push back against constraining policy spaces.

CONCLUSION

I began this book with an excerpt from Chief Justice Warren's *Brown v. Board of Education* decision, highlighting the hoped-for role of states and communities in ensuring an equitable education and the similarly aspirational role of education in sustaining democratic society in the United States. I reflected that making schools equitable has long been a preoccupation of policymakers, practitioners, and scholars of education, but that all too often, policymakers' intentions fall short in practice (e.g., Au, 2009; Trujillo &

Renée, 2013). Certainly, the rhetoric among policymakers and intermediaries in Nebraska touted aims about advancing equity through school accountability that extended to the state's intervention in Santee. What unfolded in implementation fell short of stated policy intention. The lessons learned in this flyover state have relevance far beyond its borders, as the role of education in advancing equity remains a public responsibility. It is a responsibility that requires a trust in the *demos*, commitment to social justice, and persistence. This kind of "serious democracy" (Freire, 1998) requires changing power constructs in society, reshaping policy spaces, and committing to social justice. It is not advanced in a representative democracy, however, when conceptions of democracy or trust in the *demos* among those in power (e.g., state legislator, state board of education member) are undermined by deficit ideologies. It remains necessary that the policy culture (Stein, 2004) in places like Nebraska evolve in its commitment to equity through "purposeful work on the cultural dimensions of schooling, [that] address[es] complex considerations of students' strengths and needs" (pp. 24–25), rather than pointing to "policy beneficiaries as deviant" (Stein, 2004, p. 17). It is necessary that policymakers demonstrate commitment to culturally responsive/sustaining policymaking, as is evidenced in places like Santee.

Afterword

A FINAL TRIP TO SANTEE

In January 2023, nearly 8 years to the day from my first road trip to Santee in 2016, I made my final trip before completing this book. I turned off the snow-bordered highway onto the Santee spur road and made that final crest of the bluff and descended into town. While much appeared the same as it did 7 years ago, change is also evident. I waited outside the school to be buzzed in through a new front entrance. I checked in at front office windows in a newly configured atrium. The conference room where I first met the school's steering committee is now a hallway to a new early childhood wing. Student learning and Dakota culture are evident in the work posted in hallways and the teaching and learning happening in classrooms. There were few familiar faces in classrooms, and concerns about what the new consultants will require and how a new state progress plan might disrupt the momentum happening in the district sounded all too familiar. Local consensus on hoped-for improvement in the district remains the same: a school that cultivates trust with the community, a school that has effective and stable leadership stability, a school of and for the tribe. Above all, there is hope that the state will officially recognize the positive changes that have happened in the school, activities that may not tick the box of a huge increase in state assessment outcomes, but that matter. And, some would argue, matter more.

THE *ISANTI OZUYAPI* AT STATE

In March 2023, the *iSanti* Community Schools boys' basketball team made its first appearance in the state tournament in school history. While media coverage highlighted stories about the team's leading scorer or the preparations underway for the entire town to make the trip to Lincoln for the first-round game, I reflected that in 2016 the high school could barely field a team. With graduation and attendance rates low and few students who were academically eligible, there were few students to play. In recent years, the school's graduation rate has been nearly 100% and students are showing up to school and working to make themselves eligible to participate in school activities. *iSanti* Community School's presence at the state basketball tournament signaled the progress that has happened and is continuing to happen in Santee, even if it does not yet show up on the SBOE's progress plan as improvement.

As the teams warmed up and pep bands played, the stands began to fill with people in blue *iSanti Ozuyapi* (warriors) team shirts, vastly outnumbering the opposing team's fans. Over and over there were comments about the whole reservation showing up. Other tribal nations from the state had also shown up, wearing *Ozuyapi* colors in solidarity. The two teams lined up on either side of the basketball court, and before the playing of the national anthem and player introductions, members of the tribe sang the Dakota Flag Song, a symbolic and official declaration of the Dakota people's history and sovereignty. Then, at halftime, with the team trailing by 13, the school's *TaS'unke Ska* Culture Club marched onto the floor; students sang and danced in full regalia. The drum resounded and students' voices, joined by members of the community, seemed amplified in the cavernous arena. It was a collective statement of survivance through song, and a celebration. It reminded me of Waziyatawin Angela Wilson's concluding words to her 2005 work *Remember This! Dakota Decolonization and the Eli Taylor Narratives*, where she stated that

> By putting forth our stories we are exerting this belief in ourselves, in our history, and our ability to transform the world. While faith in ourselves has faltered among many of our own people over the centuries, as a nation we must struggle to reclaim this faith as a part of our larger project to fight those who have dominated us. (p. 240)

Even though the team ended up losing in the final seconds, the pride in being an *i*CS student, in being a member of the Santee community, and in being Dakota was evident. *iSanti Ozuyapi* students made a clear pronouncement that the Dakota people and culture remain as a new generation of belief emerges. Like their ancestors and elders, they persevere through stories, songs, and daily acts of resistance that assert their right to self-education and a school for the Dakota people.

References

Adams, D. W. (1995). *Education for extinction: American Indians and the boarding school experience, 1875–1928*. University of Kansas Press.

Agbo, S. A. (2004). First Nations perspectives on transforming the status of culture and language in schooling. *Journal of American Indian Education, 43*(1), 1–31.

Ahearn, L. M. (1999). Agency. *Journal of Linguistic Anthropology, 9*(1/2), 12–15.

Alim, H. S., Paris, D., & Wong, C. P. (2020). Culturally sustaining pedagogy: A critical framework for centering communities. In N. S. Nasir, C. D. Lee, R. Pea, & M. Royston (Eds.), *Handbook of the cultural foundations of learning* (pp. 261–276). Routledge.

American Indian language teacher; requirements of 1999. Nebraska Revised Statute § 79–802.01.

Anderson, J. (2013). New Nebraska ed commissioner Matthew Blomstedt took less traditional path to job. *Omaha World Herald*. http://www.omaha.com/news/new-nebraska-ed-commissioner-matthew-blomstedt-took-less-traditional-path/article_f88ce847-9ffd-5eab-ab33-07635c6d329d.html

Anderson-Levitt, K. M. (2012). Complicating the concept of culture. *Comparative Education 48*(4), 441–454.

Anthony-Stevens, V. (2017). Cultivating alliances: Reflections on the role of non-Indigenous collaborators in Indigenous educational sovereignty. *Journal of American Indian Education, 56*(1), 81–104.

Apple, M. W. (2013). Can education change society? Du Bois, Woodson and the politics of social transformation. *Review of Education, 1*(1), 32–56.

Au, W. (2009). *Unequal by design: High-stakes testing and the standardization of inequality*. Routledge.

Austin, R. (2005). Perspectives of American Indian nation parents and leaders. *New Directions for Student Services*, 109, 41–48.

Ball, S.J. (2009). Privatizing education, privatizing education policy, privatizing educational research: network governance and the "competition state." *Journal of Education Policy, 24*(1), 83–99.

Balter, A., & Grossman, F. (2009). The effects of the No Child Left Behind Act on language and culture education in Navajo public schools. *Journal of American Indian Education, 48*(3), 19–46.

Barnhardt, R., & Kawagley, A. (2005). Indigenous knowledge systems and Alaska native ways of knowing. *Anthropology & Education Quarterly, 36*(1), 8–23.

Barnhardt, R., & Kawagley, A. (2010). *Alaska Native Education: Views from Within*. Alaska Native Knowledge Network, Fairbanks: Center for Cross-Cultural Studies, University of Alaska Fairbanks

Barth, R. (1969). *Ethnic groups and boundaries*. Little, Brown.
Bartlett, L., & Brayboy, B.M.J. (2005). Race and schooling: Theories and ethnographies. *The Urban Review*, 37(5), 361–374.
Beaulieu, B. (2006). A survey and assessment of culturally based education programs for Native American students in the United States. *Journal of American Indian Education*, 45(2), 50–61.
Beaulieu, D. (2000). Comprehensive reform and American Indian education. *Journal of American Indian Education* 39(2), 29–38.
Beaulieu, D. L., Sparks, S., & Alonzo, M. (2005). Preliminary report on No Child Left Behind in Indian country. National Indian Education Association.
Beggs, W. K. (1939). *Frontier education in Nebraska* [Doctoral dissertation]. University of Nebraska–Lincoln.
Berliner, D. C., & Biddle, B. J. (1995). *The manufactured crisis: Myths, fraud, and the attack on America's public schools*. Addison-Wesley Publishing Company.
Berliner, D. & Glass, G. (2014). *50 myths and lies that threaten America's public schools*. Teachers College Press.
Berman, P., & McLaughlin, M. W. (1978). *Federal programs supporting educational change, Vol. VIII: Implementing and sustaining innovations* (No. R-1589/8HEW). Rand Corporation. https://www.rand.org/pubs/reports/R1589z8.html
Bird, C. P., Lee, T. S., & López, N. (2013). Leadership and accountability in American Indian education: voices from New Mexico. *American Journal of Education*, 119(4), 539–564.
Bonvillain, N. (1996). *The Santee Sioux*. Chelsea House Publishers.
Brayboy, B. M. J. (2005). Toward a tribal critical race theory in education. *The Urban Review*, 37(5), 425–446.
Brayboy, B. M. J. (2013). Tribal critical race theory: An origin story and future directions. In M. Lynn, & A. D. Dixon (Eds.), *Handbook of critical race theory in education* (pp. 88–100). Routledge.
Brayboy, B. M. J., & Castagno, A. E. (2009). Self-determination through self-education: Culturally responsive schooling for Indigenous students in the USA. *Teaching Education*, 20(1), 31–53.
Brayboy, B. M. J., Faircloth, S. Lee, T., Maaka, M., & Richardson, T. (2015). Sovereignty and education: An overview of the unique nature of Indigenous education. *Journal of American Indian Education*, 54(1), 1–9.
Brayboy, B. M. J., & Maaka, M. (2015). K–12 achievement for indigenous students. *Journal of American Indian Education*, 54(1), 63–98.
Brighouse, H., & Schouten, G. (2014). To charter or not to charter: What questions should we ask and what will the answers tell us? *Harvard Educational Review*, 84(3), 341–364.
Brown v. Board of Education. 347 U.S. 483 (1954).
Butler, T. A. (2014). School leadership in the 21st century: Leading in the age of reform. *Peabody Journal of Education*, 89(5), 593–602.
Cantor, L. (1980). The growing role of the states in American education. *Comparative Education*, 16(1), 25–31.
Carjuzaa, J., Jetty, M., Munson, M., & Veltkamp, T. (2010). Montana's Indian Education for All: Applying multicultural education theory. *Multicultural Perspectives*, 12(4), 192–198.

Carr, P. (2008). Educating for democracy: With or without social justice. *Teacher Education Quarterly, 35*(4), 117–136.

Castagno, A. E., & Brayboy, B. M. J. (2008). Culturally responsive schooling for indigenous youth: A review of the literature. *Review of Educational Research, 78*(4), 941–993.

Castagno, A. E., Garcia, D., & Blalock, N. (2016). Rethinking school choice: Educational options, control, and sovereignty in Indian Country. *Journal of School Choice, 10*(2), 227–248.

Child, B. (1998). *Boarding school seasons*. University of Nebraska Press.

Cleary, L. M., & Peacock, T. D. (1998). *Collected wisdom: American Indian education*. Allyn & Bacon.

Cleary, L.M. (2008). The imperative of literacy motivation when Native children are being left behind. *Journal of American Indian Education, 47*(1), 96–117.

Clune, W. (1993). Systemic educational policy: A conceptual framework. In S. Fuhrman (Ed.), *Designing coherent education policy: Improving the system* (pp. 125–140). Jossey-Bass Publishers.

Coburn, C. E., & Stein, M. K. (2006). Communities of practice theory and the role of the teacher professional community in policy implementation. In M. I. Honig (Ed.), *New directions in education policy implementation*. State University of New York Press.

Coburn, C. E., Hill, H. C., & Spillane, J. P. (2016). Alignment and accountability in policy design and implementation: The Common Core State Standards and implementation research. *Educational Researcher, 45*(4), 243–251.

Cody, A. (2008, August 4). Doug Christensen: He fought the law. *Education Week*. https://www.edweek.org/education/opinion-doug-christensen-he-fought-the-law/2008/08

Cohen, D. K. (1995). What is the system in systemic reform? *Educational Researcher, 24*(9), 11–31.

Commissioner of Education: office; powers; duties. Nebraska Revised Statute § 79–304.

Council of Chief State School Officers. (2013). *ESEA flexibility requests: A study of states' requests for waivers from requirements of the No Child Left Behind Act of 2001*. Author. https://www.nciea.org/wp-content/uploads/2021/11/ASR-SCASS-ESEAFlexStudyPaper_CSD13.pdf

Courtney, S. (2015). Corporatised leadership in English schools. *Journal of Educational Administration and History, 47*(3), 214–231.

Cowen, R. (2014). Ways of knowing, outcomes and "comparative education": Be careful what you pray for. *Comparative Education, 50*(3), 282–301.

Cuban, L. (2003). *Why is it so hard to get good schools?* Teachers College Press.

Cuban, L., & Usdan, M. (2003). Learning from the past. In *Powerful reforms with shallow roots*. Teachers College Press.

Cuban, L. (2013). *Inside the black box of classroom practice*. Harvard Education Press.

Cullen, J. B., Jacob, B. A., & Levitt, S. D. (2005). The impact of school choice on student outcomes: an analysis of the Chicago Public Schools. *Journal of Public Economics, 89*(5–6), 729–760

Dappen, L., & Isernhagen, J. (2005). Nebraska STARS: Assessment for learning. *Planning and Changing, 36*(3&4), 147–156.

Datnow, A., Hubbard, L., & Mehan, H. (2002). *Extending educational reform: From one school to many*. Routledge.

de Certeau, M. (1984). *The practice of everyday life*. University of California.

Dee, T. S., Jacob, B., & Schwartz, N. L. (2012). The effects of NCLB on school resources and practices. *Educational Evaluation and Policy Analysis, 35*(2), 252–279.

Dehyle, D. (1992). Constructing failure and maintaining cultural identity: Navajo and Ute school leavers. *Journal of American Indian Education, 31*(2), 24–47.

Deyhle, D. (1998). From break dancing to heavy metal: Navajo youth, resistance, and identity. *Youth & Society, 30*(1), 3–31.

Dejka, J. (2013). Nebraska commissioner of education Roger Breed to retire. *Omaha World Herald*. https://omaha.com/news/nebraska-commissioner-of-education-roger-breed-to-retire/article_50c74ea0-d7b5-53f0-b3d0-a268737ade4b.html

Dejka, J. (2019). Work of a $4,000-a-day consultant at struggling schools shows promise, but some question cost. *Omaha World Herald*. https://omaha.com/news/education/work-of-4-000-a-day-consultant-at-struggling-nebraska-schools-shows-promise-but-some/article_cfc08085-2752-59ea-ac21-e62944c07c33.html

Deloria, E. (1998). *Speaking of Indians*. University of Nebraska Press. (Originally published 1944.)

Deloria, V. Jr., & Wildcat, D. R. (2001). *Power and place: Indian education in America*. Fulcrum Publishing

Demmert, W. (2001). *Improving academic performance among Native American students: A review of the research literature*. ERIC Clearinghouse on Rural Education and Small Schools. https://eric.ed.gov/?id=ED463917

Dryzek, J. (2000). *Deliberative democracy and beyond*. Oxford University Press.

Duffy, E. (2015). For retiring OPS educator Deb Frison, "It's a life thing; it's not a career." *Omaha World Herald*. http://www.omaha.com/news/education/for-retiring-ops-educator-deb-frison-it-s-a-life/article_79e1c2f1-585e-5edd-aea4-ca5deb87c344.html

Duggan, J. (2014). Sen. Scott Lautenbaugh ends term early to be lobbyist. *Omaha World Herald*. https://omaha.com/state-and-regional/sen-scott-lautenbaugh-ends-term-early-to-be-lobbyist/article_335ef8e1-0e6e-5bf5-ad82-cdbd206840a9.html

Dumas, M. J., & Anyon, J. (2006). Toward a critical approach to education policy implementation. In M. I. Honig (Ed.), *New directions in education policy implementation* (pp. 149–168). State University of New York Press.

Eastman, C. (1902). *Indian boyhood*. Little, Brown & Company.

Education Committee Hearing (2014). *Quality education and accountability act, LB438*: Public hearing. State of Nebraska.

Elmore, R. F. (2003). Change and improvement in educational reform. In D. T. Gordon (Ed.), *A nation reformed?* (pp. 23–38). Harvard University Press.

Foucault, M. (1977). *Discipline and punish*. Vintage Books.

Fox, R., & Buchanan, N. (Eds.). (2017). *The Wiley handbook of school choice*. Wiley-Blackwell.

Freire, P. (1998). *Teachers as cultural workers*. Westview Press.

Friedman, M. (1955). *The role of government in education*. Rutgers University Press.

Fuhrman, S. H. (2003). Riding waves, trading horses: The twenty-year effort to reform education. In D. T. Gordon (Ed.), *A nation reformed?* (pp. 7–22). Harvard University Press.

Fuhrman, S. H., & Elmore, R. (1990). Understanding local control in the wake of state education reform. *Educational Evaluation and Policy Analysis, 12*(1), 82–96.

Fullan, M., & Hargreaves, A. (1996). *What's worth fighting for in your school.* Teachers College Press.

Gallagher, C. (2007). *Reclaiming assessment.* Heinemann.

Gay, G. (2002). Preparing for culturally responsive teaching. *Journal of Teacher Education, 53*(2), 106–116.

Goffman, E. (1959). *The presentation of self in everyday life.* Anchor.

Goodlad, J., Mantle-Bromley, C., & Goodlad, S. J. (2004). *Education for everyone: Agenda for education in a democracy.* Jossey-Bass.

Gordon, D. T. (Ed.). (2003). *A nation reformed?: American education 20 years after a nation at risk.* Harvard University Press.

Gorski, P. C. (2014). Poverty, economic inequality, and the impossible promise of school reform. In P. C. Gorski & K. Zenkov (Eds.), *The big lies of school reform: Finding better solutions for the future of public education* (pp. 129–141). Routledge.

Gram, J. R. (2016). *Education at the edge of empire: Negotiating Pueblo identity in New Mexico's Indian boarding schools.* University of Washington Press.

Grande, S. (2015). *Red pedagogy.* Rowman & Littlefield.

Greene, M. (1985). The role of education in democracy. *Educational Horizons, 63,* 3–9.

Gunter, H.M., Hall, D., & Mills, C. (2015). Consultants, consultancy and consultocracy in education policymaking in England. *Journal of Education Policy, 30*(4), 518–539.

Gutmann, A. (1999). *Democratic education.* Princeton University Press.

Hall, J. N., & Parker, L. (2007). Rethinking no child left behind using critical race theory. In C. E Sleeter (Ed.), *Facing accountability in education* (pp. 132–144). Teachers College Press.

Hall, P. M., & McGinty, P. J. (1997). Policy as the transformation of intentions: Producing program from statute. *Sociological Quarterly, 38*(3), 439–467.

Hamann, E. T., & Lane, B. (2004). The roles of state departments of education as policy intermediaries: Two cases. *Educational Policy, 18*(3), 426–455.

Hamann, E. T., & Rosen, L. (2011). What makes the anthropology of educational policy implementation 'anthropological'? In A. U. Levinson & M. Pollock (Eds.), *A companion to the anthropology of education* (pp. 461–477). Blackwell Publishing.

Harkins, A. (2016). The midwest and the evolution of "flyover country." *Middle West Review, 3*(1), 97–121.

Heck, R. H. (2004). *Studying educational and social policy.* Lawrence Erlbaum Associates.

Hermes, M. (2005). "Ma'iingan is just a misspelling of the word wolf": A case for teaching culture through language. *Anthropology & Education Quarterly, 36*(1), 43–56.

Hermes, M. (2007). Moving toward the language: Reflections on teaching in an Indigenous-immersion school. *Journal of American Indian Education, 46*(3), 54–71.

Hill, A., Lynch, A., & Dalley-Trim, L. (2012). Positive educational responses to Indigenous student mobility. *International Journal of Education Research, 54,* 50–59.

Holman, S., Welch, G. W., & Baumfalk, B. (2014). *Evaluating the impact of Nebraska's school improvement grants*. University of Nebraska–Lincoln, College of Education &Human Sciences. https://www.education.ne.gov/wp-content/uploads/2017/07/Evaluating_the_Impact_of_Nebraska_SIG-2014-10.pdf

Honig, M. I. (2006). Complexity and policy implementation. In Mi. I. Honig (Ed.), *New directions in education policy implementation* (pp. 1–23). State University of New York Press.

Hopkins, J. P. (2020). *Indian education for all: Decolonizing indigenous education in public schools*. Teachers College Press.

H.R. & S. Rep. No. 4 (1897). https://digitalcommons.law.ou.edu/cgi/viewcontent.cgi?article=6498&context=indianserialset

Isanti Community Schools (2019). *Isanti Community Schools staff handbook*. https://www.santeeschools.org/pages/uploaded_files/2021-2022%20STAFF%20Handbook.pdf

Isom, J. (2012). *Perceptions of Nebraska teachers regarding the transition from STARS to NeSA* [Doctoral dissertation]. University of Nebraska–Lincoln. https://digitalcommons.unl.edu/dissertations/AAI3503478/

Jaffer, K. (2010). School inspection and supervision in Pakistan: Approaches and issues. *Prospects, 40*(3), 375–392.

Jenkins, L. (2008) *From systems thinking to systemic action*. Rowman & Littlefield.

Jester, T. E. (2002). Healing the "unhealthy Native": Encounters with standards-based education in rural Alaska. *Journal of American Indian Education, 41*(3), 1–21.

Kawagley, A. O. (1995). *Incorporation of the world views of Indigenous cultures: A dilemma in the practice and teaching of western science*. [Conference Session]. Interntional History, Philosophy, and Science Teaching Conference, Minneapolis, MN.

King, F. (2018). *The earth memory compass: Diné landscapes and education in the twentieth century*. University of Kansas Press.

Klug, B. J., & Whitfield, P. T. (2003). A brief history of American Indian education. *Widening the circle: Culturally relevant pedagogy for American Indian children*. Routledge.

Koyama, J. (2011). Principals, power, and policy: Enacting "supplemental educational services." *Anthropology & Education Quarterly, 42*(1), 20–36.

Kuper, H. (1972). The language of sites in the politics of space. *American Anthropologist, 74*, 411–425.

Labaree, D. F. (2010). *Someone has to fail: The zero-sum game of public schooling*. Harvard University Press.

Ladson-Billings, G. (1990). Like lighting in a bottle: Attempting to capture the pedagogical excellence of successful teachers of black students. *International Journal of Qualitative Studies in Education, 3*(4), 335–344.

Ladson-Billings, G. (1995). Toward a theory of culturally relevant pedagogy. *American Educational Research Journal, 32*(3), 465–491.

Lane, B., & Garcia, S. (2005). State-level support for comprehensive school reform: Implications for policy and practice. *Journal of Education for Students Placed at Risk. 10*(2), 87–112.

Lashaw, A. (2010). The radical promise of reformist zeal: What makes "inquiry for equity" plausible? *Anthropology & Education Quarterly, 41*(4), 323–340.

Lee, T. S. (2009). Language, identity, and power: Navajo and Pueblo young adults' perspectives and experiences with competing language ideologies. *Journal of Language, Identity, and Education*, 8(5), 307–320.

Lee, T. S. (2015). The significance of self-determination in socially, culturally, and linguistically responsive (SCLR) education in Indigenous contexts. *Journal of American Indian Education*, 54(1), 10–32.

Lefebvre, H. (1991). *The production of space* (D. Nicholson-Smith, Trans.). Basic Blackwell.

Lévi-Strauss, C. (1963). *Structural anthropology*. Basic Books.

Limoges, B. (2001). *A history of Nebraska public school accreditation* [Doctoral dissertation]. University of Nebraska–Lincoln.

Linn, R. L. (2007). Performance standards: What is proficient performance. In C. E. Sleeter (Ed.), *Facing accountability in education* (pp. 112–131). Teachers College Press.

Lipka, J. (1990). Integrating cultural form and content in one Yup'ik Eskimo classroom: A case study. *Canadian Journal of Native Education*, 17(2), 18–32.

Lipka, J., & McCarty, T. L. (1994). Changing the culture of schooling: Navajo and Yup'ik cases. *Anthropology & Education Quarterly*, 25(3), 266–284.

Lipka, J., Sharp, N., Brenner, B., Yanez, E., & Sharp, F. (2005). The relevance of culturally based curriculum and instruction: The case of Nancy Sharp. *Journal of American Indian Education*, 44(3), 31–54.

Lomawaima, K. T., & McCarty, T. L. (2006). *To remain an Indian: Lessons in democracy from a century of Native American education*. Teachers College Press.

Low, S. (2009). Claiming space for an engaged anthropology: Spatial inequality and social exclusion. *American Anthropologist*, 113(3), 389–407.

Low, S. (2014). Spatializing culture: An engaged anthropological approach to space and place. In J. J. Gieseking & W. Mangold (Eds.), *The people, place, and space reader* (pp. 68–72). Routledge.

Low, S., & Lawrence-Zúñiga, D. (2003). "Locating culture." In S. Low & D. Lawrence-Zúñiga (Eds.), *The anthropology of space and place: Locating culture* (pp. 1–50). Wiley Press.

Lusi, S. (1997). *The role of state departments of education in complex school reform*. Teachers College Press.

Madsen, J. (1994). *Educational reform at the state level: The politics and problems of implementation*. The Falmer Press.

Mahony, P., Hextall, I., & Menter, I. (2004). Building dams in Jordan, Assessing teachers in England: A case study in edu-business. *Globalisation, Societies and Education*, 2(2), 277–296.

Manuelito, K. (2005). The role of education in American Indian self-determination: lessons from the Ramah Navajo Community School. *Anthropology & Education Quarterly*, 36(1), 73–87.

McCarty, T. L. (1993). Language, literacy, and the image of the child in American Indian classrooms. *Language Arts*, 70(3), 182–192.

McCarty, T. L. (2002). *A place to be Navajo: Rough Rock and the struggle for self-determination in Indigenous schooling*. Routledge.

McCarty, T. L. (2012). Enduring inequities, imagined futures—Circulating policy discourses and dilemmas in the anthropology of education. *Anthropology & Education Quarterly*, 43(1), 1–12.

McCarty, T. L., & Lee, T. (2014). Critical culturally sustaining/revitalizing pedagogy and indigenous education sovereignty. *Harvard Educational Review*, 84(1), 101–124.

McDermott, B. (2014). *Push for charter schools in Nebraska faces uphill battle.* KVNO News. http://www.kvnonews.com/2014/08/push-charter-schools-nebraska-faces-uphill-battle/

McGuinn, P. (2011). Stimulating reform: Race to the Top, competitive grants and the Obama education agenda. *Educational Policy*, 26(1), 136–159.

McNeil, L. (2004). Creating new inequalities: Contradictions of reform. In D. Flinders & S. Thornton (Eds.), *The curriculum studies reader* (pp. 275–284). Routledge.

McNeil, L. (2000). *Contradictions of school reform*. Routledge.

Mehan, H. (2005). Commentary: The changing but underrealized roles of state education agencies in school reform. *Journal of Education for Students Placed at Risk*, 10(1), 139–146.

Mette, I., & Stanoch, J. (2016). School turnaround: A rural reflection of reform on the reservation and lessons for implementation. *The Rural Educator*, 37(2), 39–50.

Meyer, R. W. (1993). *History of the Santee Sioux: United States Indian policy on trial*. University of Nebraska Press.

Mignolo, W. D., & Walsh, C. E. (2018). *On decoloniality: Concepts, analytics, praxis*. Duke University Press.

Mills, C. (2015). Consultants, brokers, experts: Knowledge actors and knowledge exchange and flows in educational administration. *Journal of Educational Administration and History*, 47(3), 209–213.

Mira, N., & Morrell, E. (2011). Teachers as civic agents: Toward a critical democratic theory of urban teacher development. *Journal of Teacher Education*, 62(4), 408–420.

Morrill, A. (2017). Time traveling dogs (and other Native feminist ways to defy dislocations). *Cultural Studies↔Critical Methodologies*, 17(1), 14–20.

Nader, L. (1972). Up the anthropologist-perspectives gained from "studying up." In D. Hymes (Ed.), *Reinventing anthropology* (pp. 284–311). Pantheon Books.

Nayar, P. K. (2010). The postcolonial uncanny: The politics of dispossession in Amitav Ghosh's *The Hungry Tide*. *College Literature*, 37(4), 88–119.

Nebraska Revised Statute, § 79–760.03.

Nebraska's State Legislature. (1869). *Act to establish a system of public instruction for the State of Nebraska*.

Nebraska's 102nd Legislature, 2nd Sess. (2012). *For an act relating to schools: LB870.*

Nebraska's 103rd Legislature, 1st Sess. (2013a). *For an act relating to education: LB438*. State of Nebraska.

Nebraska's 103rd Legislature, 1st Sess. (2013b). *Education committee hearing*. State of Nebraska.

Nebraska's 103rd Legislature, 1st Sess. (2013c). *Legislative resolution 305*. State of Nebraska

Nebraska's 103rd Legislature, 2nd Sess. (2014a). *Working to improve Nebraska schools act, LB952*. State of Nebraska.

Nebraska's 103rd Legislature 2nd Sess. (2014b). *Quality education and accountability act, LB438: Floor debate*. State of Nebraska.

References

Nebraska's 103rd Legislature 2nd Sess. (2014c). *Quality education and accountability act, LB438: Floor debate*. State of Nebraska.

Nebraska's 103rd Legislature 2nd Sess. (2014d). *Quality education and accountability act, LB438: Floor debate*. State of Nebraska.

Nebraska's 103rd Legislature 2nd Sess. (2014e). *Quality education and accountability act, LB438: Floor debate*. State of Nebraska.

Nebraska's 104th Legislature. (2016) *Inside our nation's only unicameral*. State of Nebraska.

Nebraska Department of Education. (2004). *STARS, a summary report*. Nebraska Department of Education.

Nebraska Department of Education. (2014a). *Administrators' days: Commissioner Matthew L. Blomstedt's keynote*. Lincoln, NE: Nebraska Department of Education.

Nebraska Department of Education. (2014b). *NePAS 1.1, accountability task force synthesis*. Nebraska Department of Education.

Nebraska Department of Education. (2015a). *Commissioner's administrators' days presentation: Broader, bolder, better*. Nebraska Department of Education.

Nebraska Department of Education. (2016a). *Commissioner's report of priority school activities*. Nebraska Department of Education.

Nebraska Department of Education. (2022). *Request for proposal: Contract priority school support*. Nebraska Department of Education.

Nebraska Revised Statute § 301. (n.d.) State Department of Education; State Board of Education; Commissioner of Education; powers; duties; vacancy, absence, or incapacity; deputy commissioner; duties. State of Nebraska.

Nebraska Secretary of State. (2016). Overview of regulation process. https://sos.nebraska.gov/regulations/overview-regulation-process

Nebraska State Board of Education. (2013a). *December state board of education business meeting*. State of Nebraska.

Nebraska State Board of Education. (2014a). January state board of education work session. State of Nebraska.

Nebraska State Board of Education. (2014b). *February state board of education work session*. State of Nebraska.

Nebraska State Board of Education. (2014c). *August state board of education work session*. State of Nebraska.

Nebraska State Board of Education. (2014d) *September state board of education work session*. State of Nebraska.

Nebraska State Board of Education. (2014e). *November state board of education work session*. State of Nebraska

Nebraska State Board of Education. (2014f). *December state board of education work session*. State of Nebraska.

Nebraska State Board of Education. (2015a). *January state board of education work session*. State of Nebraska.

Nebraska State Board of Education. (2015b). *February state board of education work session*. State of Nebraska.

Nebraska State Board of Education. (2015c). *March state board of education work session*. State of Nebraska.

Nebraska State Board of Education. (2015d). *April state board of education work session*. State of Nebraska.

Nebraska State Board of Education (2015e). *June state board of education work session.* State of Nebraska.

Nebraska State Board of Education. (2015f). *August state board of education work session.* State of Nebraska.

Nebraska State Board of Education. (2015g). *September state board of education work session.* State of Nebraska.

Nebraska State Board of Education. (2015h). *December state board of education business meeting.* State of Nebraska.

Nebraska State Board of Education. (2016a). *February state board of education work session.* State of Nebraska.

Nebraska State Board of Education. (2016b). *March state board of education work session.* State of Nebraska.

Nebraska State Board of Education. (2016c). *April state board of education work session.* State of Nebraska.

Nebraska State Board of Education. (2016d). *May state board of education work session.* State of Nebraska.

Nebraska State Board of Education. (2016e). *June state board of education work session.* State of Nebraska.

Nebraska State Board of Education. (2016f). *August state board of education work session.* State of Nebraska.

Nebraska State Board of Education. (2016g). *August state board of education business meeting.* State of Nebraska.

Nebraska State Board of Education. (2017a). *March state board of education work session.* State of Nebraska.

Nebraska State Board of Education. (2017b). *June state board of education work session.* State of Nebraska.

Nebraska State Board of Education. (2018). *June state board of education work session.* State of Nebraska.

Nebraska State Board of Education. (2019). *October state board of education work session.* State of Nebraska.

Nelson-Barber, S., & Estrin, E. T. (1995). Bringing Native American perspectives to mathematics and science teaching. *Theory Into Practice, 34*(3), 174–185.

Nelson-Barber, S., & Lipka, J. (2008). Rethinking the case for culture-based curriculum: Conditions that support improved mathematics performance in diverse classrooms. In M. Brisk (Ed.), *Language, curriculum and community in teacher preparation* (pp. 99–123). Lawrence Erlbaum Associates, Inc.

Nelson-Barber, S., & Johnson, Z. (2019). Raising the standard for testing research-based interventions in Indigenous learning communities. *International Review of Education, 65,* 47–65.

Nevada Department of Education. (2017). *Nevada only state to receive $3.251 million U.S. Department of Education Native Youth Community Projects Grant.* [Press Release].

Ngai, P., & Koehn, P. (2016). Teacher/family partnerships for student learning: Lessons from *Indian Education for All* in Montana. *Journal of American Indian Education, 55*(1), 23–48.

Nichols, J., & Cuenca, A. (2014). Two roadmaps, one destination: The economic progress paradigm in teacher education accountability in Georgia and Missouri. *Action in Teacher Education, 36*(5–6), 446–459.

References

Noble, A.J., & Smith, M.L. (2000). Time(s) for education reform: The experience of two states. In P. Gándara (Ed.), *The dimensions of time and the challenges of school reform*, (pp. 181–201). State University of New York Press.

Noddings, N. (2013). *Education and democracy in the 21st century*. Teachers College Press.

Noel, J. (2002). Education toward cultural shame: A century of Native American education. *The Journal of Educational Foundations, 16*(1), 19.

O'Day, J., & Smith, M. (1993). Systemic educational policy: A conceptual framework. In S. Fuhrman (Ed.). *Designing coherent education Policy* (pp. 125–140). Jossey-Bass Publishers.

Office of Health Disparities and Health Equity. (2020). *Nebraska minority population report card*. Nebraska Department of Health and Human Services. https://dhhs.ne.gov/Reports/Minority%20Population%20Report%20Card.pdf

Office of Minority Health. (n.d.). *Profile: American Indian/Alaska Native*. U. S. Department of Health and Human Services. https://minorityhealth.hhs.gov/omh/browse.aspx?lvl=3&lvlid=62

Oklahoma v. Castro-Huerta, 597 U.S. ___ (2022).

Onosko, J. (2011). Race to the Top leaves children and future citizens behind: The devastating effects of centralization, standardization, and high stakes accountability. *Democracy and Education, 19*(2), 1.

Ozga, J. (2009). *Policy research in educational settings*. Open University Press.

Paris, D. (2012). Culturally sustaining pedagogy: A needed change in stance, terminology, and practice. *Educational Researcher, 41*(3), 93–97.

Paris, D., & Alim, H. S. (2014). What are we seeking to sustain through culturally sustaining pedagogy? A loving critique forward. *Harvard Educational Review, 84*(1), 85–100.

Parker, W. (2003). *Teaching democracy*. Teachers College Press.

Patrick, R. (2008). Perspectives on change: A continued struggle for academic success and cultural relevancy at an American Indian school in the midst of No Child Left Behind. *Journal of American Indian Education, 47*(1), 65–81.

Patrinos, H., Arcia, G., & Macdonald, K. (2015). School autonomy and accountability in Thailand: Does the gap between policy intent and implementation matter? *Prospects, 45*(4), 429–445.

Peck, C., & Reitzug, U. C. (2014). School turnaround fever: The paradoxes of a historical practice promoted as a new reform. *Urban Education, 49*(1), 8–38.

Pewewardy, C. (2022). Comanche-centered education: A quest for educational sovereignty revisited. *Multicultural Education, 29*(3/4), 2–10.

Pewewardy, C., & Hammer, P. (2003). Culturally responsive teaching for American Indian students. ERIC Clearinghouse on Rural Education and Small Schools.

Pewewardy, C., Lees, A., & Clark-Shim, H. (2018). Transformational indigenous praxis model: States for developing critical consciousness in indigenous education. *Wicazo Sa Review, 33*(1), 38–69

Phillips, A. (2017). When policy is practice: SDE effort to help/transform/label low-performing schools (Publication No. 10608328) [Doctoral dissertation, University of Nebraska at Lincoln]. Digital Commons. https://digitalcommons.unl.edu/dissertations/AAI10608328/

Phillips, A. (2019). Ways of seeing and responding to a school in Santee Sioux country. *Journal of American Indian Education, 58*(1), 62–83.

Phillips, A. (2021). "I'm here anyway": School choice in Indian country. In A. Phillips & T. Gray (Eds.), *Agency in constrained academic contexts: Explorations of space in educational anthropology* (pp. 52–68). Lexington Press.

Phillips, A., & Gray, T. (2021). Introduction. In A. Phillips & T. Gray (Eds.), *Agency in constrained academic contexts: Explorations of space in educational anthropology* (pp. 1–18). Lexington Press.

Phillips, A., & Hamann, E. T. (2021). The Lady from North Carolina: The perils and limitations of external expertise. *Anthropology & Education Quarterly*, 52(3), 335–351.

Polikoff, M., McEachin, A., Wrabel, S., & Duque, M. (2013). The waive of the future? School accountability in the waiver era. *Educational Researcher*, 43(1), 45–54.

Porter, A., McMaken, J., Hwang, J., & Yang, R. (2011). Common core standards: The new U.S. intended curriculum. *Educational Researcher*, 40(3), 103–116.

Powers, K., Potthoff, S. J., Bearinger, L. H., & Resnick, M. D. (2003). Does cultural programming improve educational outcomes for American Indian youth? *Journal of American Indian Education*, 42(2), 17–49.

Rabinow, P. (1982). Ordonnance, discipline, regulation: Some reflections on urbanism. *Humanities in Society*, 5(3–4), 267–278.

Ravitch, D. (2010). *The death and life of the great American school system*. Basic Books.

Ravitch, D. (2013). *Reign of error*. Random House.

Reist, M. (2015, January 9). State Board of Ed elects officers. *Lincoln Journal Star*. http://journalstar.com/news/local/education/state-ed-board-elects-officers/article_3117beda-c184-5f51-8112-9417cb69a6ee.html

Reyhner, J., & Eder, J. (2004). *American Indian education: A history*. University of Oklahoma Press.

Robinson, I., & Toney, D. (2021). Mi'kmaw women principals' leadership as pathways for cultural revitalization. *Journal of American Indian Education*, 60(1–2), 100–122.

Ruff, R. R. (2019). State-level autonomy in the era of accountability: A comparative analysis of Virginia and Nebraska education policy through No Child Left Behind. *Education Policy Analysis Archives*, 27(6), 1–29.

Russakoff, D. (2015). *The prize: Who's in charge of America's schools?* Houghton Mifflin.

Russell, W. (1929). School administration and conflicting American ideals. *Teachers College Record* 31(1), 17–23.

Sabzalian, L. (2019). *Indigenous children's survivance in public schools*. Routledge.

Sabzalian, L., Morrill, A., & Edmo, S. (2019). Deep organizing and Indigenous studies legislation in Oregon. *Journal of American Indian Education*, 58(3), 34–57.

Santee Community Schools (2015). *Santee history*. https://www.isanti.school/vnews/display.v/ART/537cb48e08817

Santee Community School Board (10 May 2016a). *Commissioner's report of priority school activities for the Santee Community Schools: Preliminary efforts, findings, and next steps*.

Santee Community School Board (10 May 2016b). *Business meeting*. Santee Community School.

References

Santee Community School Board. (13 June 2017). *June business meeting*. Santee Community School.
Santee Community School Board. (2 March 2020). *March business meeting*. Santee Community School.
Sexton, D. M. (2008). Student teachers negotiating identity, role, and agency. *Teacher Education Quarterly, 35*(3), 73–88.
Simola, H., & Rinne, R. (2011). Education politics and contingency: Belief, status and trust behind the Finnish PISA miracle. In M. A. Pereya, H. Kotthoff, & R. Kowen (Eds.) *PISA under examination* (pp. 223–244). Sense.
Sleeter, C. E. (2007). Democracy, equity, and accountability. In C. E. Sleeter (Ed.), *Facing accountability in education* (pp. 1–12). Teachers College Press.
Smylie, M. A., & Evans, A. E. (2006). Social capital and the problem of implementation. In M. I. Honig (Ed.), *New directions in education policy implementation* (pp. 187–208). State University of New York Press.
Soja, E. (2010). *Seeking spatial justice*. University of Minnesota.
South Dakota Department of Education (2018). *Oceti Sakowin: Essential understandings and standards*. South Dakota Tribal Relations: https://sdtribalrelations.sd.gov/docs/OSEUs-18.pdf
State Board of Education; districts; numbers; boundaries; established by maps; Clerk of Legislature; Secretary of State; duties. Nebraska Revised Statute § 79–311. (1968).
State Board of Education; powers; duties. Nebraska Revised Statute § 79–318.
Statewide assessment and reporting system for school year 2009–10 and subsequent years; State Board of Education; duties; technical advisory committee; terms; expenses, Nebraska Revised Statute § 79–760.03.
State Board of Education; members; qualifications. Nebraska Revised Statute § 79–313.
State Department of Education; State Board of Education; Commissioner of Education; powers; duties; vacancy, absence, or incapacity; deputy commissioner; duties. Nebraska Revised Statute § 79–301.
Stein, S. J. (2004). *The culture of education policy*. Teachers College Press.
Sturges, K.M. (2015). Curriculum testing on the persistent fringes: Neoliberal policy and the new regime of Title I high school reform. *Anthropology & Education Quarterly, 46*(2), 129–146.
Sturm, C. (2011). *Becoming Indian: The struggle over Cherokee identity in the twenty-first century*. University of New Mexico Press.
Sumida Huaman, E., & Valdiviezo, L. A. (2012). Indigenous knowledge and education from the Quechua community to school: beyond the formal/non-formal dichotomy. *International Journal of Qualitative Studies in Education, 27*(1), 65–87.
Sutton, M., & Levinson, B. (2001). *Policy as practice: Toward a comparative sociocultural analysis of educational policy*. Ablex Publishing.
Swisher, K., & Deyhle, D. (1989). The styles of learning are different, but the teaching is just the same: Suggestions for teachers of American Indian youth. [Special Issue] *Journal of American Indian Education*, 1–14.
Takayama, K. (2009). Politics of externalization in reflexive times: Reinventing Japanese education reform discourses through Finnish PISA success. *Comparative Education Review, 54*(1), 51–75.
Talking heads. (1978). The big country [Song]. More songs about buildings and food [Album]. Sire Records.

Timar, T. (1997). The institutional role of state education departments: A historical perspective. *American Journal of Education, 105*(3). 231–260.

Trudell, T. (2022, December 2). A reservation school graduates 100% of students. School leaders say it's because they're learning tribal culture. *Flatwater Free Press.* https://nebraskapublicmedia.org/en/news/news-articles/a-reservation-school-graduates-100-of-students-school-leaders-say-its-because-theyre-learning-tribal-culture/

Trujillo, T., & Renée, M. (2013). Democratic school turnarounds: Pursuing equity and learning from evidence. *Voices in Urban Education, 36*(Apr), 18–26.

Tuck, E., & Yang, K. W. (2012). Decolonization is not a metaphor. *Decolonization: Indigeneity, Education & Society, 1*(1), 1–40.

Tuck, E., & Yang, K. W. (2014). Unbecoming claims: Pedagogies of refusal in qualitative research. *Qualitative Inquiry, 20*(6), 811–818.

United States Census Bureau (2022, July 1). U.S. Census Bureau QuickFacts: Oklahoma. United States Census Bureau. https://www.census.gov/quickfacts/fact/table/OK/PST045222

United States Congress (1897). United States Congressional Report No. 4.

United States Department of Education. (1983). *A nation at risk.* National Commission on Excellence in Education.

United States Department of Education (7 June 2012). *ESEA flexibility: Request for window 3.* U.S. Department of Education.

United States Department of Education (13 November 2014). *ESEA flexibility: Guidance for renewal process.* U.S. Department of Education.

United States Office of Indian Affairs. (1868). *Annual report of the Commissioner of Indian Affairs to the Secretary of the Interior.* U.S. Government Printing Office.

United States Department of the Interior (1887). *Annual report of the Department of the Interior.* U.S. Government Printing Office.

United States Department of Justice (2023, March 8). District of South Dakota: Indian country. United States Department of Justice. https://www.justice.gov/usao-sd/indian-country#:~:text=Census%20data%20puts%20the%20state,at%2068%2C976%20(8.57%20percent).

Vinovskis, M. A. (2003). Missed opportunities: Why the federal response to *A Nation at Risk* was inadequate. In D. T. Gordon (Ed.), *A nation reformed?* (pp. 115–130). Harvard University Press.

Vizenor, G. R. (1999). *Manifest manners: Narratives on postindian survivance.* University of Nebraska Press.

Vizenor, G. (2007). *Literacy chance: Essays on Native American survivance.* Universitat de València.

Weick, K. E. (1995). *Sensemaking in organizations.* Sage Publications.

Weinbaum, E. H., Weiss, M. J., & Beaver, J. K. (2012, September). *Learning from NCLB: School responses to accountability pressure and student subgroup performance* [Policy brief]. Consortium for Policy Research in Education. http://repository.upenn.edu/cpre_policybriefs/42

Weiner, L. (2007). NCLB, U.S. education, and the world bank: Neoliberalism comes home. In C. E. Sleeter (Ed.). *Facing accountability in education* (pp. 159–171). Teachers College Press.

References

Welch, G., Holman, S., & Baumfalk., B. (2015, October 31). *Nebraska School Improvement Grants: A framework for evaluating fidelity and impact*. Nebraska Center for Research on Children, Youth, Families and Schools, University of Nebraska–Lincoln.

Wilkins, D. E., & Lomawaima, K. T. (2001). *Uneven ground: American Indian sovereignty and federal law*. University of Oklahoma Press.

Williams, T., & Tracz, S. M. (2016). Taking back the fire: schooling experiences of Central California Indian people across generations. *Journal of American Indian Education, 55*(2), 75–98.

Wilson, A. C., (2005). *Remember this!: Dakota decolonization and the Eli Taylor narratives*. University of Nebraska Press.

Wolcott, H. F. (1988). "Problem finding" in qualitative research. In H. T. Trueba and C. Delgado Gaitan (Eds.), *School and society: Learning content through culture* (pp. 11–35). Praeger.

Wolfe, P. (2006). Settler colonialism and the elimination of the native. *Journal of Genocide Research, 8*(4), 387–409.

Wyman, L. (2012). *Youth culture, language endangerment, and linguistic survivance*. Multilingual Matters.

Zhao, Y. (2009). *Catching up or leading the way: American education in the age of globalization*. ASCD.

Zimmer, R., Gill, B., Booker, K., Lavertu, S., & Witte, J. (2012). Examining charter student achievement effects across seven states. *Economics of Education Review 31*(2), 213–224.

Index

Accountability, 18–28; Common Core State Standards (CCSS) and, 21, 24, 59; culturally sustaining policymaking and, 9–10, 55–56; democracy and, 3–4; Every Student Succeeds Act (ESSA, 2015), 1–2, 18, 25, 91; federal-level, 1–2, 18–25. See also No Child Left Behind Act (NCLB, 2001); history in Nebraska schools, 74; nature of "good" education and, 53–54, 136–138; neoliberal narrative in, 18, 21, 30–31, 53, 58; power systems and. See Power/power systems; priority/low-performing schools and, 3–4, 30, 51–52, 58–69, 81–90, 91–113; Race to the Top (RttT) and, 19, 21, 23, 24; state-level, in Nebraska, 2–3, 8–9, 15–16, 17, 19–20, 25–28, 31–33, 56, 73–78. See also Accountability for a Quality Education System Today and Tomorrow (AQuESTT); Nebraska State Legislature

Accountability for a Quality Education System Today and Tomorrow (AQuESTT), 13, 28, 71–90, 123, 128, 130, 135, 137, 139, 140; classification/designation of schools and districts, 77, 81–90, 112; codifying, 79–80; development of, 38–41, 73, 76–79; Evidence-based Analysis (EBA) tool, 82–85, 90, 112; as expanded vision of assessment/accountability, 81–88, 112; implementation, 80–88, 115–132; space as concept and, 70; tenets of, 77, 80, 96, 99, 106–107; top-down policy culture and, 30–31, 112–113

Adams, D. W., 48

Adams, Greg (Nebraska District 24 Senator), 32, 33, 37, 38, 58–69, 72–76

Agbo, S. A., 54

Agency. See also Power/power systems; agentic acts among students, educators, and community leaders, 130–131; "incognito" improvement efforts and, 94, 118, 121, 125, 129–132, 138–139; school choice movement and, 21–23; survivance and. See Survivance

Ahearn, L. M., 28

Alaska, 2, 24, 122–123

Alexander, Lamar, 19

Alim, H. S., 54

Alonzo, M., 9, 51

America 2000, 19

American Board of Missionaries, 48–49, 111

American Indian education terminology, 4–8; decolonization and space, 6–8; education vs. schooling, 6, 48–50. See also Schooling; Indian Country/tribal lands, 5; Indigenous/Native as terms, 5; survivance, 8. See also Survivance; tribal sovereignty, 5–6, 43. See also Tribal sovereignty

American Schools Development Corporation, 19

Anderson, J., 73

Anderson-Levitt, K. M., 53

Anthony-Stevens, V., 6, 22–23, 138

Anyon, J., 17

Apple, M. W., 27, 134

AQuESTT. See Accountability for a Quality Education System Today and Tomorrow (AQuESTT)

Arcia, G., 53

Arizona, 2, 136

Assessment. See Accountability

Atkins, John A. C., 49

Au, W., 1, 141–142

Austin, R., 55, 113, 140

Ball, S. J., 128

Balter, A., 9, 112

Barnhardt, R., 9, 53, 54, 112, 113, 138

Barth, R., 28

Bartlett, L., 56

Baumfalk, B., 51, 89

Bearinger, L. H., 54
Beaulieu, D. L., 9, 51, 53, 112, 140
Beaver, J. K., 21
Becoming Indian (Sturm), 11
Beggs, W. K., 35
Berliner, D. C., 15, 20, 24
Berman, P., 16
Biddle, B. J., 15, 20
Bird, C. P., 54, 136
Blalock, N., 5, 6, 22–23, 50, 138
Blomstedt, Matthew L. (Nebraska Commissioner of Education), 33, 35–36, 40, 41, 57–58, 62, 69–70, 72–88, 91–92, 94–101, 103, 104, 106–110, 118–120, 122, 134–135, 139
Bonaiuto, John, 60–62
Bonvillain, N., 49
Booker, K., 22
Brayboy, B. M. J., 5, 6, 9, 10, 43, 51–56, 112, 123, 124, 130, 136–141
Breed, Roger (Nebraska Commissioner of Education), 40, 60, 61, 72
Brenner, B., 54, 113, 138
Brighouse, H., 22
Brookings Institution, 21–22
Brown v. Board of Education (1954), 1, 53, 141
Buchanan, N., 22
Buros Center for Testing, University of Nebraska–Lincoln, 32
Bush, George H. W., 19
Bush, George W., 20
Butler, T. A., 24

California, 25
Canada, 45–47
Cantor, L., 17, 25
Carjuzaa, J., 140
Carlisle Indian Industrial School (Pennsylvania), 48–49
Carr, P., 53
Castagno, A. E., 5, 6, 9, 10, 22–23, 43, 50, 53–56, 112, 130, 138–140
Catching Up for Leading the Way (Zhao), 24
Center for School Turnaround and Improvement, 128
Chambers, E., 63
Charter schools, 22–23, 31, 38, 59, 67, 134
Cherokee Nation, 11–12
Child, B., 49, 56
Chouart, Médard, Sieur des Groseilliers, 44

Christensen, Doug (Nebraska Commissioner of Education), 31, 32
Chubb, John E., 21–22
Cleary, L. M., 54, 113, 138
Clinton, Bill, 19
Clune, W., 16
Coburn, C. E., 16, 24
Cody, A., 32
Cohen, D. K., 19, 20
Commissioner of Education. *See* Blomstedt, Matthew L. (Nebraska Commissioner of Education); Nebraska Commissioner of Education
Common Core State Standards (CCSS), 21, 24, 59
Cook, T., 66
Council of Chief State School Officers (CCSSO), 24, 25
Courtney, S., 134
COVID-19 pandemic, 125–127
Cowen, R., 53
CREDO, 22
Critical theory, 17; Critical Race Theory (CRT), 51; TribalCrit framework, 51, 141
Cuban, L., 3, 15, 16, 20
Cuenca, A., 26
Cullen, J. B., 22
Culturally sustaining and responsive pedagogy, 53–56; characteristics of, 54; Dakota language and culture at *iSanti* Community School, 49, 50, 55, 93–99, 101, 107, 109–110, 112–113, 116, 118, 121–125, 127, 129–132, 137–139, 143–144; decolonizing work of, 6–8, 139–141, 144; democracy in, 139–141, 142; "incognito" improvement efforts at *iSanti* Community School, 94, 118, 121, 125, 129–132, 138–139; nature of culturally responsive schooling (CRS), 53–54; nature of culturally sustaining pedagogy (CSP), 54; nature of culturally sustaining/revitalizing pedagogy (CSRP), 54–55; Nebraska compared with other states, 2; policy culture and, 4, 9–10, 12, 15, 26–28, 30–31, 55–56, 90, 110–113, 137–138, 140–142; power/power systems and, 54–55, 112–113, 139–141
Culture of Education Policy (Stein), 10

Dalley-Trim, L., 138
Daniels, Kari, 124
Dappen, L., 20, 31–32
Datnow, A., 18, 134

Index

de Certeau, M., 28, 52, 139
Decolonization; in culturally sustaining/ responsive education, 139–141, 144; education policy in, 7; nature of settler colonialism, 6–7; space and, 6–8; survivance as strategy in. *See* Survivance
Dee, T. S., 21
Deficit frame, 10, 27, 56, 69, 110, 111, 131–132, 135, 141
Dehyle, D., 54
Dejka, J., 61, 135
Delaware, 136
Deloria, E., 49
Deloria, V., Jr., 54
Demmert, W., 9, 54, 55, 112, 113, 138, 140–141
Democracy; in culturally sustaining/ responsive education, 139–141, 142; education policy development and, 4, 16, 18; equity and, 3, 10; evolution of, 15; school accountability education reform and, 3–4; serious democracy (Freire) and, 3, 4, 12, 18, 131, 139–140, 142
Denman, Hampton, 48, 111
Deyhle, D., 54, 113, 138
District of Columbia, 25
Druid Hill Elementary School, 86, 87
Dryzek, J., 3
Duffy, E., 83
Duggan, J., 59
Dumas, M. J., 17
Duncan, Arne, 23, 24
Duque, M., 25

Early childhood programming, 64–66, 143
Eastman, Charles *(Hakadah; Ohíye S'a)*, 45–47
Eder, J., 48–50
Edmo, S., 9, 52
Education. *See also* Schooling; schooling vs., 6, 48–50
Education Committee Hearing, 62
Education policy, 15–28; accountability and, 18–28. *See also* Accountability; critical theory and, 17, 51, 141; criticism of, 16–18; culturally sustaining/responsive education and. *See* Culturally sustaining and responsive pedagogy; educational spaces and, 28, 70; evolution of, 15; as expression of democracy, 4, 16, 18; federal government role in, 16, 17–19; history of Nebraska schooling and governance and, 35–36; implementation study and, 17, 18; Indigenous/Dakota language and, 49, 50, 55, 129–132; intention and context in implementing, 41; *A Nation at Risk* (1983) and, 16, 18; nature of "good" education and, 53–54, 136–138; Nebraska as education policy "renegade," 2, 12, 29–31, 133; Nebraska education policy landscape and key figures, 36–41. *See also* Nebraska Department of Education (NDE); Nebraska State Board of Education (NSBOE); Nebraska State Legislature; Nebraska public schools governed by locally elected school boards, 2–3, 6, 17, 37, 50, 51–52; "Nebraska Way" of engaging multiple voices, 13, 31–34, 41, 72, 76–78, 81, 90, 133; neoliberal narrative and, 18, 21, 30–31, 53, 58; policy culture (Stein) and, 4, 9–10, 12, 15, 26–28, 30–31, 55–56, 90, 110–113, 137–138, 140–142; policy intention vs. policy enactment and, 89–90; policy spaces and, 28, 70, 90; power/power systems and, 15, 27–28, 53–54, 110–113, 136–141; school as policy tool, 48–50; state departments of education and, 17–18, 25–28, 40–41, 51–52; wave metaphor for (Honig), 16, 17
Elementary and Secondary Education Act (ESEA), 20; reauthorizations, 19, 21, 23, 84; *Request for ESEA Flexibility*, 24–25, 58, 62–63, 72
Elmore, R. F., 17, 19, 20
Estrin, E. T., 54, 113, 138
Evans, A. E., 16
Every Student Succeeds Act (ESSA, 2015), 1–2, 18, 25, 91

Faircloth, S., 5, 6, 9, 43, 52, 123, 137–138
Feis, Polly (Deputy Commissioner of Education), 31
Flint, Glen (SBOE District 2), 38, 73, 108
Flyover country, as term, 2–3, 12, 29–30, 141–142
Foucault, Michel, 4, 28, 70, 124
Four Domains of School Improvement (Center for School Turnaround and Improvement), 128
Fox, R., 22
Freire, Paulo, 3, 4, 12, 18, 131, 139–140, 142
Friedman, Milton, 21

Frison, Deborah A. (Nebraska Deputy Commissioner of Education), 40, 83, 87, 88, 91, 93–98, 100, 103, 107–109, 115, 118–120
Fuhrman, S. H., 17, 19
Fullan, M., 26

Gallagher, C., 12, 20
Garcia, D., 5, 6, 22–23, 50, 138
Garcia, S., 17, 19, 26
Gay, G., 53
Gill, B., 22
Glass, G., 24
Goals 2000: Educate America Act (1994), 19
Goffman, E., 7, 28
Goodlad, J., 6
Goodlad, S. J., 6
Gordon, D. T., 20
Gorski, P. C., 27
Gradual release of instruction model, 117, 119–120
Gram, J. R., 52
Grande, S., 7
Gray, T., 7, 12, 28
Greene, M., 17, 139
Greysolon, Daniel, Sieur du Luth, 44
Grossman, F., 9, 112
Gunter, H. M., 134
Gutmann, Amy, 3, 18, 140

Hall, D., 134
Hall, J. N., 3, 20, 21
Hall, P. M., 4
Hamann, Edmund T., 17, 20, 25, 26, 134
Hammer, P., 53–54, 138
Hargreaves, A., 26
Harkins, A., 29
Harms, J., 64–66
Hayes, Justin, 125
Heck, R. H., 15–17, 25, 26, 36, 37
Heineman, Dave, 38–39, 69
Hennepin, Louis, 44
Hermes, M., 56
Hextall, I., 134
Heycock, Kati, 102
Hill, H. C., 24
Hill, A., 138
Ho-Chunk (Winnebago) tribe, 2
Holman, S., 51, 89
Honig, M. I., 16, 17
Hopkins, John P., 2, 5–8, 50, 52, 136, 140
Hubbard, L., 18, 134
Hwang, J., 24

Improving America's Schools Act (1994), 19
Indian Boyhood (Eastman), 45–47
Indian Country/tribal lands; nature of, 5; school policy reform in, 2–3, 8–9
Indian Education for All (Hopkins), 5–8
Indian Education for All Act, 29
Indigenous Children's Survivance (Sabzalian), 8
Indigenous/Native students; agency and school choice, 22–23; Indigenous/Dakota language and, 49, 50, 55, 129–132; Indigenous/Native, as terms, 5; population relative to other Plains states, 2, 12, 29
iSanti Community School (formerly Santee Community School, SCS), 2–3, 10–12, 91–139; administrator and staff turnover/churning, 103, 109, 118–120, 122, 123, 126–128, 130; continued compliance with state programs, 124–129; COVID-19 pandemic and, 125–127; Dakota language and culture and, 49, 50, 55, 93–99, 101, 107, 109–110, 112–113, 116, 118, 121–125, 127, 129–132, 137–139, 143–144; deficit approaches and, 10, 27, 56, 69, 110, 111, 131–132, 135, 141; described, 3, 50, 91; diagnostic reviews by external consultants, 94, 95–98; gradual release of instruction model and, 117, 119–120; history as Santee Community School (SCS), 2, 49–50, 127, 139; implementation of state-level reforms, 115–132; "incognito" improvement efforts, 94, 118, 121, 125, 129–132, 138–139; lack of culturally responsive/sustaining interventions and, 110–113; lessons learned, 133–142; methodology of study. *See* Methodology of study; outside consultant/Lady from North Carolina, 40, 93–112, 115–124, 128–129, 134–136, 138; outside consultants/Big City Professor and Big City Board Consultant, 124–128, 129, 134–136; outside consultants/New Teacher Project (NTP), 128–129, 134–136; Phillips (author) as NDE liaison, 10–12, 30, 79, 85–88, 91–98, 99–124; Phillips (author) final visit to, 143–144; Phillips (author) initial thoughts about improvement, 92–94; as priority/low-performing school, 30, 51–52, 63–64, 66, 67, 69, 86, 87, 88–90, 91–113; progress plan approval and implementation, 106–113; progress plan development,

98–106; progress plan final results (2023), 143–144; progress plan interim results and revisions (2016–2023), 122–129; renaming (2021), 2, 50, 127, 139; "Santee DNA–the school and community" and, 93–94, 130–131, 137–138; school choice and, 22–23; school governance and, 37; School Improvement Grants, 51, 64, 89, 97; in state basketball tournament (2023), 143–144; state intervention in public school, 2, 7, 30–31, 37, 50, 51–52, 98–100; Warrior Improvement Team (WIT), 120–121, 126; *yes, and* approach of, 130–132, 139

iSanti (Santee) tribe, 2. *See also* Santee Dakota Sioux

Isernhagen, J., 20, 31–32

Isom, J., 32

Jacob, B. A., 21, 22
Jaffer, K., 53
Jenkins, L., 16
Jester, T. E., 53, 122–123, 140
Jetty, M., 140
Johnson, Z., 9, 53, 54, 112, 113

Kawagley, A. O., 9, 53, 54, 56, 112, 113, 138
Kentucky, 25–26, 40–41, 71–72
King, F., 50
Klug, B. J., 54, 113
Koehn, P., 140
Koyama, J., 135
Kuper, Hilda, 7–8, 27

Labaree, D. F., 3, 15, 20, 27
Ladson-Billings, Gloria, 53
Lane, B., 17, 19, 20, 25, 26
Larson, Lillie (SBOE District 1), 38, 63–64, 66–67, 69
Lashaw, A., 1
Lautenbaugh, Scott (Nebraska District 18 Senator), 38, 59–62, 64–65, 67–68
Lavertu, S., 22
Lawrence-Zúñiga, D., 7, 28, 70, 138
LB438 (2014, statewide accountability system for schools and districts), 33, 34, 37–40, 58–70, 72–79, 88, 137. *See also* Accountability for a Quality Education System Today and Tomorrow (AQuESTT); becomes law, 69–70, 73–74, 79, 88–89; codified as Neb. Rev. Stat. § 79-760.06.-.07, 36, 69–70,

74, 79–80, 83, 88–89; Final Reading and vote, 69–70; financial concerns and, 60–61, 63; floor debates, 62–69, 136–137; implementation process, 38–39, 40, 41, 61–69, 72–88; introduction to Unicameral, 37–38, 58–59; public hearings, 59–60, 80–81; as Quality Education Accountability Act/Quality Education Postponement Act (Nebraska, 2000), 31, 61–62, 65

Lee, T. S., 5, 6, 8, 9, 43, 52–55, 112, 123, 136–138

Lefebvre, Henri, 27

Legislative process. *See* Nebraska State Legislature

Lenger, John F., 118

Levinson, B., 2–3, 17, 18, 55–56

Lévi-Strauss, C., 70

Levitt, S. D., 22

Limoges, B., 35

Lincoln, Abraham, 45

Linn, R. L., 19, 20

Lipka, J., 9, 54, 113, 138, 140

Lomawaima, K. T., 2, 3, 5–9, 41, 43, 48, 50, 52, 54–56, 113, 131, 139

López, N., 54, 136

Loup County Elementary School, 86, 87

Low, Setha, 7, 28, 70, 138

Lusi, Susan Follett, 19, 25–26, 40–41, 71–72

Lynch, A., 138

Maaka, M., 5, 6, 9, 43, 52, 123, 136–138
Macdonald, K., 53
Madsen, J., 26
Mahoney, P., 134
Maine, 20
Mantle-Bromley, C., 6
Manuelito, K., 6, 137–138
MAP (Measures of Academic Progress), 125
McCarty, T. L., 2, 3, 5–9, 41, 43, 48, 50, 52–55, 112, 113, 131, 138–140
McDermott, B., 38
McEachin, A., 25
McGinty, P. J., 4
McGuinn, P., 23
McLaughlin, M. W., 16
McMaken, J., 24
McNeil, L., 21, 53
McPherson, Patrick, 39, 108–111
Mehan, H., 17, 18, 26, 134
Mello, Heath, 65–66, 68
Menter, I., 134

Methodology of study, 10–12; positionality of author. See Phillips, Aprille J.; pseudonym use, 14, 37
Mette, I., 51, 112
Meyer, R. W., 44–45, 47–49
Mignolo, W. D., 141
Mills, C., 128, 134
Minnesota, 21, 44, 47–48
Mira, N., 3
Moe, Terry M., 21–22
Montana, 2, 7, 8, 25, 29, 140
Moore, John, 45
Morrell, E., 3
Morrill, A., 8, 9, 52
Multi-Tiered Systems of Support, 125
Munson, M., 140

Nader, Laura, 11
National Governors Association Center for Best Practices, 24
A Nation at Risk (1983), 16, 18
Nayar, P. K., 6
Nebraska; American Indian/Alaska Native population size, 2, 12, 29; capitol building in Lincoln, 57–58; flyover country, as term, 2–3, 12, 29–30, 141–142; history of schooling and governance in, 35–36. *See also* Education policy; legislative process. *See* Nebraska State Legislature
Nebraska Administrative Code (N.A.C.), 79
Nebraska Association of School Boards (NASB), 60–61
Nebraska Commissioner of Education, 31–33, 35–36; Matthew Blomstedt. *See* Blomstedt, Matthew L.; Roger Breed, 40, 60, 61, 72; Doug Christensen, 31, 32
Nebraska Council of School Administrators (NCSA), 60–61
Nebraska Department of Education (NDE), 30–33, 35–36, 73–78, 83, 95, 128; Accountability Coordinator, 40, 78, 80, 93, 99, 100–104, 106, 107; Accreditation and School Improvement Administrator, 71, 80, 99; components of, 39–40; deficit frame and, 10, 27, 56, 69, 110, 111, 131–132, 135, 141; Director of Statewide Assessment, 73–76, 81–82; early childhood programming, 64–66, 143; expanded vision of assessment/accountability, 76–79; methodology of study. *See* Methodology of study; passage of LB438 and, 72–77; positionality of Phillips (author). *See* Phillips, Aprille J.; role in education policy, 25–28, 30; shifting roles of, 40–41; STARS (School-based, Teacher-led, Assessment and Reporting System, Nebraska), 31–32, 74; state-level accountability. *See* Accountability for a Quality Education System Today and Tomorrow (AQuESTT)
Nebraska Deputy Commissioner of Education; Polly Feis, 31; Deborah A. Frison. *See* Frison, Deborah A.
Nebraska Office of Minority Health, 2
Nebraska Office of Public Instruction, 35
Nebraska Performance Accountability System (NePAS/NePAS 1.1), 32–33, 73–78. *See also* Accountability for a Quality Education System Today and Tomorrow (AQuESTT)
Nebraska Rural Community Schools Association, 40
Nebraska Secretary of State, 79
Nebraska State Board of Education (NSBOE), 12, 35–39, 58–69, 74–90, 91–113, 116–128, 130, 133–137; Blomstedt as Commissioner of Education. *See* Blomstedt, Matthew L.; composition of, 38–39; "consultocracy" and, 134–136, 138; Frison as Deputy Commissioner of School Improvement and Support. *See* Frison, Deborah A.; history of, 35–36; LB438 implementation and, 38–39, 40, 41, 61, 72–88; nature of "good" education and, 53–54, 136–138; policy intention vs. policy enactment and, 89–90; priority/low-achieving schools, 3–4, 30, 51–52, 58–69, 81–90, 91–113; state-level accountability. *See* Accountability for a Quality Education System Today and Tomorrow (AQuESTT); Rachel Wise as President, 38, 77, 80, 86–87
Nebraska State Educators' Association (NSEA), 39, 60
Nebraska State Legislature, 57–70; 102nd, 2nd Sess. (2012), 32, 33, 62, 73; 103rd, 1st Sess. (2013), 58, 59–61; 103rd, 2nd Sess. (2014), 61–69; 104th (2016), 33–34; bill progression in, 34; capitol building in Lincoln and, 57–58; history of the Nebraska State Board of Education and, 35–36; LB438. *See* LB438 (2014, statewide accountability system for schools and districts); LB870 (2012, statewide accountability system for schools and districts), 32, 33, 62; LB952

(2014, Working to Improve Nebraska Schools Act), 62; LB972 (charter schools), 38; LB1157 (2008, single statewide assessment of reading, math, and science), 32; Nebraska Revised Statute § 79-301, 35–36; Nebraska Revised Statute § 79-802.01, 49; Nebraska Revised Statute § 79–760, 32, 36, 69–70, 74, 80, 83, 88; Unicameral (one-house state legislature) and, 31, 33–34, 37–38, 52, 56, 57–59, 61–62, 68–69, 79–80
Nebraska State Superintendent, 35
Nebraska Statewide Assessments (NeSA), 32, 73–76, 81–82
Nelson-Barber, S., 9, 53, 54, 112, 113, 138
Nevada, 140
New Teacher Project (NTP), 128–129, 134–136
Ngai, P., 140
Nichols, J., 26
Nickels, Maureen (SBOE District 6), 39
Noble, A. J., 136
No Child Left Behind Act (NCLB, 2001), 1–2, 12, 17–19, 28, 30–31, 50, 76, 135; accountability in Nebraska. *See* Accountability for a Quality Education System Today and Tomorrow (AQuESTT); Adequate Yearly Progress (AYP) and, 21, 31, 73; components of, 20; "failing" schools, 22, 27, 29, 58–60, 65–69, 85, 107, 130, 133–135; limbo status and, 21–25; *Request for ESEA Flexibility* and, 24–25, 58, 62–63, 72; school choice and, 21–23; school classification under, 51, 89; School Improvement Grants (SIGs), 19, 51, 55, 64, 85, 89, 97; unintended consequences of, 21
Noddings, N., 3, 21, 22, 139
Noel, J., 8–9
North Dakota, 12, 25, 29, 47
Northwest Evaluation Association (NWEA), 125

Obama, Barack, 21–24, 39
O'Day, J., 16
Office of Health Disparities and Health Equity, U.S. Department of Justice, 2
O'Holleran, Molly, 39, 72, 76, 77, 81, 91, 94, 99, 110
Oklahoma, 2, 6, 11–12, 29
Oklahoma v. Castro-Huerta (2022), 6
Onosko, J., 23

Oregon, 2, 8
Ozga, J., 16, 17

Paris, Django, 54, 55
Parker, L., 3, 20, 21
Parker, W., 3
Partnership for Assessment of Readiness for College and Careers (PARCC), 23, 24
Patrick, R., 51
Patrinos, H., 53
Peacock, T. D., 54, 113
Peck, C., 1
Pennsylvania, 48–49
Pewewardy, C., 6, 53–54, 138
Phillips, Aprille J., 7, 8, 22, 26, 28, 134; final visit *to iSanti* Community School, 143–144; initial thoughts about improvement at *iSanti* Community School, 92–94; as NDE liaison with *iSanti* Community School, 10–12, 30, 79, 85–88, 91–98, 99–124; as NDE Student Achievement Coordinator, 30, 79
Pike, Zebulon, 44
Policy culture (Stein), 4, 9–10, 12, 15, 26–28, 30–31, 55–56, 90, 110–113, 140–142
Polikoff, M., 25
Politics, Markets, and America's Schools (Chubb & Moe), 21–22
Ponca tribe, 2
Porter, A., 24
Potthoff, S. J., 54
Power/power systems. *See also* Agency; Tribal sovereignty; and culturally sustaining/revitalizing pedagogy (CSRP), 54–55, 112–113, 139–141; decolonizing work and, 6–8, 139–141; education policy and, 15, 27–28, 53–54, 110–113, 136–141; space and, 7–8, 27–28, 70, 90; state differences in, 15–16; structures of, 15–16; subjects vs. objects in (Foucault), 4
Powers, K., 54
Pratt, Richard Henry, 48–49
Professional learning communities (PLCs), 125, 139
Pseudonym use, 14, 37

Quality Education Accountability Act/ Quality Education Postponement Act (Nebraska, 2000), 31, 61–62, 65. *See also* LB438
Quandahl, Mark, 38, 72

Rabinow, P., 28
Race to the Top (RttT), 19, 21, 23, 24
Radisson, Pierre Esprit, 44
Ravitch, D., 21–24
Reagan, Ronald, 21
Reed, Wayne O., 35
Reist, M., 39
Reitzug, U. C., 1
Remember This! (Wilson), 144
Renée, M., 1, 141–142
Resnick, M. D., 54
Reyhner, J., 48–50
Richardson, T., 5, 6, 9, 43, 52, 123, 137–138
Riggs, Alfred L., 49
Rinne, R., 53
Robinson, I., 54
Rosen, L., 17
Ruff, R. R., 12
Russakoff, D., 23
Russell, W., 17

Sabzalian, Leilani, 2, 8, 9, 52, 131
Santee Community School (SCS); establishment as K-12 public school (1976), 2; founding (1971), 49–50; renamed *iSanti* Community School (2021), 2, 50, 127, 139. *See also iSanti* Community School (formerly Santee Community School, SCS)
Santee Community School Board, 98, 99–100, 122, 125
Santee Dakota Sioux. *See also* Santee Sioux Reservation; Bureau of Indian Affairs and, 2, 44–45, 48, 49, 53; Dakota War (1862), 45–46, 47; descriptions of Santee life and tribal education, 45–47; as federally recognized Indian Tribal Nation, 9, 43; interactions with European colonizers, 44, 47; interactions with the U.S. government, 44–45, 47–48; missionaries and, 44, 48–49, 111; relocation to Nebraska from Minnesota, 44, 47–48; Santee Normal Training School, 48–49; school as policy tool and, 48–50
Santee Sioux Reservation, 4, 10–12, 43–56, 91. *See also* Santee Dakota Sioux; concept of space and, 7–8; descriptions of Santee life and tribal education, 45–47; relocation to Nebraska from Minnesota, 44, 47–48; Santee Normal Training School, 48–49; school as policy tool and, 48–50; state intervention in public school on, 2, 7, 30–31, 37, 50, 51–52. *See also iSanti* Community School (formerly Santee Community School, SCS); village of Santee. *See* Village of Santee
SBOE. *See* Nebraska State Board of Education (NSBOE)
School choice, 21–23
School Improvement Grants, 19, 51, 55, 64, 85, 89, 97
Schooling; agency and, 52; education vs., 6, 48–50; equity and, 3, 10; history of, in Nebraska, 35–36; nature of "good" education and, 53–54, 136–138; school as policy tool, 48–50; school choice and, 21–23; as space containing power and constraint, 7; survivance and. *See* Survivance
Schouten, G., 22
Schwartz, N. L., 21
SDEs. *See* Nebraska Department of Education (NDE); State departments of education (SDEs)
Sears, Jay, 60
Self-determination, 5–6, 12, 14, 43, 50–52, 123, 131
Self-education, 5–7, 12, 36–37, 41, 43, 50–52, 56, 88, 112, 131–132, 137–138, 139, 141, 144
Self-governance, 5–6, 9, 43, 51–52, 123
Serious democracy (Freire), 3, 4, 12, 18, 131, 139–140, 142
Settler colonialism, 6–8; decolonization and, 6–8; dominant colonizing voice and, 7; Indigenous survivance and, 8. *See also* Survivance; nature of, 6–7; ongoing influence of, 7; schooling and, 7
Sexton, D. M., 28
Sharp, F., 54, 113, 138
Sharp, N., 54, 113, 138
Simola, H., 53
Sleeter, C. E., 20, 32
SMARTER Balanced Consortium, 23, 24
Smith, M. L., 16, 136
Smylie, M. A., 16
Soja, E., 7
South Dakota, 2, 3, 12, 29, 121
Sovereignty. *See* Agency; Power/power systems; Tribal sovereignty
Space; concept of space vs. experience of space (Kuper), 7–8; decolonization and, 6–8; defined, 7; educational, 28, 70; Indian Country/tribal lands and, 5. *See also* Santee Sioux Reservation; policy, 28,

70, 90; power systems and, 7–8, 27–28, 70, 90; spatial tactics as resistance, 28
Sparks, S., 9, 51
Spillane, J. P., 24
Stanoch, J., 51, 112
STARS (School-based, Teacher-led, Assessment and Reporting System, Nebraska), 31–32, 74
State departments of education (SDEs); in Alaska, 2, 24, 122–123; in Arizona, 2, 136; in California, 25; in Delaware, 136; in the District of Columbia, 25; in Kentucky, 25–26, 40–41, 71–72; in Maine, 20; in Minnesota, 21; in Montana, 2, 7, 8, 25, 140; in Nebraska. See Nebraska Department of Education (NDE); in Nevada, 140; in North Dakota, 12, 25; in Oklahoma, 2, 6, 11–12; in Oregon, 2, 8; policy culture and, 4, 9–10, 12, 15, 26–28, 30–31, 55–56, 90, 110–113, 137–138, 140–142; power and, 15–16. See also Power/power systems; requests for flexibility under ESEA, 24–25, 58, 62–63, 72; role in education policy, 17–18, 25–28; in South Dakota, 2, 12, 121; standards-assessment approach and, 17–18; in Texas, 24; in Vermont, 25–26, 40–41, 71–72; in Virginia, 24; in Washington state, 2
Stein, M. K., 16
Stein, Sandra J., 4, 9–10, 12, 15, 26–28, 55–56, 110–113, 140–142
Sturges, K. M., 134
Sturm, Circe, 11
Sullivan, Kate (Nebraska District 41 Senator), 37–38, 61–64, 68, 69, 72, 74–76
Sumida Huaman, E., 56
Survivance; Dakota language and culture and, 49, 50, 55, 93–99, 101, 107, 109–110, 112–113, 116, 118, 121–125, 127, 129–132, 137–139, 143–144; nature of, 8, 52; renaming Santee Community School as, 2, 50, 127, 139; as strategy in decolonization, 8, 52, 144
Sutton, M., 2–3, 17, 18, 55–56
Swisher, K., 54, 138

Takayama, K., 53
Taylor, Edward B., 47
Texas, 24
Timar, T., 26
Timm, Patricia (SBOE District 5), 39, 72
Toney, D., 54

Tracz, S. M., 136
TribalCrit framework, 51, 141
Tribal sovereignty. See also Culturally sustaining and responsive pedagogy; agency and, 52. See also Agency; comparison of states and, 2; defined, 5–6, 43; nature of "good" education and, 53–54, 136–138; recognition of, 50; self-determination and, 5–6, 12, 14, 43, 50–52, 123, 131; self-education and. See Self-education; self-governance and, 5–6, 9, 43, 51–52, 123
Trudell, T., 129–130
Trujillo, T., 1, 141–142
Tuck, Eve, 6–8, 141

UMÓ"HO" (Omaha) tribe, 2, 75–76, 77
Unicameral (one-house state legislature), 31, 33–34, 37–38, 52, 56, 57–59, 61–62, 68–69, 79–80
United States Bureau of Indian Education/Indian Affairs, 2, 44–45, 48, 49, 53, 111
United States Census Bureau, 2
United States Congress, 45
United States Department of Education, 16, 18, 25, 32; No Child Left Behind. See No Child Left Behind Act (NCLB, 2001); Race to the Top (RttT), 19, 21, 23, 24; STARS (School-based, Teacher-led, Assessment and Reporting System, Nebraska) and, 31–32, 74
United States Department of Justice, Office of Health Disparities and Health Equity, 2
United States Department of the Interior, 49
United States Office of Indian Affairs, 48, 111
University of Nebraska–Lincoln, 32
Usdan, M., 20

Valdiviezo, L. A., 56
Veltkamp, T., 140
Vermont, 25–26, 40–41, 71–72
Village of Santee, 43–56; described, 43, 91; descriptions of Santee life and tribal education in, 45–47; *iSanti* Community School. See *iSanti* Community School (formerly Santee Community School, SCS); methodology of study and. See Methodology of study
Vinovskis, M. A., 19, 20
Virginia, 24

Vizenor, Gerald R., 8, 52
Voucher programs, 22–23

Walsh, C. E., 141
Warren, Earl, 1, 141
Warrior Improvement Team (WIT), 120–121, 126
Washington state, 2
Weick, K. E., 18
Weinbaum, E. H., 21
Weiner, L., 20
Weiss, M. J., 21
Welch, G. W., 51, 89
Welch, Roger, 29
WestEd, 128
Whitfield, P. T., 54, 113
Wildcat, D. R., 54
Wilkins, D. E., 6, 8–9, 50, 56
Williams, T., 136

Wilson, Angela C., 144
Wise, Rachel (SBOE District 3), 38, 77, 80, 86–87
Witte, J., 22
Witzel, John (SBOE District 4), 39, 73, 110
Wolcott, H. F., 14
Wolfe, P., 6–7
Wong, C. P., 54
Working to Improve Nebraska Schools Act (LB952), 62
Wrabel, S., 25
Wyman, L., 8–9, 50

Yanez, E., 54, 113, 138
Yang, K. Wayne, 6–8, 141
Yang, R., 24

Zhao, Yong, 24
Zimmer, R., 22

About the Author

Aprille J. Phillips is an associate professor in the Department of Educational Administration at the University of Nebraska at Kearney in Kearney, Nebraska. Her research explores the intersection of theory and practice as they relate to advancing equity in educational spaces. She interrogates how school reform is or is not responsive to Indigenous people and policy as a sociocultural practice in its development and implementation across tiers (e.g., state departments of education, local schools).